THE RIGVEDA

THE RIGVEDA:

THE OLDEST LITERATURE OF THE INDIANS

ADOLF KAEGI

TRANSLATOR

ROBERT ARROWSMITH

GYAN

Published by

Gyan Publishing House
5, Ansari Road
Daryaganj, New Delhi-110002
Phone: 011-47034999, 9811692060
E-mail: books@gyanbooks.com

Distribution Network
gyanbooks.com
India, USA, Canada, UK, Australia

ISBN: 978-93-6920-458-8 (PB)

First Published, 1886

2nd Impression 2025

Printed at: Gyan Press, Delhi.

THE RIGVEDA
Author: ADOLF KAEGI, Translator: ROBERT ARROWSMITH

THE RIGVEDA:

THE OLDEST LITERATURE OF THE INDIANS.

BY

ADOLF KAEGI,

PROFESSOR IN THE UNIVERSITY OF ZÜRICH.

AUTHORIZED TRANSLATION WITH ADDITIONS TO THE NOTES

BY

R. ARROWSMITH, PH.D.,

INSTRUCTOR IN SANSKRIT, RACINE COLLEGE, RACINE, WIS.

BOSTON:

GINN AND COMPANY.

1886.

TRANSLATOR'S NOTE.

THE translation of the present work was undertaken in order to place at the command of English readers interested in the study of the Veda a comprehensive and, at the same time, condensed manual of Vedic research. It has been the aim to make the translation as close as possible; especially in the metrical quotations the author's renderings have nearly always been adhered to, though with continual reference to the text of the hymns.

Since the second German edition appeared, in 1880, much work has been done in the study of the Veda, and many additions made to the literature. These PROFESSOR KAEGI kindly offered to incorporate in the Notes, and, to some extent, to remodel the latter, but was prevented from doing as much as he had intended by stress of work and ill-health. The translator has endeavored to complete the references to the literature to date, and has extended a number of the Notes in some particulars. All such additions are designated by brackets [ ]. The only addition to the text is the Frog Song on p. 81 f.

The thanks of the translator are due to DR. KAEGI for his ready consent and interest in the undertaking, to PROFESSORS WHITNEY and LANMAN for suggestions and material, and to DR. A. V. W. JACKSON, of Columbia College, for revising the portions of the Notes pertaining to the Avesta.

The references have been verified as far as practicable, and it is believed that a reasonable degree of accuracy has been attained. It is requested that the translator be notified of the discovery of any mistakes which may have been overlooked.

R. A.

RACINE COLLEGE,
RACINE, WIS., February, 1886.

PREFACE TO THE SECOND EDITION.

THE invitation of my publishers to have my treatise on the Rigveda (Two Parts, Wissenschaftliche Beilage zum Programm der Kantonsschule in Zürich, 1878 and 1879) published in a somewhat revised and extended form, seemed to me the more to be accepted, since I had repeatedly been urged to do so from the most varied sources, and the article was frequently inquired for in the trade. It is plain that to specialists in the subject, to investigators in the field of the Veda, it cannot offer anything really new; its aim is to embrace the results of Vedic investigation, as well for beginners in the study as for all those who have a more special interest in this literature, the importance of which is perceived and admitted in ever-widening circles, especially for theologians, philologists and historians. That, however, it is founded throughout on personal investigation of the sources and examination of the investigations of others will be easily perceived by every one who takes the trouble to subject the text and notes to a more minute survey.

Here let me once more call attention to the fact that, in the sections upon the Vedic Belief and the Divinities, I have confined myself as closely as possible to the language of the hymns, so that almost the whole of this text (pp. 28–32, 34–71) is made up of the words of the poets. The quotations from the *Siebenzig Lieder* (*cf.* pp. 34 and 92) being given throughout in Italics, make it possible even for the non-Sanskritist to prove the method by which this is accomplished, at least in some short portions.

If, especially in the treatment of Varuṇa, I have somewhat more fully followed out the similarities of the Vedic and the Biblical language (*cf.* now A. Holzman in the Zeitschrift für Völkerspsychologie und Sprachwissenschaft, 1880, p. 251 f.), I shall now hardly have to meet the criticism that in so doing non-Indian, or even Christian, conceptions are put into the Veda; translation stands beside translation; it is left to the reader to prove similarity, as well as difference.

The great extent of the notes is explained by the fact that they are intended not only to prove, sustain and amplify the material presented in the text, but also to facilitate for others the survey of Vedic literature, and to point out the historical significance of the Rig. If some may criticise here too much or too little, others perhaps will be glad to utilize what is presented, even if only the references to the literature, for which the Indices may be welcome. On the letter, as well as on the correction, much care has been expended; if, notwithstanding, mistakes are discovered, it will surely be pardoned, especially in the very large quantity of numbers, by those who are experienced in such matters.

May the work in its new form serve to carry the knowledge of this ancient and highly important poetry and the interest in our studies into further circles.

DR. ADOLF KAEGI.

ZURICH, November, 1880.

TABLE OF CONTENTS.

INTRODUCTION: p. 1.

Vedic Literature and Exegesis: p. 2; the Vedic People and its Civilization: p. 11.

THE RIGVEDA: p. 21.

The Collection: p. 21; Language and Form of the Hymns: p. 22; Contents: p. 24.

Religious Poetry: p. 26; Religious Thought: p. 27; The Vedic Belief: p. 32.

THE DIVINITIES: p. 34.

On Earth: Agni: p. 35;

In the Air-region: Ṛbhus: p. 37; Vâta: p. 38; Rudra: p. 38; Maruts: p. 39; Parjanya: p. 40; Indra: p. 40.

In the Bright Heaven: Açvins: p. 49; Uṣas: p. 52; Sûrya: p. 54; Pûṣan: p. 55; Viṣṇu: p. 56; Savitar: p. 56.

The Âdityas: p. 58; Varuṇa: pp. 61–69.

Belief in Immortality: p. 69.

Soma: p. 72; Bṛhaspati: p. 73; All Gods: p. 74.

SECULAR POETRY: p. 74.

Wedding Hymn: p. 74; Funeral Hymn: p. 76; Historical Compositions: p. 78; Humorous: p. 81; Didactic-gnomic: p. 84; Incantation and Exorcism: p. 85; Poetical Riddles: p. 86; Philosophical: p. 87.

NOTES: p. 92.

Index of Matters, Names, and Words: p. 181; of Bible Passages: p. 197.

INTRODUCTION.

It is well known with what enthusiasm Voltaire, in his writings, especially in the *Essai sur les mœurs et l'esprit des nations*, repeatedly praised the ancient wisdom of the Brâhmans which he thought to have discovered in the *Ezour-Veidam*, brought to his notice from India about the middle of the last century.[1] But even Voltaire's eloquence persuaded but few of his contemporaries of the authenticity of the book. Although scholars were not in a position to disprove its genuineness,[2] they preserved a suspicious and skeptical attitude toward it. Soon after Voltaire's death, J. G. Herder, in the tenth book of his *Ideen zur Geschichte der Menschheit*, unhesitatingly expressed his opinion that whatever knowledge Europeans had hitherto gained of the mysteries of the Indians, was plainly only modern tradition; "for the real Weda of the Indians," he adds, "as well as for the real Sanskrit language, we shall probably have long to wait."[3] Although, happily, Herder's prophecy as to the language itself was not fulfilled,[4] yet in fact a number of decades passed before more trustworthy and detailed information was gained of these oldest literary memorials of the Indians. Colebrooke's celebrated Essays *On the Vedas*[5] did indeed (in 1805) give a valuable survey of the whole territory of Vedic literature, with some scattered quotations from various Vedic books; but it was not possible for Colebrooke to examine all the extraordinarily extensive works which are embraced in India under the name *Veda*, to distinguish properly the individual writings, or to determine their mutual relations.

About twenty years later a German, Friedrich Rosen, recognized in the rich collection of Vedic manuscripts which had come to London, in great part through the efforts of Colebrooke, the true worth of this literature, and the need of making it accessible to European scholarship. He undertook with zeal the editing of the oldest portion, the Rigveda, but died in 1837, before the first eighth was published.[6]

The first enduring impulse was given by the small but epoch-making *Zur Litteratur und Geschichte des Weda, Drei Abhandlungen* von Rudolph Roth, Stuttgart, 1846.[7] It inaugurated a movement which since then has irresistibly led all Sanskritists to the study of the Veda. As early as 1852, aided by the recent purchase of a rich collection of Sanskrit manuscripts by the Royal Library of Berlin, A. Weber was enabled to give, in his *Academische Vorlesungen über indische Literaturgeschichte*, a very detailed and valuable survey of the Vedic books, which was afterwards supplemented in many points, especially for the later periods, by Max Müller's *History of Ancient Sanskrit Literature*, London, 1859. During the last twenty years, through the efforts of Benfey, Weber, Roth and Whitney, and Aufrecht, the most important texts, since followed by many more, have been accessible in printed form; and this investigation opens to the historical sciences, in the broadest sense of the word, sources of unexpected wealth.

VEDIC LITERATURE AND EXEGESIS.

Veda is primarily 'knowledge' in general, and among the Indians designates knowledge κατ' ἐξοχήν — the sacred knowledge, — the sacred writings, of which a brief survey follows.

The oldest division, the **Mantra** (saying, song), is distributed in four Sanhitâs (collections), — the Rig-, Sâma-, Yajur-, and Atharva-Sanhitâs. The oldest and most valuable portion of these collections, the foundation of the whole Vedic literature, is composed of songs, in which, in primeval times, at the first stage of their history as an independent nationality, still at the threshold of the land which they afterward filled with their culture, — more than 1000 years before the expedition of Alexander the Great in the same regions, centuries before the production of the Indian Pantheism or of the gods Brahma, Viṣṇu, Çiva, — in which that people in childlike simplicity praised and entreated their gods, with which they accompanied their sacrifices and strove to propitiate the revered ruler of their destiny, to gain for themselves and their flocks prosperity and secure habitations. From the whole treasury of song which, as its best possession, the Indian race had brought with it from earlier homes to the land of the Ganges, learned men and teachers in later centuries made a selection of the hymns, which had already become partially unintelligible ; these they divided, arranged, and used in their schools (*caraṇa*). Such a selection (*çâkhâ*, recension), has been preserved to us, viz.:

The Rigveda; the knowledge of the hymns, which will be considered more at length below.[8] It was made with the intention of protecting this heritage of ancestral times from further corruption, and from destruction ; and is therefore, to an extent, a scientific, historical collection, while the two following sanhitâs had their origin in practical, liturgical uses.

The Sâmaveda, the knowledge of the songs, contains about 1800 separate verses, for the greater part taken from the hymns of the Rig, but here torn out of their original relation and put together almost without any internal connection. Remodeled with certain musical modifications, they are called *sâman*, songs, in which form they were recited at the Soma sacrifice * by a special priest-class, whose song-book therefore this Veda is. By the musical modification of single verses, the whole number of Sâman could naturally be greatly increased.[9]

* This is the favorite sacrifice of the Vedic period, at which the sap of the Soma plant, mixed with milk or barley, was offered; of which more below.

The Yajurveda contains the knowledge of the prayers. When in time the sacrifice became no longer a simple act of divine worship and offering, left to the free-will and impulse of the individual, but when more and more in every detail an established ritual was set up, the exact observance of which fell to various priest-classes, not only the verses to be recited during the ceremony, but also a quantity of formulas and phrases of explanation, of excuse, blessing, etc., for practical use, began to be put together. Such words, formulas, and passages, partly in connected, partly in unconnected form, among them, too, not a few verses from the Rig, were called yajus; and the books containing the yajus for the whole sacrificial ceremony, Yajurveda. We hear of a considerable number of such prayer-books; two of them, related in contents, but differing in arrangement, have already been edited; a third, in all probability the oldest of the existing ones, has been disclosed only within the last few years.[10] The composition of all these books belongs to a period when the priest-class had already gained a decided ascendency over the other classes.

It was only at a time considerably later than these collections (*trayî vidyâ*, threefold knowledge), that a fourth attained to canonical recognition, the Atharva- or Brahma veda, knowledge of incantations. This probably contained originally the poetry more properly belonging to the people and current among them, which only secondarily was admitted into the circle of the priests, and distributed among their productions.[11] As a historical collection of songs it has most similarity to the Rigveda, though the spirit of the two collections is quite different. 'The Rig is permeated by a lively sympathy and love of nature; in the Atharvan rule only shrinking dread of its evil spirits and their magic powers.' The word bráhman (whence Brahmaveda), here means no longer, as in the Rig, 'devotion, prayer,' but 'charm, spell, enchantment (carmen, incantamen, devotio).' By the use of such a formula the skilled priest is enabled to attain everything, and to force even the gods to the fulfillment of his will. Side by side with later passages are found here many formulas, whose perfect agreement with Old-Germanic spells reveals their origin from the ancient Indo-Germanic period.[12] Of this Veda too a new recension has lately become known, and with it a considerable quantity of new Vedic texts.[13]

The second grand division of Vedic literature is formed by the **Brâhmaṇa,** *i.e.*, writings relating to brâhman, to prayer and sacrificial ceremony.[14] These clearly belong to a much later period, when the old hymns were regarded as ancient and sacred revelation, acquaintance with which was confined to a small number of wise priestly teachers, among whom, however, even at this period, its interpretation was a matter of strife, because the language had meantime become a different one. The Brâhmaṇas, all of them marvelous products of priestly knowledge and perverted imagination, are throughout in prose, and for the greater part, like the Sanhitâs, furnished with accents. They develop the theories of celebrated teachers concerning the sense of the old hymns, their relation to the sacrifices, the symbolic meaning of the latter, etc. Dogma, mythology, legend, philosophy, exegesis, etymology, are here interwoven in reckless confusion. Since these works furnish the oldest prescriptions for the ritual and explanation of the language, as well as the oldest traditions and philosophical speculations, they are not without value for the history of language and civilization; but the gold is largely hidden under a mass of dross.

The Brâhmaṇas themselves, of which a considerable number are preserved,[14a] are in later times looked upon as inspired, and united with the hymns as *çruti*, revelation, excepting only the youngest portions, the Âraṇyakas, writings for the wood-dwellers (*ὑλόβιοι*),[15] and the Upanișads, instructions. Both classes of works show a method of thought totally different from that of the old Vedic books; and with their speculations on cosmogony and eschatology lead into the midst of the system of the Vedânta ('aim or end of Veda').[16]

The third and youngest stage of Vedic literature is the **Vedânga** ('members of the Veda'), also called **Sûtra.** The more Vedic study gained in extent, the more difficult it became to master it. 'The mass of material became too large; the fullness of description in details had to yield to a short survey of the sum of these details, in which the greatest brevity was necessary.' Therefore the most concise rules were invented with a conventional system for the designation of termini technici, expressed in algebraic formula. These rules, as well as the books embracing them in almost unbroken succession, are called Sûtra (thread, guide, rule); they do not confine themselves to one school or recension, and, especially in later times, attain the last imaginable degree of brevity. How far this principle was pushed may be seen from the saying of the Indian scholars, that "an author should rejoice as much over the saving of half a long vowel as over the birth of a son"; in which it must be remembered that without a son to perform the death rites, a Brâhman was not thought capable of gaining heaven.[17] We must confine ourselves to mentioning the six Vedânga- or Sûtra-groups in the traditional order, and to pointing out briefly their signification. They are:

1. Çikṣâ: pronunciation.
2. Chandas: metre.
3. Vyâkaraṇa, (lit. 'analysis'): grammar.
4. Nirukta (word-explanation): etymology.
5. Kalpa: ritual.
6. Jyotiṣa: astronomy.

The first four are chiefly occupied with the reading and understanding of the sacred texts; the last two principally with the sacrifice and its seasons.[18]

As from the study of Homer the Greek grammar rose, so from the study of the Veda grew the Indian; but the investigations of the Indians, favored by the constitution of their language, were incomparably deeper and more lasting than those of the Greek grammarians. Prominent among the grammatical writings are the Nirukta, a collection of strange or obscure words (γλῶσσαι) of the Veda, together with the interpretation of the Vedic investigator Yâska (about 500 B.C.),[19] and the Prâtiçâkhyas, each of which contains, for the various recensions of a single Veda, the most precise statements of phonetic changes, pronunciation, accentuation, metre, etc.[20] In connection, they display a number of delicate observations in phonetics, such as only the science of our own day has begun to institute and turn to account.* The above named works therefore do not treat of grammatical forms; of older works on this subject little has been left us, clearly because a later work, in its comprehensive and practical presentation surpassed all earlier ones and made them superfluous; namely, the grammar of Pâṇini, who probably lived in the third century B.C.[21] "In them is presented the scientific treatment of a single tongue in a perfection which arouses the wonder and admiration of all those who are more thoroughly acquainted with it; which even now stands, not only unsurpassed, but not even attained, and which in many respects may be looked upon as the model for similar work. In this presentation of the Sanskrit the method of the Indian grammarians was displayed; and it found so much the more speedy acceptance, since it is nearly allied to the tendency which since the beginning of this century has made itself felt with ever increasing power in other sciences. This is the method applied to the natural sciences; the method which seeks to gain knowledge of a subject from itself, by analysis into its elements. It views language as a natural phenomenon, the character of which it strives to determine by analysis into

* I believe I shall not be contradicted by Helmholtz, or Ellis, or other representatives of phonetic science, if I say that, to the present day, the phoneticians of India of the fifth century B.C. are unsurpassed in their analysis of the elements of language.—*Max Müller*, OGR. 150.

its component parts and investigation of their functions; by this method and its wonderful results the linguistic labors of the Indians have pre-eminently, — indeed, almost alone, — made it possible for modern philology to take up its problem and work it out to its end with the success which is universally conceded to it." — (*Benfey.*)[22]

The treatises on Ritual, the Kalpasûtras, specially called Sûtra,[23] are either:

1. Çrautasûtra (pertaining to *çruti*, revelation); *i.e.*, they contain the prescriptions for the solemn ceremonies to be performed with the assistance of the priests and with exact observance of the ritual[23 a]; or

2. Smârtasûtra (pertaining to *smṛti*, tradition); *i.e.*, they teach the observances prescribed by tradition, and are divided into *a*) Gṛhyasûtra, giving the models for acts of domestic piety which must accompany the individual and his family in all special circumstances of life from the cradle to the grave; these books, though made later, preserve many ancient characteristics;[24] and into *b*) Dhârmasûtra, which fix the rules of daily life in act and attitude toward others;[25] from these last arose later the metrical law-books (Dharmaçâstra) of Manu, Yâjnavalkya, and others.[25 a]

There are, finally, a number of additions (Pariçiṣṭa, *i.e.*, *παραλιπόμενα*), among which I mention the Purâṇas ('old tales'), which in their present form date at the earliest from the eighth century A.D., only because, up to the fourth decade of the present century, — (with some "historians" even later!) — they ranked with the Upaniṣads as the most important source of 'Indian' and 'Vedic' religious conceptions.[26]

Upon the whole of this rich literature, which in extent at least equals all the preserved monuments of the Greek literature, essentially rest the commentaries of Mâdhava and Sâyaṇa, still preserved and highly regarded in India, which however were only composed in the fourteenth century A.D. About 1350, in the middle of the

Dekkhan, in the Karnâta territory, a man of humble, non-Aryan descent succeeded in throwing off the Mohammedan yoke and in setting up in those regions once more and for the last time a magnificent Indian nation, by founding the dynasty of Vijayanagara (city of Victory). At the court of the third king of this dynasty, Bukka, the prime minister, Mâdhava, and his brother Sâyaṇa instituted an intense and widespread scientific activity, to which we owe, among many other works, these Vedic commentaries or paraphrases.[27]

What then is more natural than, at the time when the Veda was beginning to be understood, when a wholly new world was here unfolding to view, the understanding of which however presented at the outset the very greatest difficulties, — what more natural than that aid should eagerly be sought, which might serve for the interpretation of this unknown material! It was a matter of rejoicing that works were at once found explaining or paraphrasing every word of the foundation text; and as they appeal at every step to old authorities, it was believed that in them lay not *a* tradition or traditional explanation, but *the* tradition, — the true interpretation from ancient times. The problem of Vedic investigation was considered to be the search for and discovery of that interpretation which was current in India a few centuries ago, *i.e.*, the interpretation presented in the Commentaries.[28] On the other hand, Roth insisted from the beginning that these commentaries could by no means be taken as the chief guides, for we have to seek not the sense which these books attribute to the hymns, but that which the composers themselves intended; that these works might indeed be excellent guides to the understanding of the theological books and the ritual, but altogether insufficient in the far older and entirely different territory of the hymns; that concerning the latter there was nowhere a trace of views handed down by tradition, *i.e.*, of continuity in the interpretation, but only a tradition among investigators. But that any other tradition was not imaginable; for it only began to be asked how one point or another in the old hymns was to be interpreted, when they were no longer, or at least no longer clearly, understood;* that we have in the so-called tradition only attempts at a solution, not the solution itself; that in discovering the latter, European scholars would succeed much better than Indian theologians, having the advantage in freedom of judgment, as well as in a larger range of view and historical faculty. However, Roth expressed himself thus only on occasion,[29] but boldly and independently began to build anew. By the aid of grammatical and etymological comparison, by confronting all passages related in sense and form, he endeavored, keeping in view the tradition, to evolve the meaning of single words, and so created a broad and firm foundation for Vedic exegesis;[30] while others, partly in more negative manner proved the impracticability of the native interpretation, partly went forward on the road newly pointed out.[31] The correctness of the method is to-day no longer challenged by any non-Indian scholar;[32] even in India itself within a few years the publication of an edition of the Rigveda has been undertaken which more and more makes independent use of the results and methods of European scholarship.[33] But no one disputes that we have not yet by far reached the foundation; and none better know this than those who are zealously striving, on the path pointed out and with continual observance of the native tradition, to further, by minute investigation of particulars, the understanding of these ancient hymns. All these corrections will in no measure detract from the services of the founder of Vedic exegesis. 'That Roth has cut his way through the fog of Indian misinterpreta-

* The degree to which the understanding of these texts had been lost may be illustrated by a literary strife between Yâska and another Vedic scholar, Kautsa. The latter insisted that explanation of the words was useless, since the hymns had no meaning at all; to which Yâska responded, that it was not the fault of the rafter that the blind man did not see it; that was the fault of the blind man.

tion straight to the kernel of the Veda, that he has seized with sure historical sense the spirit of Indian antiquity, that he has taught us to recognize the power and freshness of expression, of which the Indians knew little more,—this is one of the most brilliant achievements of modern philology.'—(*Delbrück.*)[34]

THE VEDIC PEOPLE AND ITS CIVILIZATION.

After this general literary and historical introduction, we must preface our special subject, the examination of the Rigveda, with some account of the people among whom the book arose, of its life and occupation, its manner of action and thought. In this we may throughout rely on Zimmer's excellent work, *Altindisches Leben*, Berlin, 1879, which presents a masterly picture of the culture of the Vedic Aryans, drawn from all the Sanhitâs.[35]

To comparative philology we owe the indisputable proof of the fact that the ancestors of Indians and Iranians and Greeks, of Slavs and Lithuanians and Germans, of Italians and Celts, in far distant ages spoke one language, and as a single people held dwelling-places in common, wherever that home may have been situated;[36] and further, that for a considerable period after their separation from their brothers living further to the west, the Indians and Iranians lived together, and distinguished themselves from other tribes by the common name of Aryan.[37] After their separation from the Iranians, the Eastern Aryans, the later Indians, wandered from the west into the land afterward called *India*, descending from the heights of Iran, probably over the western passes of the Hindukush. As to their place of abode at the time of composition of most of the hymns of the Rig—about 2000–1500 B. C.[38]—the names of rivers mentioned in the hymns give definite information. According to these, the chief settlement of the Vedic people was then in the territory of the Sindhu (to-day *Indus*, *Sindh*), the banks of the mighty stream itself being probably most thickly populated, the river, after receiving all its tributaries, reaching so great a width that boats midway between its shores are invisible from either. The singers in inspired strains sing its greatness: "With nourishing waves it rushed forth, a firm stronghold and brazen fortress for us; like a fighter in his chariot, the stream flows on, overtaking all others. It alone among the rivers flows with pure water from the mountains to the sea; with regard for riches, for many men, it brings fatness and a refreshing draught to the dwellers on the shore."

Simple tribes, like the Gandhâri (Γανδάριοι) still remained in the valley of the Kubhâ (*Kabul*) and the Suvâstu (*Swat*), a northern tributary; to the south the settlements had been pushed beyond the mouths of the Krumu (*Kurum*) and Gomatî (*Gomal*), but not far beyond the union of the Sindhu with the *Pancanada*,* though they knew of the Sindhu's emptying into the ocean. In the north, the western and middle Himâlaya formed an impassable wall; to the east the Çutudrî (*Satlaj*) must for a long time have formed the boundary, across which from time to time they moved forward to the Yamunâ (*Jumna*) and Gangâ (*Ganges*), enticed by the beauty of the land and pressed on by advancing tribes behind.[39]

In East Kabulistan and the Panjab, therefore, where the condition of climate and soil was about the same as now,[40] the Aryan colonists lived in their houses; for they had already changed the movable tent of the shepherd and nomad for a more fixed shelter. "Columns were set up on firm ground, with supporting beams leaning obliquely against them, and connected by rafters on which long bamboo rods were laid, forming the high roof. Between the corner-posts other beams were set up, according to the size of the house. The crevices in the walls were filled in with straw or reeds, tied in bundles, and the whole

* Pancanada, the five rivers, signified primarily the union of the five rivers, Vitastâ, Asiknî, Paruṣṇî or Irâvatî, Vipâç, and Çutudri; then the whole region, as to-day, the *Panjab*. See Note 39.

was to some extent covered with the same material. The various parts were fastened together with bars, pegs, ropes and thongs." The house could be shut in by a door, which, as in the Homeric houses, was fastened with a strap.[41] A number of such dwellings form the village; fenced and enclosed settlements give protection against wild animals; against the attacks of enemies and against inundations large tracts were arranged on higher ground, protected by earthworks and ditches. But of cities, *i.e.*, of collections of adjoining houses, surrounded by wall and moat, there is no mention.[42]

The principal means of sustenance was cattle-keeping. Repeatedly in the hymns we meet with the prayer for whole herds of cows and horses, sheep and goats, heifers and buffaloes, but especially of milch-cows, which are to more than one singer the sum of 'all good which Indra has created for our enjoyment.' By divine power the red cow yields the white milk, from which is prepared mead and butter, 'the favorite food of gods and men,' and perhaps also cheese.[43] After the cattle, the most important interest is the cultivation of the soil. The ground is worked with plough and harrow, mattock and hoe, and when necessary watered by means of artificial canals. Twice in the year the products of the field, especially barley, ripen; the grain is threshed on the floor, the corn, separated from husk and chaff by the winnowing, is ground in the mill and made into bread. Men still engage in hunting game with bow and arrow, snares and traps, but this occupation has no importance as a means of livelihood, and fishing still less.[44] The chief food consists, together with bread, of various preparations of milk, cakes of flour and butter, many sorts of vegetables and fruits; meat, cooked on the spit or in pots, is little used, and was probably eaten only at the great feasts and family gatherings. Drinking plays throughout a much more prominent part than eating. "The waters are indeed pre-eminently praised; in them lie all healing properties, and they secure to the body health, protection and long-continued sight of the sun; — but it no more occurred to the Vedic people to quench their thirst with water than to the ancient Germans. They bathed in it, and the cattle drank it; man had other beverages," — surâ, a brandy made from corn or barley, and above all, the sorrow-dispelling Soma, which, on account of its inspiring power, was raised to the position of a god, and will therefore be considered below.[45]

Among occupations that of the wood-worker is most frequently mentioned; he is still carpenter, wheelwright and joiner in one, and is skilled not only in building war-chariots and wagons with all their parts, but also in more delicate carved work, such as artistic cups, etc. The tanner prepares leather from the hide of the slaughtered cattle, and uses it for water-bottles, bow-strings, slings and other articles. Metal-workers, smiths and potters ply their craft for the purposes of common life. Navigation, being confined to the streams of the Panjab, could not be very important, and trade exists only as barter, the foundation of which, as well as the money unit, is the cow, in reference to which all things are valued. But the transition to the use of coined money was being prepared by the various golden ornaments and jewelry; active tradesmen and usurers come to view; while the occurrence of the Babylonian mina as an accepted gold standard proves, in connection with other facts, a very early intercourse between India and the western Semitic colonies.

The women understood the plaiting of mats, weaving and sewing; they manufactured the wool of the sheep into clothing for men and covering for animals, and were especially occupied with their many ornaments and decorations.[46]

The foundation of the state was formed by the Family, at the head of which stood the father as lord of the house. The foundation of a family proceeded from the man. At festal gatherings and similar occasions there were often opportunities for forming acquaintance between youth and maiden, and even then careful mothers did not neglect, at such times, to come to their daughters' assistance with advice and action. If such an acquaintance proved lasting, permission for the marriage had to be sought from the father or, after his death, from the eldest brother. This office was assumed by a friend of the suitor, who is always the oldest unmarried son of a family, for it was a settled custom for the children of a family to marry in order of age. If the suitor was acceptable, he had to purchase his bride by rich gifts to his future father-in-law. Thereupon the marriage was celebrated in traditional form in the presence of both families and their friends in the house of the bride's parents. Further on we shall have opportunity for a fuller description of the ceremony. That a marriage portion was given with the young wife is not distinctly stated but is yet indicated, as also that a rich inheritance helped many a girl to gain a husband, who otherwise would have remained in her father's house. In the new home the young wife is subject to her husband, but at the same time mistress of the farm-laborers and slaves, and of parents- and brothers-in-law. The Vedic singers know no more tender relation than that between the husband and his willing, loving wife, who is praised as "his home, the darling abode and bliss in his house." The high position of the wife is above all shown by the fact that she participates in the sacrifice with her husband; with harmonious mind at the early dawn both, in fitting words, send up their prayers to the Eternals.[47] These relations are comprehensible only if monogamy was the rule; and to this the texts point directly. Though there were instances of polygamy, especially among kings and nobles, yet the ordinary condition was "a united pair, with one heart and one mind, free from discord." Marriage was looked upon as an arrangement founded by the gods, the aim of which was the mutual support of man and wife and the propagation of their race; therefore it is the often-repeated wish of the Vedic singer to beget a son of his own flesh, whose place could never be filled by adoption; while the birth of a daughter is nowhere distinctly desired, but is even plainly asked to be averted.[48] That exposure of new-born children[49] and of old people enfeebled by age[50] occurs offends our feelings no more than the well-known custom of burning the widows, for thousands of years demanded by the Brâhmans. The latter, it is true, is nowhere evidenced in the Rigveda; only by palpable falsification of a hymn, which will be examined later, has the existence of the custom been forcibly put into the texts, which, on the contrary, prove directly the opposite, — the return of the widow from her husband's corpse into a happy life, and her re-marriage. Yet from other indications we have to accept the probability that the custom, which in the oldest times was wide-spread, of causing the widow to follow her husband to death, was also observed now and then in the Vedic period.[51] Such features might easily modify our general verdict regarding the stage of morality and culture of the Vedic Aryans; but we must not forget that "people in a condition of nature are not sentimental, as to-day peasants are not; and that the death of a relative, or the thought of their own, leaves them indifferent."[52] When, in addition to what has been said above of the tender relation between husband and wife, we learn that violence to defenceless maidens and unfaithfulness on the part of a married woman belong to the heaviest offences, we must infer that true womanliness and morality generally prevailed. It is a matter of course that the picture had its shadows. Even at that time the woman was charged with fickleness, light-mindedness, and lack of judgment; mention is here and there made of the sons of unmarried women; fallen ones tried to free themselves from the consequences of their misdeeds in criminal manner, and even prostitutes were not wanting.[53]

On the foundation of the family rests the State, the organization of which in the Vedic period is very near that of the primitive times. For protection against threatened attacks and for the purpose of marauding incursions into the territory of other peoples, coalitions were formed between tribes; but having returned home after a victory, in times of peace the individual people or tribe formed the highest political unit, which was divided into districts, which in turn were composed of single clans or hamlets. The latter were originally, as the expressions in the texts make evident, each a single kindred, a number of families more nearly connected among themselves. This tribe division was applied not only in time of peace but also, as among the Afghans to-day, in battle; warriors of the same families, localities, districts, and tribes fought side by side, in the manner which Tacitus describes as characteristic of the Germans, and as Nestor advises Agamemnon to make his arrangement.[54]

The government of the Aryan states thus organized was naturally, in consequence of their origin in the family, a monarchical, at the head of which the king stands as leader, his dignity being in many instances hereditary. In other cases, he was elected by all the districts in assemblies of the tribe, or in times of peace several members of the royal family exercised the power in common. At all events the kingship was nowhere absolute, but everywhere limited by the will of the people, which made its power felt in assemblies of the nation, the district, and the tribe. In peace the king was "judge and protector" of his people, who owed him lasting obedience but no settled tribute; only voluntary gifts were brought to him. In war he held the chief command and it was his duty, at serious junctures, *e.g.*, before a battle, to prepare a sacrifice for the tribe, either performing it himself or causing a priestly singer to perform it.[55] In this custom of the kings to be represented by a priestly substitute, is to be recognized the beginning of the historically unique Indian hierarchy and the origin of the castes, the existence of which in the oldest Vedic times, in spite of all assertions to the contrary, must be denied.[56]

That developed ideas of Law were present in the oldest period is taught by the common legal terms existing in the various languages of our family. The Vedic texts present a further list of such terms, and the hymns strongly prove how deeply the prominent minds in the people were persuaded that the eternal ordinances of the rulers of the world were as inviolable in mental and moral matters as in the realm of nature, and that every wrong act, even the unconscious, was punished and the sin expiated. But the same hymns also show that the relations of the various members of the community among themselves were not always the best. Deceitful men strove to injure in every way, by slander, lying, and fraud; thieves plied their vocation under the concealing shadow of night; daring swindlers, highwaymen, and robbers terrorized the peaceable and embittered the life of the upright. In cases of doubt as to guilt or the guilty one, recourse was had to oath, on more serious occasions to the decision of the gods in various forms; unworthy men were expelled from the clan and became fugitives.[57] But there are also more pleasing features. Praise is given to those who from their abundance willingly dispense to the needy, to those who do not turn away from the hungry, but who by deeds of kindness to the poor increase their own possessions, and who in change of fortune never swerve from their faithfulness to old friends.[58]

When business is despatched in the assembly, the shrewd men gather together; "they sift their words like corn in a sieve and remember their friendship." Others engage in sport and joking over their drinking, and pour forth irony and boasts or indulge in play with dice, which was passionately loved, and at which many a man gambled away his possessions, and finally even his own person. "Of no effect is the father's punishment of the dissolute son; the player is unmoved by the destruction of his home; he remains indifferent though his wife become the property of others; he rises early and indulges in the passion of play till evening; defeat in play is equivalent to starvation and thirst." [59] Wives and maidens attire themselves in gay robes and set forth to the joyful feast; youths and girls hasten to the meadow when forest and field are clothed in fresh verdure, to take part in the dance. Cymbals sound, and seizing each other lads and damsels whirl about until the ground vibrates and clouds of dust envelop the gaily moving throng.[60]

A more earnest trait appears in the favorite contests in the chariot race,[61] for it is the peaceful preparation for the decisive struggle on the battle-field, for the joyous war in which they delighted, and which plays so large a part in the songs as well as the life of the people. In the battle Indra seeks his friend, battle and struggle give the hero experience and renown, when with his fellow-warriors he helps to conquer new homes or to protect those already won, whether against other Aryans or the hosts of aborigines (*dasyu*), from whom the colonists were sharply separated by different color, different customs, and above all, by different religion.[62] When an enemy approaches the Aryan boundaries, earthworks are thrown up, a barricade of timbers erected, impassable bulwarks of bronze made, and sacrifices offered to the gods to secure their help. Then the army advances with loud battle-songs, with the sound of drums and trumpets, with waving banners, against the opposing force. The warrior stands at the left of the chariot, and beside him the charioteer, and the foot-soldiers fight in close lines, village beside village, tribe beside tribe (cf. page 17). The warrior is protected by brazen coat of mail and helmet; with the bow he hurls against the enemy feathered arrows with poisoned tips of horn or metal, or presses on with spear and axe, lance and sling. And when the enemy is conquered, loud rejoicing resounds with the beat of drums, like the noise of the rising storm; the sacred fire is kindled to offer to the gods a song and sacrifice of thanksgiving, and then to divide the spoil.[63]

In arts and sciences the race still stood on the lowest stage. The art of writing it did not possess (and even for a long time afterward),[64] and little was known of the ideas of number or of measure.[65] The theories of cosmogony are altogether childish.[66] Among the countless stars certain ones had already been observed and named, before all, the Bear, followed by Sirius and the five planets.[67] The lunar year of 354 days was in various ways brought into harmony with the solar year; either the twelve extra days were added yearly (cf. below, p. 37 *), or they were allowed to accumulate, and a thirteenth month from time to time was added to the twelve.[68] — Their medical art distinguished quite a number of diseases, but almost the sole curatives and preventives known were charms and the use of amulets and healing herbs, whose power was brought forth and made effectual only by the sacred formula.[69] Deeper natures indeed only hoped to be freed from their ills by repentance and reformation; for sickness was to them "divinely sent chains" with which Varuna, the world's ruler, bound those who transgressed his eternal laws.[70]

Only one art had long been in full bloom, that of poetry; of this we have the most convincing evidence in that collection of songs, to the more detailed examination of which we now proceed.

THE RIGVEDA.

THE COLLECTION.—FORM AND CONTENTS OF THE HYMNS.

THE recension which has come down to us, the received text of the Çâkala school (Çâkalaçâkha), contains in ten books (Maṇḍala)[71] 1017 (or 1028) hymns,[72] the extent of which about equals that of the Homeric poems. As a rule, the oldest hymns are contained in Books 2–7; these show only portions, each assigned by tradition to a single family,[73] in which they were long preserved as a family inheritance. These are in order the hymns of Gṛtsamada, Viçvâmitra, Vâmadeva, Atri, Bharadvâja, Vasiṣṭha and their descendants. The internal arrangement of these Maṇḍalas bears distinct traces of the work of a single school; the hymns in each are arranged in groups according to the gods addressed; and these groups always follow the same order,—first the hymns to Agni, then those to Indra, etc. Inside the groups the position of the hymns is determined by the number of verses in diminishing order; where this principle seems violated, the hymns are either to be separated into shorter ones or they found a place in the collection only at a later date.[74] The eighth book contains chiefly hymns of the Kaṇva gens, but shows no prevailing principle in their arrangement. Book 9 seems to betray a different origin, all its hymns being addressed to one divinity, the inspiring Soma, honored as a god, and being arranged with reference to the metres. The youngest portion is Books 1 and 10, which, with beautiful examples of Vedic lyrical poetry, also show productions of the latest period of Vedic time, and even of the time of compilation. The fourteen groups of the first book, each hymns of one family, show the same principle in their arrangement as the family books; the tenth shows smaller collections (*e.g.*, liturgical); the whole Maṇḍala gives the impression of a subsequent compilation of religious and secular pieces not collected before.

Since the time at which our collection was closed, about the year 1500 B.C.,[75] the text has been handed down, though for centuries orally,[76] with the most painstaking care, so that since that time, nearly 3000 years ago, it has suffered no changes whatever; — with a care such that the history of other literatures has nothing similar to compare with it. The Indians were not satisfied with one form of the text, but made several;[77] grammatical treatises were written upon the mutual relations of the various forms[78] and other like precautions taken. But it is true that at the period of compilation much had become unintelligible; a method of exposition had gained currency which to a certain extent replaced the text, and it is probable that only few hymns then preserved exactly the same form in which they were composed. For example, it is easy to show that in many hymns the order of the verses is changed and that in others verses not belonging to the hymn have been interpolated. Many such erratic portions were collected by the scholiasts in places where from the occurrence of the same or similar words they inferred a similar sense (cf. p. 10*); others show themselves to be modern, and in part very senseless, variations of old hymns or additions made by the priests for the support of their doctrine.[79]

Little need be said of the **external form of the hymns**; this language is an exceedingly ancient popular dialect,[80] which differs, in all grammatical points (accentuation, phonetics, word-formation, declension, conjugation, syntax) and in its vocabulary, from the later artificial Indian language, the Sanskrit * of the law-books, epics, dramas, etc.,

* Sanskrit is the *artificial, adorned speech* of the three higher castes and the learned literary language in distinction to the *popular dialect, Prâkrit.*

in a much greater degree than, *e.g.*, the language of Homer from the Attic. Here the wonderful imagery of the language shines out in transparent clearness and exuberance of sparkling brilliancy; its forms of expression are poured forth as from an inexhaustible spring; we meet everywhere originality, richness of diction, pushing growth and buoyant life, which, not yet fettered as in later Sanskrit by the iron-bound canons of a learned grammar, give us glimpses of the development and history of the language, in the laboratory of that immense intellectual product, through which the languages of our family have become the most cultivated of all tongues.[81] In a certain sense this dialect too is artistic; it is, like the language of Homer, though to a smaller degree, a popular artistic or poetic speech developed in the guilds of singers, and the many conventional turns of expression in it plainly prove that the art of song had long been fostered and practised among the people.[82] Here, as in Homer, we often find fixed epithets, formulaic expressions confined to certain connections, rhetorical adornments, idioms and whole passages which repeatedly re-occur unchanged or with slight variations. Assonance, Homoioteleuta, Parachesis and other rhetorical figures, and especially the most varied play upon words, are of frequent application; the refrain, repeating some principal thought, is used with great freedom.[83]

The syntactical relations are usually clear; in the use of case and mode much more of the original fullness of the language is preserved than in Sanskrit or the classical tongues. But since pure Syntax, the developed structure of periods, was not yet matured, it is sometimes impossible to fix upon one or another translation and explanation of a verse as the sole possible and only correct one, even in passages where every individual word is fully clear.[84]

It is used in the Indian drama only by gods and male members of the first two castes, priests and warriors, while all females (including goddesses), children, and people of lower class speak Prâkrit.

The metrical laws are simple; the stanzas consist throughout of three or more, generally of three or four verses; the latter contain eight, eleven, or twelve syllables, seldom five, more seldom four or more than twelve, and are therefore usually dimeter, trimeter, or trimeter catalectic; the cæsura occurs after the fourth or fifth syllable. The first syllables of the verse are not fixed in regard to quantity (*ancipites*), while the last four are in general strictly measured, iambic in verses of twelve syllables (⏑ – ⏑ ⏓), trochaic in those of eleven (– ⏑ – ⏒); only a few older hymns with verses of eight syllables show a trochaic cadence.[85]

In many hymns two or three stanzas are more closely connected, and thus form a *strophe*; in others a kind of chain-structure is noticeable, in which the beginning of a stanza or strophe takes up the closing thought of the last stanza or strophe. There are, even at this early date, isolated instances of *lyrical dialogue*; of which there are also forms which picture the progress of the action and describe past events, and which therefore correspond in nature to the ballad.[86]

As to the **contents**, it has already been pointed out above (page 3), that the far greater proportion of hymns belongs to the religious lyric; a small number only of secular songs is preserved in the tenth book. The great majority of the hymns are invocations and adoration of the gods respectively addressed; their keynote is a simple outpouring of the heart, a prayer to the eternals, an invitation to them to accept favorably the gift reverently consecrated. Of the later theory of inspiration the hymns recognize nothing. The singer's wish is to give eloquent expression to the sentiments which a god has placed in his soul,— to give vent to the crowding emotions of his heart. "As a skilled workman builds the wagon, like well-adorned and fitted garments he forms his song as best he can according to his knowledge and ability."[87]

Therefore the hymns vary greatly in value; by the side

of the splendid productions of divinely inspired poets we find a large number of unimportant, tiresome, and overburdened compositions. But this does not appear strange, when we remember that the Rigveda furnishes us the works of the most various poets of a whole people, some of whom are separated by a period of at least 1000 years; that individual genius is confined neither to locality nor age, and that these productions at the time of compilation, even then partially unintelligible, were looked upon as ancient, divinely inspired wisdom, and therefore protected against all human criticism. Even the flower of the Vedic lyric suffers from monotony and endless repetition, since almost all the hymns are variations of the same theme; but through them all we feel the fresh breath of a vigorous poetry of Nature. If one will only take the trouble to project himself into the life and thought, the poetry and action of a people and age, which best display the first development of intellectual activity in our own race,* he will find himself attracted by these hymns on many sides, now by their childlike simplicity, now by the freshness or delicacy of their imagery, and again by the boldness of their painting and their scope of fancy. And most certainly these truly unique literary remains, which throw the strongest light on the most varied conditions of life, of classical as well as present peoples, will remain sealed for all who do not take that trouble, — who are used to recognize a common humanity and pure beauty only when clothed in the most modern forms. They will be closed for all who have never experienced the delight of following back to its distant mountain-sources the mighty river of human thought, on whose surface we ourselves are hastening toward the Future, who no longer have any soul for that which has freed the minds of millions of human beings with their noblest hopes, fears, and endeavors; who lack the sense for the History of Humanity.[88]

Turning now to the

* "In so far as we are Aryans in speech, that is, in thought, so far the Rigveda is our own oldest book." — *Max Müller.*

RELIGIOUS POETRY,

we shall not, from what has preceded, expect to find any unified views or defined prevailing conceptions. Each one of the poets so far separated in time follows his own imagination, his individual feeling, his momentary perception, which may conform with those of most of his contemporaries, or may be centuries ahead of them. The whole significance of the Rigveda in reference to the general history of religion, as has repeatedly been pointed out in modern times, rests upon this, that it presents to us the development of religious conceptions from the earliest beginnings to the deepest apprehension of the godhead and its relations to man. "Very differently," says L. Geiger, "from all others of the oldest literatures known to us, which show new forms rising on the ruins of a past sunk in oblivion or produced by the contact and commingling of the spiritual characteristics of various peoples, we have in these hymns the picture of an original, primitive life of mankind, free from foreign influences, not restored in new forms from the destruction of the past, but springing forth new and young from the bosom of Nature, — a spiritual form still unspoiled in word and deed; and that which everywhere else we see only as complete and finished, is here presented in process of formation. Therefore in these hymns lies the key to understanding not only the subsequent development of the Indians, nor alone that of all peoples in part springing from the same root, but also, from the unity of nature recognized in the whole process of development of our race, the key to the productions of all speculative power on earth, or to the whole contents of mind, *i.e.*, its lasting acquisitions, from the period when convictions formed from impressions retained in memory first took shape among men, and manifold opinions, beliefs, or knowledge were at all possible."[89]

THE RELIGIOUS THOUGHT

is here in greater part filled with the productions of sense. A maze of marvellous stories and myths reveals the mighty influence of the ever-changing phenomena of nature upon the son of earth. The forces of nature impress him now as friends, again as enemies, and he views the wonders of the great creation with the unaccustomed eyes of the child. As a German nursery rhyme asks: "Tell me how white milk can come from the red cow,"—so an Indian sage is struck with wonder that the rough red cow gives soft white milk, and this miracle is praised again and again as an evidence of divine power.[90] There is of course no recognition of the laws of nature, and science does not, as now, spring up at every step as an obstacle to imagination. Now we calculate at what moment a certain star will be visible at a certain spot on the earth, and the rising of the sun causes us no astonishment,—we *know* that it happens necessarily. Not so the man of that time; when he sees the sun moving freely through the heavens, so evidently producing all life upon the earth, seen and known by all, and yet to all a mystery from beginning to end, what it is, whence it comes, whither it goes,—then he asks:

> "Unpropped beneath, not fastened firm, how comes it
> That downward turned, he falls not downward?
> The guide of his ascending path,—who saw it?"—**4**. 13. 5.

Full of wonder he begins to conjecture "whither the Pleiades, that show themselves in the night, go by day," and it seems a miracle to him that "the sparkling waters of all rivers flow into one ocean, without ever filling it." *[91] Such expressions of wonder, if we try to place ourselves in sympathy with the childlike mental conditions of that primitive time, we shall not find childish; we shall rather wonder at the happy and graphic expressions with which man is able to clothe his thoughts when beginning

* Cf. Eccles. 1. 7: All the rivers run into the sea; yet the sea is not full.

for the first time to grope about him, to perceive, to observe, and from repeated observations to draw conclusions. In all the phenomena of nature he observes movement and action similar to his own or those of his immediate surroundings; but because he never sees movement or action here behind which a moving or acting person does not stand, he logically refers these occurrences in nature to acting persons, who for him coincide with the phenomena. The bright all-containing heaven is him the "Lightener" (*Dyaus*) or the "Surrounder" (*Varuṇa*); the moon is the "Measurer" (*Mâs*, Gr. μήν, μείς); the sun, the "Illuminator" (*Sûrya*) or the "Enlivener" (*Savitar*) or the "Nourisher" (*Pûṣan*), etc. This silent "wanderer" through space,—this majestic ruler of the firmament,—this friend, departing in the dark West and returning in the shining East, in its daily and yearly courses first showed men an unbroken rule, a strict, unchanging order (*ṛta*).[92] And as the "thinking one" (*mânuṣa*, Mensch, man) looks further about him, he observes that, while his own plans are so often crossed and destroyed, while nothing in his daily life has permanency, throughout the whole realm of Nature order, unchangeable and "inimitable," prevails. "In ever-varying alternation with the day-star, the moon light-giving moves through the night; solitary it wanders through the gathering of many; it waxes and wanes; the breathing being of yesterday dies to-day and returns living to-morrow." "Every day, in unceasing interchange with night and her dark wonders, comes the dawn with her bright ones, to reanimate the worlds, never failing in her place, never in her time,—both ever entering on their paths with renewed youth." "Day and night know their seasons, when the dark sister must give place to the bright; they halt not, nor stand still; unlike in color but of like mind both pursue their endless way," and unchangingly the hot and cold seasons follow each other.[93]

All these occurrences and the forces behind them, these natural phenomena conceived of as personal, are pictured by man as being similar to himself; human in their thinking, feeling, and acting; but, since their order is never disturbed, their will never bent, and their power never broken, infinitely more powerful and exalted and wise; to him they are creatures against whose will no one on earth can contend.[94] As light is to him the symbol of all happiness and blessings, he calls these wise powers, these infallible guardians of the eternal order of the worlds the Shining Ones (*devâs, dîvi*), and he adores them as givers of good,[95] as *gods*. In pressing need there rises in his heart a yearning for a helper; he looks about among his kinsmen and companions for aid, but in vain. "Who will take pity, who will give us refreshment, who will come nigh with help? The counsels counsel, the thoughts in the hearts, the wishes wish, they fly out into the worlds; no other merciful one is found but them: therefore my longing lifts itself to the gods."[96] Anxiously the hopeful ask:

"Who is it knows, and who can tell us surely
Where lies the path that leads to the Eternals?
Their deepest dwellings only we discover,
And hidden these in distant secret regions."—**3**. 54. 5.

That path the experienced singer has seen, "who sees further than others; he, who has learned to mark the Eternals and in the course of nature to perceive their might and wisdom."[97] He says to mortals that not without effort can gods be gained for friends; the idle and negligent are not pleasing to them; they desire Soma-pressers, constant in prayer and zealous in sacrifice; when the tribes meet in conflict over their possessions, they come as allies to those who offer sacrifices; the Mighty Ones have no friendship for such as bring no gifts.[98] And so man gladly offers the sacrificial food and freely pours the Soma for their enjoyment, and the "span" of his pious songs, that perchance the god may heed and accomplish the singer's wish. With the most pleasing hymns he lays hold on the hem of the Exalted's garments, as a son touches the father's;

with loud rejoicing, as the streams rush from the heights, he sends up his devotion to heaven, that the god implored may take it up as the mother clasps the darling son; that he may bind the long rows of songs about him for adornment like the stars in heaven, and rejoice in them as a bridegroom in his bride.[99] Superficial natures, indeed, naïvely think to talk the gods over: "If I possessed as as much as you, O God, I would not give the singer over to poverty, and day by day would give my adorer rich possessions, wherever he might be." "If you were a mortal and I immortal, I would not abandon you to misfortune nor poverty; my singer would not be needy, not in evil case, not lacking his deserts."[100]

Another, oppressed by heavy trouble, turns to the lord of the old home, to whom his father called, — to that god who has so often aided before, the support of the sacrificer and the friend of his ancestors, who rejoices in being implored, and who cares for him like a loving father; for he knows from experience: "If I asked again and again, the ever victorious Indra fulfilled all my prayers."[101]

And if unable to offer an ox or cow, he hopes that even small gifts from the heart, a fagot, a libation, a bundle of grass, offered with reverence, or a specially powerful verse, will be more acceptable to the god than butter or honey.[102] Therefore men honor the gods as frequently as they can; to them, the mighty ones above, they pray at early morning, at midday, and at the setting of the sun, for wealth and happiness, for health and long life, for a hundred autumns without the burdens of old age, which causes the beauty of the form to disappear like mist;[103] for the blessing of offspring and an honorable position among friends and the whole people; for protection against all dangers and adversaries, at home and abroad; for victory and rich booty from every enemy, Aryan and barbarian.[104] "Grant me," cries Gṛtsamada to Indra, —

"Grant me, O God, the highest, best of treasures,
A judging mind, prosperity abiding,
Riches abundant, lasting health of body,
The grace of eloquence, and days propitious."[105]—2. 21. 6.

And others in the people pray to the Highest, to "the gods, bright and clear as a spring, superior to blemish, deceit, and harm," that to their former benefactions they may add the protection which frees even the guilt-laden from his guilt, like the captive from his bonds; "for every one," cries a singer, "returning from his sins, you, wisest gods, make live again."[106] They are besought from guilt incurred or unaccomplished to guide to well-being and to protect from sins great and small. Man hopes that in the presence of these pure ones he shall again see his father and mother, and be united with his ancestors who have gone before.[107]

Beside this purer conception, which regards the gifts of sacrifice as the free-will offerings of a heart filled with thankfulness, though perhaps hoping too for new aid, the calculating spirit, here as elsewhere, shows itself from the very beginning, which regards the god as under obligation for the gifts, and permits the sacrificer to expect, or almost to demand, a gift in return.[108] "I give to thee, — do thou give to me," is the keynote of many hymns; and many a singer declares that only the songs and sacrifices, and above all the Soma, first gave the gods the courage and power for their saving deeds of might. But when once such results were confidently awaited from such gifts, it was only a step to the further conclusion that these deeds of the gods had been made possible *only* by the men's gifts, and that the gods were therefore dependent upon the acts and will of men, especially of those men who were familiar with the ancient songs and the conduct of the sacrifice, — the *priests*. In *their* hands remained the knowledge of the hymns and the ritual connected with them, while the mass of the people had in general far too much to do in waging war against the aborigines to be able to occupy themselves with other matters; all their energy was employed in maintaining their position and conquering new homes. In the strange land, where the customs of home are always invested with a sacred charm, the guardians of the old worship came more and more into the foreground.[109] A creation and at the same time a personification of priestly action is seen in Bṛhaspati or Brahmaṇaspati, *i.e.*, the Lord of Devotion. To him are ascribed by later singers the deeds for which formerly other gods, notably Indra, were celebrated, and in very many old hymns interpolations and additions are plainly recognizable for the purpose of confirming the superiority of the human lords of prayer, the priests, over all the other classes, because only they knew how to present the effectual song and sacrifice, and therefore alone could secure the aid of the gods. Even in the second period of Vedic literature, in the Brâhmaṇa, we read that "there are two kinds of gods, the *devas* and the *brâhmaṇas* (*i.e.*, the priests), who are to be held as gods among men." "The wise Brâhman has the gods in his power," etc.[110] Such a conception is naturally foreign to the old hymns; on the other hand, even then success and a continuance of prosperity seem to have led to a denial of gods who ordered all things with strong hand. "The sun and moon in turn fulfill their course, that man may look and believe in God," but the people living in prosperity does not heed this. "Nowhere, Indra," cries a singer, "canst thou find a rich man for thy friend; men insolent from drinking hate thee; but when thou thunderest loud, thou bringest them together; then as a father thou art called upon." "When he hurls hither and thither his lightning, then they believe on the gleaming god."[111]

THE VEDIC BELIEF.

The individual gods, corresponding to their origin from the personification of natural phenomena, are depicted as supreme in their own spheres, and in the Rigveda a younger race of gods stands plainly in the foreground. The old Father of Heaven, Dyaus (Zeus, Diespiter, Tyr, Zio), the divine parents, Heaven and Earth (Dyâvâpṛthivî), Trita and others have almost entirely disappeared [112] and have been superseded by new forms, the representatives of those phenomena which in their new homes made a specially vivid impression on the minds of the Aryans, or exercised a special influence on their manner of life. Thus in one tribe we find one god pre-eminently reverenced, in another, another. And since there are many phenomena, and hence many gods, we are at first impelled to designate the Vedic religion as polytheism; it is not, however, polytheism in the usual sense, but it presents to us throughout a stage of religious thought which, elsewhere hardly observed, in India developed partly into monotheistic, partly into polytheistic conceptions, and which Max Müller has proposed to designate by the name Henotheism or Kathenotheism;—a belief in single gods, each in turn standing out as the highest. And since the gods are thought of as specially ruling in their own spheres, the singers, in their special concerns and desires, call most of all on that god to whom they ascribe the most power in the matter,—in whose department, if I may say so, their wish comes. This god alone is present to the mind of the suppliant; with him for the time being is associated everything that can be said of a divine being;—he is the highest, the only god, before whom all others disappear, there being in this, however, no offense or depreciation of any other god.[113]

Since that which was told of one god could so easily be spoken of others, it was natural to combine individual related gods, possessing certain qualities or rights in common, into dual divinities. Thus Indra (the conqueror of every enemy) and Agni (the conqueror of darkness and the dark hostile demons), the two lords, "Indra, the hero, and Varuṇa, the king," Indra and Vâyu, Rudra and Soma, and others, are praised and reverenced together. Later on the composers of a large number of hymns sought to win a unified expression for the numerous individual gods by grouping them together under the comprehensive name of *viçve devâs*, i.e., *all gods*. Others distinguish older and newer gods whom they try to systematize, or declare openly that a given god is identical with several others, and show in this an inclination toward a monotheistic conception, which will occupy us later on in the philosophical poetry.[114]

THE GODS.

Passing on to the consideration of the individual gods, I remark that I do not propose to give a complete Vedic mythology, examining all the mythological representations contained in the Veda with respect to their origin, history, chronology and order;[115] but on the other hand, I have been careful to collect all the essential characteristics given in the hymns into a general view of each divinity. In this I have confined myself as closely as possible to the words of the hymns, so that the whole work is, so to speak, made up of the words of the poets themselves. The metrical citations are for the greater part taken from *Siebenzig Hymnen des Rigveda*, übersetzt von Karl Geldner und Adolf Kaegi. Mit Beiträgen von R. Roth, Tübingen 1875, which give the reader a general view of the poetry of the Rigveda.[116]

In the classification of gods I follow a very old division of the universe, contained in the hymns themselves, into the three realms of the Earth, the Air and the bright Heaven.[117] The basis of this threefold division is the separation of air and light. The realm of light is not in the air-region, but beyond it, in the infinite space of the heaven; it is not confined to the shining mass of the sun, but is an independent, eternal force. Between this world of light and the earth lies the region of the air, which is under the control of gods, in order to keep the path of the light to earth unobstructed, to give passage to its enlivening force, and at the same time to allow the heavenly waters, whose home is also in the light region, to fall on the fields of the earth.[118]

The **Earth** was given by the gods to men for a dwelling-place. But aside from the fact that all the gods, in heaven and on earth, everywhere reveal their power in the waters, herbs and trees, and have implanted Will in man's body, they have chosen a representative from their midst to dwell here, among mortals immortal. Like a loving friend they have placed in the dwellings of men **Agni,** the god of fire.[119] Born from the floods of heaven (the clouds), he first came down to earth as lightning, and when he had disappeared and remained hidden, Mâtariçvan, a demi-god, another Prometheus, brought him back again from afar from the gods to men, to the tribe of Bhṛgus.[120] From that time the latter have been able to create him anew for themselves; in a multitude of hymns and innumerable images is sung his production from two sticks rubbed together, — his "parents." He lies concealed in the softer wood, as in a chamber, until, called forth by the rubbing in the early morning hour, he suddenly springs forth in gleaming brightness. The sacrificer takes and lays him on the wood; greedily he stretches out his sharp tongue and melts the wood. When the priests pour melted butter upon him, he leaps up crackling and neighing like a horse, — he whom men love to see increasing like their own prosperity.[121] They wonder at him, when, decking himself with changing colors like a suitor, equally beautiful on all sides, he presents to all sides his front.

> "All-searching is his beam, the gleaming of his light,
> His, the all-beautiful, of beauteous face and glance,
> The changing shimmer like that floats upon the stream,
> So Agni's rays gleam ever bright and never cease." — 1. 143. 3.

Although the first of the gods, he is yet, because every morning kindled anew, the youngest; gleaming with brightness he whirls upward the sacred, light-red smoke; growing from his flames, which never age, from himself, he mounts on high, sweeps the heavenly vault with his flowing locks, and mingles himself with the sunbeams. Then they offer to him prayer and song, the devout sacrificial gift, that he may carry it on his gleaming chariot to the Immortals; or he can bring down the gods, ready to give aid, to the pious worship of men, to the drinking of the Soma at the sacred place of sacrifice; for gods and men have chosen him, who rules over heavenly as well as earthly things, for their messenger, the sacrificial carrier.[122] Once, it is said, he was weary of the service, so that he refused longer to fulfill the office; from Varuṇa, who tries to persuade him, he demands remuneration for his labor:

> "Then give me all the first and last libation,
> And give the juciest sacrificial portion, —
> The cream of water and the herbs' aroma,
> And long, O Gods, shall Agni's life continue." — **10.** 51. 8.

As Varuṇa grants all this, Agni yields and remains thereafter the High Priest of men, who above all knows the sacred institutions and times.[123] If at any time men unknowingly transgress the laws of the knowing (gods), or if in foolishness mortals, weak in discernment, neglect the sacrifice, he, the best sacrificer, makes everything right. And when the light of day, the sun, has departed, Agni is visible through the darkness of night, and by this divine power he proves himself the victorious conqueror of gloom and its evil spirits, the ghosts and goblins, the magicians and witches.[124] So the god becomes a visible savior, a strong fortress for the devout. He drives away the noxious tribes from their dwelling-places; he burns them down like dry bushes, and the Immortal, bringing joy to mortals, finds a home in their midst. He orders their hosts and protects their settlements; from fear of him, whom the gods placed as a light to the Aryans, the black tribes fled; scattering, they abandoned their possessions, and the god breaks their strongholds. He overthrows barbarian and Aryan enemies, and sweeps away their wealth from field and mountain.[125] In him, the lord of riches, lies all wealth, as the rays lie hid in the sun; like a king he protects all treasures, whether they are contained in the mountains, in the plants, in the waters, or among men. From him proceed all gifts of fortune, as branches from the tree, and to him are directed the thoughts of the devout as man's eyes turn to the sun. He may be looked upon as father and relation, dear friend and brother; called upon and reverenced, he brings with bounteous hands rich wealth into the house of the highly-favored singer. Therefore he is a welcome guest to all men, and in every place a beloved family friend.[126]

In the middle realm of the **Air,** various divinities of the wind and storm are supposed to live, as well as the genii of the seasons, the **Ṛbhus.**[127] These three skillful men by their dexterity gained divine honors, a share in the sacrifice and immortality. Since they made the chariot of the Açvins, the daily course of these gods, bringing blessing to man, is their deed; by them too were formed Bṛhaspati's miraculous cow and Indra's obedient team, which harness themselves at his command.[128] They cherished and cared for their parents, long since broken down by age, with miraculous powers, until their youthful vigor returned;[129] and many other wonderful deeds they accomplished on their journey, until they were received as guests in Agohya's * house. Here they spend twelve days in enjoyment; then the course begins anew, and anew the earth brings forth fruit, the streams flow; plants cover the heights, and waters the depths.[130] Impressed by all these things, the gods wish to try their skill and send Agni as messenger to commission the Ṛbhus to fashion, from the one cup of the gods, the masterpiece of the gods' work-

* *Agohya* is the "unconcealable" sun-god, with whom the Ṛbhus rest after their year's course; *i.e.*, the year is at an end; the three seasons and the sun, which has reached its lowest point, apparently rest twelve days, — the twelve intercalary days of the winter solstice; *vid.* above, p. 20 and Note 68.

man Tvaṣṭar, four others like it. They at once accomplish the work and more, so that Tvaṣṭar, overcome by jealousy, hides himself. But the gods rejoice in the work, looking at it with understanding and appreciation; and they search everywhere for the Ṛbhus and lead them to the company of the gods, where they find the reward of their zeal.[131]

Vâta (Vâyu), the wind, first arises in the early morning to drink the Soma and leads in the dawn. Then all the winds follow him like maidens to the feast. His approach is perceived by the waving of the flame; he is recognized hastening along the paths of the air in his swift car, never stopping; but each one asks:

"In what place was he born, and from whence comes he?
The vital breath of gods, the world's great offspring,
The God where'er he will moves at his pleasure:
His rushing sound we hear — what his appearance, no
one."[132] * — 10. 168. 3. 4.

Rudra, the god of the destroying storm,[133] is loudly sung because he, most beautiful of those that were born, strongest of the strong, with the lightning in his hands from his high seat looks out upon the inhabitants of the earth and the heavenly race. Where he sees a wrong, there he casts his mighty spear or sends a swift arrow from his strong bow and strikes the evil-doer.[134] But he is glad to be called upon by the upright, who look for his coming as the child seeks his father's embrace. From them he wards off all affliction and hurt; purifying the air from all harmful miasmas, he furnishes to men and cattle the best nourishment; therefore he is called the very best of physicians.[135]

"Let me through thy best medicines, O Rudra,
My life on earth prolong a hundred winters;

* The same Zeugma is in the text. St. John 3. 8: "The wind bloweth where it listeth, and thou hearest the sound thereof, but canst not tell whence it cometh, and whither it goeth." — *Cf.* Note 132.

From us dispel all hatred and oppression,
On every side calamity drive from us.

Where then, O Rudra, is thy hand of mercy,
The hand that healing brings and softens sorrow,
That takes away the ills even which the gods send?
Let me, O mighty one, feel thy forgiveness.

The hero gladdened me amid the tumult
With greater might when I his aid entreated.
Like some cool shade from the sun's heat protected,
May I attain to Rudra's grace and refuge."—**2**. 33. 2. 7. 6.

Rudra's sons and companions are the richly-adorned, well-armed **Maruts,** the gods of the thunder-storm, "the heavenly singers." [136] Loudly thundering, they are visible far off as the stars of heaven, and deck their forms like a prosperous wooer. On their heads golden helmets gleam, on their shoulders they carry gaily-colored skins and spears, on their breasts golden breast-plates, about their ankles golden bracelets and clasps, in their hands gleaming, fire-darting weapons, and in their strong arms rich wealth for the worshiper.[137] Now they set out with battle-axe and spear, with bow and arrow, as the active and daring allies of Indra; again, they equip themselves for battle alone, rushing forth in golden chariot borne through the air untiringly by golden-hoofed horses or dappled mares. When they approach roaring and throw out their lines to measure the sun's path, when the rivers reverberate with the rumbling of their wheels,—when they raise their song of the storm-clouds and down upon the earth the lightnings smite,—then both men and the mighty, lofty mountains are terrified; the heavenly canopy trembles at their raging, the immovable rocks quake, the earth is moved, and like elephants the heroes destroy the forests; the mountains yield to their coming and the streams to their command. Even in bright daytime they make darkness when they shake down the milk of the clouds,[138] or when they summon the rain-god **Parjanya.**[139] Like as a driver whips and urges his horse, he rouses up his rain-messengers with wild uproar, deep as the distant roar of the lion. Swiftly Parjanya collects his clouds for rain; the winds rush, the lightnings fall stroke on stroke, with which the mighty one smites the blasphemer and terrifies even the pure; the heaven strains and swells; then at once the floods rush down,

> "And every creature then receives the quickening draught,
> When o'er the land Parjanya's grateful stream descends.
>
> The thirsty fields he covered with the waters
> Of plenteous falling rains; but 'tis enough now.
> He caused the herbs to spring for our refreshment,
> And what his people sought of him has granted."[140]
>
> 5.83.4.10.

But the chief figure in the air-space is **Indra,**[141] the most celebrated god of the Vedic period. During this time he assumes a more and more dominating position, and becomes the real national god of the Indians.[142] In numberless hymns his deeds are celebrated, above all his conquest of the demons, Vṛtra ("surrounder"), Ahi ("confiner"), Çuṣṇa ("parcher") and others, who, in the form of mighty serpents or dragons, encompass the waters and shut off their path, as well as that of the light, from the heights of heaven to man's earth. The ever-recurring celebrations of this victory are often tiresome, but their explanation is found in the climatic conditions of the land. These descriptions and images, as, *e.g.*, John Muir, the accomplished investigator, assures us, are perfectly natural and easy of comprehension, especially for those who have lived in India and witnessed the phenomena of the various seasons there.[143]

The heavens themselves, the songs say, shrink back at the roaring of the dragons; even the gods, all of them Indra's friends, at Vṛtra's snorting leave their champion to his fate, and the young hero's mother is concerned for him. But he, inspired by the songs of his adorers, strengthened by deep draughts of Soma and rich sacrificial gifts, armed with the thunder-bolt, which Tvaṣṭar made for him, advances boldly with his companions, the warlike Maruts;[144] he encompasses the Encompasser; him, relying on his wiles, fighting without hands or feet against Indra, he overpowers by his craft, striking him in the face and back with his swift lightning; he finds the vulnerable parts of him who thought himself invulnerable, and with mighty blows smites the lurking encompasser of the waters. Like the branch hewn off by the axe, Ahi lies prone on the earth; and over his body the mighty waves rush joyfully; while Indra's enemy sinks into lasting darkness, the god, the Thunderer, brings the sun to believing mortals.[145]

At another time the fight goes thus. The gods have all declined on account of old age and put him forward as the only strong one, giving over to him all their power and intelligence; even the Maruts, who on other occasions remain true, stay behind.[146] The demon shatters the god's cheek; but he, though wounded, soon masters the enemy; as soon as Indra becomes really earnest in his wrath, he who believed himself alone unconquerable, who considered himself a little god and immortal, finds a mightier, who does not yield in defiance even to the Defiant, whose might no one has attained, now or formerly. He whets his thunderbolt like a sharp knife on the rock, and the weapon rings loud when man's friend strikes down man's enemy, like the oak struck by the lightning, 'on wide meadow shortening the demon's days.'[147] The foaming of the waters rushing forth carries away the demon's head; then the god first holds the floods together, that they may not (unnecessarily) flow asunder, but afterward lets them run freely in streams and sets the sun in the heavens. The victor, into whose own heart fear has crept at the thought of the avenger of the evil, receives the god's jubilations; the wives of the gods bring him a song of praise; mortals praise him with music and song and at their feasts loudly celebrate the Mighty's mighty deeds.[148]

In another account the story tells that the Paṇis (the avaricious ones) have driven off the rainclouds, pictured as herds of cows, and are keeping them in the caves of the rocks. To them comes Indra's messenger Saramâ, to demand the return of the stolen herds. When they defiantly mocking ask:

"Who is he? What does he look like, this Indra,
Whose herald you have hastened such a distance?
Let him come here, we'll strike a friendship with him;
He can become the herdsman of our cattle,"

Saramâ answers warningly:

"Ye cannot injure him; but he can injure,
Whose herald I have hastened such a distance.
Deep rivers cannot cover him nor hide him;
Ye Paṇis soon shall lie cut down by Indra!"—**10.** 108. 3. 4.

In vain;—trusting in their sharp weapons they remain defiant: "You have come to no purpose; nothing is to be found here." But now, united with the Angiras,* the mighty god draws near, at whose breath both worlds tremble. He drives asunder the mountain strongholds and sweeps away the cunningly built walls. Fearing his blow the cavern opens and from its depths Indra drives forth the herds on pleasant ways; as the trees grieve over their plumage (foliage) stolen by the cold, so Vala (the cave-demon) laments the stolen cattle.[149]

And in the mighty strife of the elements he is always victor:

"When heaven and earth together join in battle,
Marshalled by thee, like men that call upon thee,—
For surely thou wert born to might and power,—
Thou active dost destroy the slothful demon."—**7.** 28. 3.

The immovable, too, he moves, and shakes everything that is to its deepest foundation; even the mighty mountains from fear of him are moved like atoms:

* Demigods, mediators between gods and men (ἄγγελοι).

Through fear of thee upon the earth is shaken
E'en the immovable, — the ether, — all things,
The earth, the heavens, mountains, forests tremble;
The firm foundation trembles at thy going. — 6. 31. 2.

But he calms them all again; he hews down the summits of the mountains; demons stealthily climbing up, seeking to mount up to heaven, he shakes off and thrusts them back. He steadies the trembling earth and brings the staggering mountains to rest; at his command they stand fast; the great heaven bows in reverence to Indra and this earth to his might.[150]

Indra is thus a god of battle, the ideal of an ever-fighting, never conquered hero, and, therefore, the favorite of the race fighting for new homes and rich herds; for, as in the battle with Vṛtra all power was yielded to him, so in subduing men, lordship and victory were given him by the gods.

The man who trusts him in the decisive hour carries off the spoils of victory: in him the Aryan has found an ally able to contend with the barbarians, who overthrows fifty thousand of the dark race, and casts down their strongholds as the cloak slips from the shoulders of old age.[151] Men seek to draw the "son of mighty deeds" near with the most pleasing song, the richest sacrifice, and the strongest draughts of Soma. For he is no friend or companion of the man who provides no Soma, and has no favor for the rich miser who grudges gifts; but gladly he enters the house where the sacrificial straw is prepared for him, where songs rise to heaven, and the Soma is cheerfully pressed, and where the god is sought with the whole heart. Such a man's herds he never allows to perish; for the sacrificing hero he secures freedom, and plenteous riches for the singer who praises him.[152]

On him all men must call amid the battle;
He, high-adored, alone has power to succor.
The man who offers him his prayers, libations,
Him Indra's arm helps forward in his goings.

They cry aloud to him amid the contest,
Rushing to deadly combat, to protect them,
When friend and foe lay down their lives in warfare,
In strife to conquer peace for child and grandchild.

They gird themselves, O Mighty, for the conflict,
Provoking each the other to the quarrel;
And when the hostile armies stand opposing,
Then each would have great Indra for his ally.

Then their oblations all they bring to Indra,
And freely then the meats and cakes are offered;
Then they who grudged before come rich with Soma, —
Yea, they resolve to sacrifice a bullock.

Yet still the god gives him success who truly
With willing mind pours out the draught he longs for,
With his whole heart, nor feels regret in giving; —
To him great Indra joins himself in battle. — 4. 24. 2–6.

So he allied himself with the Indian race in their expedition and conquered their enemies; he alone subdued the nations under the Aryans and gave them the land; the barbarians he put aside to the left, gaining far-spread brightness (great happiness) for the Aryan, and increasing his power, so that he can lead his enemies hither and thither at pleasure. He turned the broad-spreading floods into an easily passable ford for Sudâs, the pious Tṛtsu king, and, in the battle of the ten kings, rescued him from the onslaughts of innumerable enemies. With Suçravas, who was without allies, he crushed with fatal chariot wheel twice ten chieftains and their 60,099 warriors.[153]

"The mighty stream, with flood o'erwhelming all things,
Thou heldest back for Vâyya and Turvîti;
Obedient stood the rapid flood, O Indra,
And through its bed thou mad'st an easy pathway."
4. 19. 6.

And Indra restrained the waters also for Yadu and Turvaça when they desired to cross the stream; * and even all the gods could not withstand Indra when he prolonged day into the night, and the sun unharnessed his chariot in the midst of heaven (day).† [154]

From these acts men grew to see in him the creator and sustainer of the world, the leader of the races of men and gods, the mighty, unrestricted lord and master, the harsh punisher of the godless, and the unfailing shield of the righteous. He made the heaven, the sun and the dawn and the earth as a likeness of heaven; he placed bounds to the air and pillars to the heavens; like two wheels upon one axle he set heaven and earth apart, and fixed them both. He placed the moon in the sky, he bids the sun traverse the wide space, and brings it to rest when it has finished its course. He created the matchless lightning of heaven, and the cloudy vault around; on earth, he divided the brooks according to their order, and in the field the plants bearing flowers and those with fruits; relying on him, the farmer puts his hand to the sickle.[155] From him come right thoughts, and every good intention in man; he is the king of the worlds and peoples, seeing and hearing all; he leads the human and divine hosts, and none equals him; — how should any surpass him? [156]

The poets never tire of praising his greatness and might; one doubts whether before him wise men ever reached the whole of all Indra's greatness, and another, rescued from great need, declares that he does not know the whole greatness of the god, the might of the mighty one, and that no one comprehends the divine power of his present favor. He overtops both heaven and earth; both together cannot reach his greatness; the air, and the depths of the

* Exodus 14. 21. Ps. 78. 13: He divided the sea and caused them to pass through; and he made the waters to stand as a heap. Is. 63. 12.

† Joshua 10. 13. Lo, the sun stood still in the midst of heaven and hasted not to go down about a whole day. And there was no day like that, before it or after it.

sea, the winds and the ends of the earth cannot contain him. Indra rejoices far out beyond stream and land.[157] Both worlds (earth and heaven) form ideas of his sublimity, but they cannot comprehend it; his half equals both of them; when he grasps both these unbounded worlds together, they are but a handful; as a skin his power rolls heaven and earth together; they both roll after him (by the necessity of nature) as the wheel after the horse.[158] His days do not pass in human fashion; * neither years nor moons make him old; the course of days do not cause him to fade, and when he thinks, "I shall not die," with him even this remains true.[159] Not the heavens can restrain his, the Mighty's, might; not days, not years, not moons: the work the hero sets about he accomplishes, and no one is able to hinder him. To-day he performs one act, to-morrow another; he calls that which does not exist into being, and even through weakness accomplishes wonderful deeds.[160] In his two hands he holds the nations and their possessions; he causes their hosts to war and again leads them to peace; he animates the spirit of heroes in battle against their enemies, though unnoticed by the wise and by the hosts, numerous as the stars.[161] He gives over the great into the hand of the small; those who think themselves great he entangles in battle, and is the subduer of the haughty. The powerful one hurls aside the proud fool; the Mighty overthrows him who decks his body, who joins himself to the niggardly, and trusts in his own arm. One he makes homeless, to another he gives a home; as a man puts his feet in turn one before the other, he makes the first last; he breaks friendship with the former, joins himself in turn to the latter, and shakes off those who are not devoted to him.[162]

The hero — listen — overcomes the mighty,
Now to the front brings one and now another;

* Job 10. 5. Are thy days as the days of man? Are thy years as man's days?

The lord of both the worlds hates all the haughty,
He cares for those who feel themselves but human.*
6. 47. 16.

All those who are guilty of great crime he strikes with his arrow when they least expect it, and smites down every one who does not keep his promise, who perverts the truth, the scheming, foolish mocker. The rich man, who presses no Soma for him, he drags forth from his concealment, unsummoned he destroys the haters of prayer; he disperses the assemblies of the unsacrificing on all sides; even in unapproachable strongholds those who have enkindled his wrath, all together cannot withstand his strength.[163] For them there is no help if they turn to the god in the day of need and promise him the richest gifts.

"I never knew a man to speak so to me,
When all the enemies are safely conquered;
Yea, when they see how fierce the battle rages,
They even promise me a pair of bullocks.

When I am absent far in distant places,
Then all with open hand their gifts would bring me;
I'll make the wealthy niggard needy,
Seize by the foot, and on the hard rock dash him." [164]
10. 27. 3. 4.

But to the upright man, whose strength rests on Indra, who has never led another aside to godlessness, and has never knowingly neglected the god's songs; whose hope ever seeks the god anew, calling to him at morning and evening, by day and night; who from love toward him relinquishes his desire, [165] — to him the world's lord offers riches with his left hand and is not doubtful with his right; to him he shows himself as his friend and savior and liberator, as his present and future protector by day and night, as the pitying supplier of his needs, who wards

* *i.e.*, who acknowledge their weakness in relation to the gods. Dis te minorem quod geris, imperas: *cf.* Note 162.

off want and hunger and frees even from great guilt.[166] The singer is dear to the god, who loves above all to listen to prayer; not the deep stream and not the lofty firm rock, no mortal and no god can hinder him when he desires to grant the upright man his desires, to give him protection and bestow rich herds upon him. Sometimes, indeed, he keeps his adorers in suspense, so that they anxiously ask when he will heed their words.

"What now shall be with hymns thy fitting service?
How shall we honor thee aright, O Indra?
I bring in love to thee all my devotion;
Hear therefore now, O Indra, this my crying."[167]—7.29.3.

Then the skeptic scoffingly seeks to undermine the faith of the believer when he exerts himself in holy acts, asking him if the god has ever stood by him.

"How then can Indra hear when men entreat him?
How, if he hears, could he find means of succor?
And where is all his wondrous consolation?
How can men call him generous to the singer?

How does the man who serves him, even zealous
And full of piety, obtain his promised bounty?"
"*The god be witness of my deeds' devotion,*
My prayer receiving and rejoicing in it." *[168]—4. 23.3.4.

And when the man, now wavering in his trust, cries out:

"Lift up loud songs of praise to gain his favor,
Real praise to Indra, if there really be one.
'There is no Indra,' many men are saying;
'Who ever saw him? Why should we adore him?'"

—then the god appears to him and speaks:

"I am, O singer, look on me, here am I,
And I am greater than all living creatures.
The service of the sacred rite delights me,
Destroying, I creation hurl to ruin." †—8. 89. 3. 4.

* *i.e.*, let my devotion please the god, so that he may not let me come to shame before the mockers.

† He helps the devout, but destroys the godless.

So men seek more and more to win **Indra** for a friend, whether praising him in the dwelling of the singer or in the stillness with a song.[169] Whoever strives to gain anything chooses Indra for an ally:

> The former, middle, latter call upon him,
> On Indra, wanderers and the home-returning,
> On Indra, those in peace and those in warfare,
> On Indra, heroes striving after booty.[170]—**4.** 25. 8.

The voice of all is:

> "Praise the great praiseworthy Indra,
> Ruler of the world, with singing,
> Him the richest man, the victor.
>
> Him let every creature honor,
> Him in works and him in action;
> Indra 'tis who brings us freedom.
>
> All the mortals, all the peoples,
> Ever in their hymns praise Indra,
> Him in songs and him in measures.
>
> Who to highest weal conducts us,
> Lends success and fame in battle
> And our foes subdues in conflict.
>
> Carry us across as boatman,
> Often praised, on ships to fortune,
> Indra over every rival.
>
> Help us, Indra, with refreshing
> Paths prepare us through thy goodness
> And to happiness conduct us."—**8.** 16. 1. 6. 9. 10–12.

Among the divinities of the **light heaven** we have first to mention the two **Açvins,** the "horse-guiders."[171] These Aryan Dioskuroi are the earliest light-bearers in the morning sky. As soon as the first beams shine in the east at break of day, the sacrifice is made ready for the two sons of heaven, two eternally young and beautiful heroes of miraculous power and deep wisdom.[172] With uplifted hands the singer sends up his devout song of praise as a messenger to the twins, who overcome all darkness; he calls to these two helpers as a son to his parents.[173] At their signal the golden sun-like chariot is harnessed, which stretches over all peoples, and with its wheels touches the ends of heaven and earth. The skillful Ṛbhus fashioned his chariot with three seats and three wheels; without horse and without bridle it glides sure and unwavering, as though on wings, to the house of the upright, bringing prosperity like a stream from the mountain;[174] or, drawn by gold-winged steeds like eagles, it hastens daily with the speed of wind through all the regions of air, through sea and rivers, swift as thought, — swifter even than a mortal's thought, swifter than the twinkling of an eye.[175] Toward the end of the night, the noble drivers mount the chariot, and with them Sûryâ, the fair daughter of the Sun-god; she yielded herself to the beauteous heroes and chose both youths for husbands, — and all the gods assented from the heart. The journey begins; day and night divide; the limits of darkness gradually become visible; the Helpers approach from night and need, rich in joy and rich in wealth, the two guardians of treasure, with abundant, never-failing aid.[176] As divine physicians they drive away sickness, bring medicines from far and near, and heal all that is hurtful; they give sight to the blind and make the lame walk; they help onward the outcast and the slow, even though left far behind. Like rotten cords they snap asunder the net of calamity, and at the feasts their deeds of wonder in the fathers' times are loudly praised among the people.[177]

Upon your chariot ye brought to Vimada
The daughter fair of Purumitra for his wife.
The eunuch's wife sent up her prayer to you, — ye came,
And made Puraṁdhi happily bring forth a child.[178]

Ye gave to Kali, when he had grown old in years,
To him, the singer, all his youthful strength again;

And Vandana ye rescued from the deep abyss,[179]
And quickly Viçpalâ the maimed ye made to walk.[180]

To Pedu ye, O Açvins, gave the snowy steed,
The runner strong, whose ninety-nine fold wondrous strength
Bears on his rider in his flight; they cry to him
As to the goodness of a rich and kindly lord.[181]

10. 39. 7. 8. 10.

The wise Atri, through the wiles of a hostile monster, has fallen with all his host into a burning chasm; at his entreaty the Açvins approach with eagle's speed, bringing a cooling and quickening draught; they protect him from the glowing flames, and finally lead him and his followers out to the life-giving air in full youthful strength.[182] The Helpers took the body of the aged Cyavâna like a cloak, made it young and beautiful again, prolonged the life of the lonely one, and made him the husband of a young maiden.[183] Rogues had kept Rebha hidden like a horse in the water, bound, wounded, overwhelmed by the flood; ten nights and nine days he lay there, till the Açvins, with their wonder-working power, brought the dead forth and revived him.[184] To the Pajrid Kakṣîvant they grant blessings in abundance; from the strong horse's hoof as from a sieve, they poured him forth a hundred jars of wine;[185] and to Ghoṣâ, remaining in her father's house, they gave a husband in her old age.[186] The quail, seized by the wolf, they free from his jaws,[187] and bring the sweet honey to the bees.[188]

But among the many wonders for which they are celebrated,—and there are very many,—none is sung so loud and so often as the rescue of Bhujyu, whom his father Tugra left behind, in the midst of the swelling waves, as a dead man abandons his possessions. Tossed about in the darkness he calls upon the youthful heroes, and they again are mindful of him, according to their wont, and hasten up with their red, flying steeds, self-harnessed, in their chariot, swift as thought. In the sea, which is without support, unceasing and unresting, they accomplish their heroic work: the struggling man is drawn into the hundred-oared craft, and the heroes, with miraculous power, bear the exile in the ship floating in mid-air to his home on the other side of the rolling sea, journeying three nights, and thrice by day.[189] What wonder that every oppressed one longs for such helpers, who so often since the fathers' times, in every need, have stretched forth a saving hand, and that his desires look to them? As the wind drives the clouds, so the singer drives his songs of praise toward the lords of light; he calls upon them at home and on the journey; he seeks to attract them from far and near, from east and west, with the pleasing draught of milk;[190] like buffaloes panting for the water's gleam, they are besought at milking-time, early in the day, at noon and at sunset, by day and night, to draw near the devout with blessing and support in his necessity.[191] Since their former deeds never flag, they are both, for all time, the helpers of all men; ever regarding ancient friendships and relations, they ward off evil from their adorers, chase away hate and envy, lengthen their life, and overthrow their contemners. The man who reverences and praises them they bring to old age with seeing eye; they reward him with riches and the blessing of children, song for song, so that he enters into old age as into his own house.[192]

After these much-praised lords of light, the Açvins, in the far East, out of the darkness from the boundary of heaven and earth, rises the friendly **Uṣas**, Eos, Aurora,* the golden daughter of heaven, with kindly countenance, to show herself to the dwellings of men.[193] The two sisters, Night and Dawn, are unlike in color, but of harmonious mind; in fixed succession they follow each other in daily interchange; as soon as the dark sister descries the light, she willingly gives place to her.[194] Now, the fairest light of lights puts to flight the darkness of the night with

* The Dawn; v. Max Müller in Note 193.

its terrors; the pure goddess drives away haters and evil-doers.* [195] She makes the undesired darkness give way to sight, she opens the gates of heaven for every creature, and begins then to fill the wide spaces.[196] White steeds, or bullocks, draw the well-adorned chariot of the goddess, self-yoking; in it she clears a goodly road and way first upon the mountains, then everywhere in the paths of men.[197] She awakens all creatures, — only the miser must sleep on in the midst of darkness, without waking, — she brings renewed life and impels all things that live to motion; the winged flocks of birds fly forth; two-footed and four-footed creatures arouse themselves at her light; men take their morning meal and all the five peoples,† whom daily she encircles, go forth to their occupations.[198]

"The goddess radiant bringing every splendor
Appeared in light, and threw the portals open;
All life arousing, she has shown us treasures, —
The Dawn has wakened every living creature.

The sleeping man the goddess wakes to motion,
One to enjoyment, one to gathering treasure,
The dim in sight to gaze afar about them, —
The Dawn has wakened every living creature.

To lordship one, to win renown another,
One to get gain, one to his occupation,
Through all the various paths of life to journey, —
The Dawn has wakened every living creature."

1. 113. 4–6.

Like a dancer the goddess puts on rich adornment; in all her form gleaming with fullness of beauty, like a maiden whom her mother has decked out, the radiant one with gracious smile displays her charms to the adorer, and brings rich treasure into the house of the man of upright mind: much life-sustaining wealth, in which the mortal rejoices, from which his fame grows wide among men.[199]

* Job 38. 12 f. Hast thou commanded the morning since thy days, and caused the dayspring to know his place; that it might take hold of the ends of the earth, that the wicked might be shaken out of it?

† A frequent designation for "the whole world"; Note 198.

Through two things, especially, this much-sung goddess awakened the astonishment of the Vedic singers. Knowing precisely the first sign of day, daily she accomplishes faultlessly her long journey, never transgressing the ordinance of the right and of the gods; skillfully she follows straight the path laid down, never failing in the direction, but appears day by day at the place appointed by the gods' commands.* [200] And when the singer sees these dawns come again and again, ever with the same beauty, old as time, yet eternally young, in appearance to-day alike, and alike to-morrow, following the path of those preceding, at the same time the first of all that shall come after,[201] — then, full of sadness, he reflects:

"Vanished and gone long since are all the mortals
Who looked of old upon the dawn's bright radiance;
To-day she shows herself to us; and others
Shall come in future time to gaze upon her.

So oft before has goddess Uṣas risen,
And now the rich one clothes the world with glory,
And still in later days will gleam her brightness,
As pleases her, unaging, never-dying." — 1. 113. 11. 13.

"She comes in radiant colors, never fading,
And leads to age the life of every mortal;
Even as a gambler hides the dice with cunning,
So she removes the human generations." [202] — 1. 92. 10. 11.

Then soon **Sûrya** himself follows the shining goddess of the morning, as the youth the maiden's footsteps; the God-born light visible from afar, the son of heaven with golden hair, the Sun.[203] Streaming forth in beams from the bosom of the dawn, the arouser of all men rises, saluted by the joyful exultation of the singers; he throws off the black cloak, his beams shake the darkness from him like a skin, and the stars with their gleam slink away like thieves.[204]

* Hosea 6. 3. His going forth is prepared as the morning. *Cf.* Job 38. 12.

Whom they, whose home is fixed, their aim unwavering,*
Have made to drive away the hostile darkness,
The sun-god, all the ends of earth surveying,
By seven steeds, all light and swift, is carried. — 4. 13. 3.

The light and bright and beauteous steeds of Sûrya,
The gleaming steeds, by songs of joy saluted,
They reverently climb the heights of heaven,
In one day all the realm of light traversing.[205] — 1. 115. 3.

The golden ornament of heaven far-seeing
Mounts, pressing to his distant goal, bright gleaming.
Impelled by Sûrya's power, let all the mortals
Pursue their aims and carry on their labors.† — 7. 63. 4.

So Sûrya rises every morning, an all-seeing searcher, mounts the high plains, looks down on right and wrong among men, guards the path of the upright, observes at bidding the occupation of each, and when at evening, his journey accomplished, he unharnesses his mares from the chariot, he commands to lay aside the work assigned in the morning, even though it be uncompleted; then Night spreads her veil over all. Unceasingly Sûrya's steeds carry now the bright gleam, now the dark, over the dome of the sky.[206]

It is evident that the sun, this vital breath of animate and inanimate things, this bright divine countenance, imperishable in the heavens, prospering mankind without distinction, — this eye all-seen and all-seeing, which above all publishes the Immortals' might and wisdom, since it exalts them high in the heavens,[207] — that the sun should be honored and sung in a very special manner; and we find its variously displayed activity praised under various names.[208]

In **Pûsan**, *i.e.*, the 'Nourisher,' the great bringer of sustenance and lord rich in treasure is praised. As be-

* The highest gods, the Âdityas: p. 58 f.

† Ps. 104. 22. The sun ariseth. . . . man goeth forth unto his work and to his labor until the evening.

stower of riches, making all men prosper, he also brings hidden treasure to light, compels the niggardly to give, and softens the heart of the miserly; he paves the way to gaining wealth, pierces the niggards' heart with his spear, and brings what was dear to them to his adorer.[209] Filling both the broad spaces, the flame-radiating god sits in the midst of heaven, and as shepherd of the world overlooks all creatures, accurately distinguishing them and surveying them all; as guardian of the herd, who governs animate and inanimate life, he weaves the sheep's dress and smoothes her coat; he follows the cattle and guards the steeds, that none of them may be lost or come to harm, none be dashed to pieces in the ravine, and that all may return unharmed.[210] As guardian of every road he clears and makes level the paths, goes before, sends on the skillful man and protects on every journey.[211] And since he knows the ways of heaven as well as earth and all the spaces, he goes before the souls of the dead on their journey to the abodes where the upright have gone, where they dwell.[212]

The far-striding ruler of the heights, **Viṣṇu**, *i.e.*, the 'Worker,' is ever and anon praised for his great heroic deed, because he measured the whole wide earth in three strides, made supports for the kingdom on high and fastened the earth all about with pegs.[213] His footprints are full of sweetness, a never-ceasing source of joy; he gave the vast expanse of earth with rich pastures to man for a sure dwelling-place.[214] Two steps of the Sun-like we can recognize, though a mortal who would see them must diligently exert himself; but the third highest none dare approach, not even the winged birds in their flight; it is known only to the Savior full of mercy. Toward this highest footprint, placed like an eye in heaven, the wise ever look; there, at the spring of sweetness, the men devoted to the gods dwell in happiness.[215]

Closely connected with Sûrya is **Savitar**, the 'Inciter, Inspirer, Enlivener'; the two words are, indeed, employed without distinction.[216] But with Savitar the etymological meaning especially stands out clearly[217]; the difference in the use of the names is usually this, that Sûrya signifies more the sun-body, Savitar the divine power behind it; *e.g.*, when we read,

> With golden hands comes hastening Savitar the god,
> Pursuing busily his work twixt heaven and earth;
> He drives away oppression, leads the sun-god forth;
> Through the dark realm of air he hastens up to heaven.
> **1. 35. 9.**

Or, in another passage,

> The sun's uprising floods the air with brightness;
> God Savitar sends all men forth to labor, etc.[218] — **1. 124. 1.**

Of Savitar it is described, in even more glowing colors than of Sûrya, how he with care and ceaselessly conducts day and night, defining their limits. Cunningly enveloped in the brilliancy of every color, Savitar follows the path of Uṣas; first the beloved god passes through this lower realm of air; enlivening, he stretches aloft his beauteous, slender golden arms, and, as he yesterday laid them to rest, to-day he awakens all creatures, — whatever has two feet or four, whatever is mortal and immortal, — to new life; man and beast must move again.[219] With golden steeds in golden chariot he drives up the heights to the light world of the heavens and rests there, enjoying the brightness of the sun's beams. Wherever the faithful god appears with his golden radiance he drives away all oppression and brings contentment for man and beast.[220] He sends infallible guardians about the house and home; he inspires courage, and with full hands brings rich store and comfort for man. Yet his best gift is that he awakens first immortality for the exalted gods, but for men, as their portion, life that follows life; he frees them from the guilt of sin and guides them to the resting-places of the blessed.[221] So he blesses daily; in the morning he brings life and at evening rest; then he cloaks himself in brown-red mantle and hastens down the heights on well-paved, dustless paths; in the dark night, following his settled custom, Savitar guides the great host of stars.[222]

The god his mighty hand, his arm outstretches
In heaven above, and all things here obey him;
To his commands the waters are attentive,
And even the rushing wind subsides before him.*

Driving his steeds, now he removes the harness,
And bids the wanderer rest him from his journey.
He checks the serpent-smiter's eager onset;
At Savitar's command the kindly Night comes.

The weaver rolls her growing web together,
And in the midst the workman leaves his labor;
The god arises and divides the seasons,
God Savitar appears, the never resting.

In every place where mortals have their dwelling,
The house-fire far and wide sheds forth its radiance.
The mother gives her son the fairest portion,
Because the god has given desire of eating.

Now he returns who had gone forth for profit;
For home the longing wanderer's heart is yearning;
And each, his task half finished, homeward journeys.
This is the heavenly Inciter's ordinance.

The restless, darting fish, at fall of evening,
Seeks where he may his refuge in the waters,
His nest the egg-born seeks, their stall the cattle;
Each in his place, the god divides the creatures.

2. 38. 2–6. 8.

THE ÂDITYAS.

The personifications of light already named, the Açvins, Uṣas, the Sun-gods, dwell in the highest realm, in the clear space of the heaven, but they are not the highest

* St. Matth. 8.27: But the men marvelled, saying, What manner of man is this, that even the winds and the sea obey him! Ps. 104.7; 107. 29. Is. 50. 2.

gods. Almost always their activity is pictured as bound to special phenomena, therefore confined to a relatively narrow sphere and not at all independent and unlimited. When Uṣas each day intelligently appears at the right spot, she only follows higher laws, and when Savitar, like a spirited warrior swings high his banner, it is still Varuṇa and Mitra who, according to their decree, cause the sun to mount high in the heavens.[223] While the poet praises Sûrya in inspired songs, he still knows that the divinity is only an instrument in the hands of higher powers, — that he is only the eye of Varuṇa and Mitra; like an eagle soaring Sûrya follows the path where these immortals laid out the road for him. Therefore the libation and songs at sunrise are homage to Varuṇa and Mitra and Aryaman,[224] the most celebrated among the Âdityas, the sons of Aditi.

To Aditi, 'eternity,' no hymns are directed; but she is often praised as the friend of all men, the glorious, heavenly sustainer of the nations, the rich bestower of blessings, who gave life to Varuṇa and Mitra, the most mighty lords, as a revelation of the highest divine power. Men entreat her for sure protection and defense, and desire to be freed by her from the debt of sin.[225] But her sons, the seven Âdityas, are the absolute, the highest.

> "The gods, all light and clear as flowing fountains
> Uplifted above harm, deceit and blemish."[226] — 2. 27. 2.

From some of their names, in part of rare occurrence,[227] one might be inclined to infer that, excepting Varuṇa, they had their origin not, as the other gods, in natural phenomena, but in moral ideas; but we have rather to see in them deep spiritual personifications of the heavenly light and its various developments. They, the righteous rulers, created the eternal order in the realm of nature as well as spirit, and they watch over it, that this their ancient ordinance of the world's government may ever have eternal continuance.[228] In the hymns to these 'living spirits of the gods' the religious feeling finds expression in the greatest depth, fervency and purity.

All the gods together chose these pure-minded, wise sons of wise parents for the highest divine power, and gladly gave over the dominion to them, so that they embrace both the wide worlds.[229]

The Âdityas, through depth and breadth extending,
Unharmed by any, harming at their pleasure,
They, many-eyed, discern the straight and crooked;
For them all things are near, the furthest even.[230]

Inanimate and animate sustaining,
The heavenly guardians of the whole creation[231]
Watch over their divinity, far-seeing;
Each evil deed with justice strict they punish.[232]

No right or left, no back or front, Âdityas,
By mortal eyes in you can be distinguished.*
No weariness can dim your eyes, nor slumber;
Afar your guardianship protects the upright.†[233]

2. 27. (v. Note 229.)

Ever the pure ones, whose very breath suffices to hold the world in bounds, assert their dominion; as the unharmed, infallible heads of the races of men, they guard everywhere their firm decrees which no god dares to disturb, and woe to the mortal who should attempt to violate them.[234] They see into the hearts of men and their thoughts,‡ the false and those without deceit; to him who, clean from any sin, never practises what the good ones punish, the spotless sons of Aditi bring freedom out of need and oppression.[235] They are his providers and his strength;

* *i.e.*, ye are not visible to human eyes. *Cf.* Note 233 and Job 9.11: Lo, he goeth by me, and I see him not; he passeth on also, but I perceive him not.

† *i.e.*, accompanies and protects him everywhere. Ps. 121.4: Behold, he that keepeth Israel shall neither slumber nor sleep.

‡ 1 Samuel 16. 7: Man looketh on the outward appearance but the Lord looketh on the heart. Jer. 17. 10: I the Lord search the heart.

when he trembles at danger and death, he flees for refuge to their heart; in them he finds protection and defense and comfort, and he entreats the infallible for their alliance. When he turns back from his sin, then they put far away the evil done openly or in secret, and prolong the life of the penitent. Although as man he is subject to death, yet the arrow of the death-god shall not strike him before a ripe old age, shall not hurry him away before his time in the midst of his work.* [236]

I pray for your protection, ye Âdityas,
I seek your strengthening power in hours of danger.
Led by your hand, Varuṇa-Mitra, may I
Escape from need as from a yawning chasm.[237]

Your path is easy, Aryaman and Mitra,
And thornless, Varuṇa, it leads straight onward.
On it, Âdityas, lead us with your blessing,
And cover us with a defence enduring.[238]

He dwells in peace in richly watered regions,
The pure one, rich in sons and armed with power.†
No hostile weapons, far or near, can reach him
Who dwells defended by the great Âdityas.[239]

Forgive, O Aditi, Varuṇa, Mitra,
If we in anything have sinned against you.[240]
Let me attain the realms of peace and brightness,
Led by your hand, in folly or in wisdom.‡

2. 27 (v. Note 229).

The might and greatness of these eternal highest beings, their wisdom and justice, their sublimity and kindliness are united in the chief Âditya, **Varuṇa,** originally the

* Psalm 102. 24: I said, O my God, take me not away in the midst of my days.

† Psalm 1. 3: And he shall be like a tree planted by the rivers of water, that bringeth forth his fruit in his season; his leaf also shall not wither; and whatsoever he doeth shall prosper. Jerem. 17. 8.

‡ *i.e.*, let me enter the bright world of the blessed, who according to my powers now err, now do right.

personification of the all-embracing heaven.[241] In the preserved hymns he stands, compared with the national Indian god of battle, Indra, more in the background, and in many places the contrast appears prominently between the governing king of peace Varuṇa and the warlike martial hero Indra, loved and celebrated by the warlike nation;[242] but the relatively few hymns to Varuṇa belong to the most exalted portions of the Veda. They recall especially the tone of the Psalms and the language of the Bible in general; to this point more attention will be directed hereafter. They picture the god as the all-wise creator, preserver and regent of the worlds, the omniscient protector of the good and avenger of the evil, holy and just, yet full of pity.

Like a cunning artist * the all-wise god called all things, the heaven and the earth here, into existence.† Through his might the broad, deep, double realm of air stands fast; he propped the heavens and marked out the spaces of earth †; as the butcher stretches a hide, he spread out the earth as a carpet for the sun,‡ which itself he created in the heavens, a golden swinging light.§ He fills both worlds with his greatness,‖ and bestows on every mortal that which gives him his value and worth.[243]

His works bear witness to his might and wisdom,
Who fashioned firm supports for earth and heaven,
Who set on high the firmament uplifted,
And fixed the stars and spread out earth's expanses.

7. 86. 1.

* Eccl. 11. 5: God who maketh all.

† Jerem. 10. 12; 51. 15: He hath made the earth by his power, he hath established the world by his wisdom, and hath stretched out the heavens by his discretion.—Is. 44. 24. That stretcheth forth the heavens alone; that spreadeth abroad the earth by myself. Job 9. 8.—Job 38. 4: Where wast thou when I laid the foundations of the earth? Declare if thou hast understanding. Ps. 104. 5; 89. 12; 102. 26.

‡ *Cf.* Ps. 104. 2: Who stretchest out the heavens like a curtain. Is. 40. 22.

§ Jerem. 31. 35: Which giveth the sun for a light by day. Ps. 136. 8.

‖ Jerem. 23. 24: Do not I fill heaven and earth? saith the Lord. Job 38. 33.

He mingled with the clouds his cooling breezes,
He gave the cow her milk, the horse his spirit,*
Put wisdom in the heart, † in clouds the lightning,‡
The sun in heaven, on the rock the Soma.§ [244] — 5. 85. 2.

The sun's sure courses Varuṇa appointed, ‖
He sent the streaming waters flowing onward,¶
The mighty path of days he first created,
And rules them as the riders guide their horses.[245] — 7. 87. 1.

Enveloped in golden cloak, in robes of glory,** the lord of all stands in the air; with the cord he measured the ends of heaven and earth and with the sun as with a measuring staff he laid out the spaces of the earth,†† on which he places his mountains.[246]

And the world which he created the lord of all life supports and carries; his breath blows as wind through the air; his eye, the sun, is the soul of the animate and inanimate; he gives drink to all creatures, as the rain to the fruits of the field.‡‡[247] Sitting in his house with

* Job 39. 19: Hast thou given the horse strength?

† Job 38. 36: Who hath put wisdom in the inward parts? or who hath given understanding to the heart?

‡ *i.e.*, the lightning in the clouds; above, p. 35. 64. Jerem. 10. 13; 51. 16: He causeth the vapors to ascend from the ends of the earth; he maketh lightning with rain.

§ Ps. 147. 8: Who maketh grass to grow upon the mountains; *cf.* Ps. 104. 13. 14.

‖ Ps. 74. 16; 104. 19: Thou hast prepared the light and the sun; the sun knoweth his going down.

¶ *i.e.*, since Varuṇa showed them the path; Note 245. Ps. 104. 10: He sendeth the springs into the valleys, which run among the hills. Ps. 74. 15, etc.—Job 38. 25: Who hath divided a water-course for the overflowing of waters? Job 26. 10, etc.

** Ps. 104. 2: Who coverest thyself with light as with a garment; Note 246.

†† Job 38. 5: Who hath laid the measures of the earth, if thou knowest? or who hath stretched the line upon it? Verse 18: Hast thou perceived the breadth of the earth?

‡‡ Job 5. 10: Who giveth rain upon the earth and sendeth water upon the fields.—Ps. 72. 6: He shall come down like rain upon the mown grass; as showers that water the earth. Hosea 6. 3.

a thousand doors, he holds sway over the broad earth and high heaven,* over gods and mortals, as absolute, unrivalled prince; in the foundations of the earth as in the air his dominion extends to the boundaries of the world, and nothing can withdraw itself from his sway.[248] Immovably he protects his ancient, inviolable laws, his infrangible decrees in nature as well as in the life of men; for firmly on him as on a rock the ordinances are fixed eternally; for he is the omniscient ruler of all.[249] He knows where the Pleiades, which show at night, go by day; he knows the secret hidden names of the dawn,† the path of the birds that soar in the spaces of the air, the ships upon the sea,‡ the twelve moons rich in children and the moon born after. Even the path of the wind, the gloriously mighty,§ and those who dwell beyond,—in short, every wonder, complete or to be completed, past and future, is revealed before him.[250] And among men he looks upon right and wrong; he watches over the thoughts of mortals ‖ as the shepherd over his herds; yea, away from him and without him no one is master even of the winking of his eye.[251]

It is admissible to insert here a fragment of the Atharvaveda, which gives expression to the divine omniscience more forcibly than any other hymn of the Vedic literature.[252]

* Ps. 89. 11: The heavens are thine, the world also is thine, the world and the fullness thereof, etc.

† Job 9. 7: Which sealeth up the stars.—Ps. 147. 4: He telleth the number of the stars; he calleth them all by their names.

‡ Ps. 50. 11: I know all the fowls of the mountains, and the wild beasts of the field are mine.—Prov. 30. 18: There be three things that are too wonderful for me: the way of an eagle in the air; the way of a serpent upon a rock; the way of a ship in the midst of the sea.

§ *Cf.* p. 38* with John 3. 8.—Ps. 104. 3: Who walketh upon the wings of the wind. Ps. 135. 7 = Jerem. 10. 13.

‖ I. Kings 8. 39: Thou only knowest the hearts of all the children of men. Prov. 21. 2. Jerem. 17. 10.

"As guardian, the Lord of worlds
Sees all things as if near at hand.
In secret what 'tis thought to do
That to the gods is all displayed.*

Whoever moves or stands, who glides in secret,
Who seeks a hiding-place, or hastens from it,
What thing two men may plan in secret council,
A third, King Varuṇa, perceives it also.†

And all this earth King Varuṇa possesses,
His the remotest ends of yon broad heaven;‡
And both the seas in Varuṇa lie hidden,§
But yet the smallest water-drop contains him.

Although I climbed the furthest heaven, fleeing,
I should not there escape the monarch's power; ‖
From heaven his spies descending hasten hither,
With all their thousand eyes the world surveying.¶

Whate'er exists between the earth and heaven,
Or both beyond, to Varuṇa lies open.**

* Ps. 33. 13: The Lord looketh from heaven; he beholdeth all the children of men.—Ps. 113. 5. Jerem. 23. 23: Am I a God at hand, saith the Lord, and not a God afar off? Can any hide himself in secret places that I shall not see him?—Ps. 139. 2: Thou understandest my thoughts afar off. 138. 6, etc.

† Ps. 139. 3: Thou compassest my path and my lying down, and art acquainted with all my ways. For there is not a word in my tongue but lo, O Lord, thou knowest it altogether. Jerem. 32. 19. Job 34. 21; 31. 4: Doth not he see all my ways and count all my steps?—Matth. 18. 20: For where two or three are gathered together (in my name) there am I in the midst of them.

‡ Deut. 10. 14: Behold, the heaven and the heaven of heavens is the Lord's thy God, the earth also with all that therein is. Job 28. 24: For he looketh to the ends of the earth and seeth under the whole heaven. Ps. 24. 1; 89. 12.

§ The "two seas" are the sea in the air and that on earth; *cf.* Gen. 1. 7: And God made the firmament and divided the waters which were under the firmament from the waters which were above the firmament.

‖ *Cf.* the highly poetic description of Ps. 139. 7–12.

¶ For the sentries of Mitra-Varuṇa, Note 230; for the messengers of Varuṇa, p. 67.

** *Cf., e.g.,* Amos 9. 1–3. Hebrews 4. 13.

The winkings of each mortal eye he numbers,*
He wields the universe, as dice a player."—**AV. 4.** 16. 1–5.

Whoever here upon earth honors Varuṇa and submits willingly to his commands and his eternal ordinances, from him he takes away all anxiety and fear and spreads over him a threefold protecting roof;† he is at hand with a hundred, a thousand remedies; he sharpens the courage and the understanding of the truly devoted,—the prayer which he himself inspired in his heart; even deep hidden secrets he imparts to the wise singer.[253] With confidence the pious may look for his pity: the kind god gives him a hundred harvests and his desire, joyful and pleasant old age,‡—and after death a new and blessed life united with the gods and his own people in the highest heaven.[254]

But whoever through any error, or any sin,§ even without intention, offends against these eternal ordinances of the All-knowing, he arouses the anger of the Sinless, him

* Matth. 10. 30. Luke 12. 7: But even the very hairs of your head are all numbered.

† Ps. 91. 1 ff. v. 14: Because he hath set his love upon me, therefore will I deliver him, I will set him on high because he hath known my name. Ps. 59. 16: For thou hast been my defence and refuge in the day of my trouble. Gen. 15. 1. Is. 41. 10.

‡ Ps. 91. 16: With long life will I satisfy him and show him my salvation.

§ "We must admit that in no other natural religion, with the single exception of the Iranian, which is only another branch of the same family, were the nature and the guilt of sin fixed more firmly and weighed more gravely. A religion which makes its highest divinity gaze into the deepest secrets of the human heart,—how could a recognition of the nature and guilt of sin escape it? Sin is a consequence of human weakness as well as of human wickedness, but as sin it is not less punishable in one case than in the other; and forgiveness is sought of Varuna even for sins which have been done in ignorance. And more than once we find in these old hymns penitent confessions of sin, united with prayer for forgiveness, expressed in the speech of simple faith. The guilt of sin is felt as a burdensome fetter, and freedom from its servitude is prayed for; here as elsewhere human power can accomplish nothing without divine assistance, for by himself man has not the power even to open or close his eyes." —*Roth.*

messengers at the command of the Just punish, and bind him with the bonds of the god,—with calamity, with sickness and death.* No deceivers' deceit, nor the wily plans of man dare to approach the pure one:[255] through reverence and prayer, through libation and sacrificial gifts every mortal seeks to allay the wrath of the Mighty.[256] And the rigorous one is yet a god who pities the sinner and who therefore is the chosen recipient of prayer.[257] To other gods men turn most for success and riches, for respect among the people and a numerous family, for victory and spoils; from Varuṇa is sought continually forgiveness of sin of every kind, since He has the power.[258]

"If we to any dear and loved companion
Have evil done, to brother or to neighbor,
To our own countryman or to a stranger,
That sin do thou, O Varuṇa, forgive us."—5. 85. 7.

"Forgive the wrongs committed by our fathers,†
What we ourselves have sinned in mercy pardon;
My own misdeeds do thou, O god, take from me,
And for another's sin let me not suffer."[259]—7. 86. 5 and 2. 28. 9.

"If ever we deceived like cheating players,
If consciously we've erred, or all unconscious,[260]
According to our sin do not thou punish;‡
Be thou the singer's guardian in thy wisdom." §
5. 85. 8 and 7. 88. 6.

* "It is nowhere clearly and distinctly expressed as the teaching of this religion, that the wages of sin is death in the sense that men die only in consequence of their guilt, and that without it they would live eternally; but the thought is often very nearly touched. Immortality is the free gift of divine mercy to men."—*Roth.*

† Ps. 79. 8: Remember not against us former iniquities. Exodus 20. 5. Ps. 109. 15. Jerem. 32. 18: *cf.* Ezek. 18. 20.

‡ Ps. 19. 13: Who can tell how oft he offendeth? Cleanse thou me from my secret faults. Job 13. 23.—Ps. 103. 10: He hath not dealt with us after our sins, nor rewarded us according to our iniquities. Ezra 9. 13. Ps. 51. 3.

§ Ps. 31. 2: 71. 2: Deliver me in thy righteousness and cause me to escape. Ps. 143. 1. 11.

The singer Vasiṣṭha is filled with pious grief, because daily, against his will and without knowledge, just as it often happens to men in their actions, he offends the god and in ignorance violates his decree.[261] Full of woe, when the hand of the god lies heavy upon him, he recalls the time when, as his most intimate friend, he held close intercourse with the Lord,* and had free approach to his high stronghold, the house of a thousand doors.[262] Anxiously he searches after the heavy sin for which the just king now visits him, his constant, loving companion. Freed from sin he yearns to be permitted, full of reverence, to approach the merciful one, and he consults the wise men by day and in the night season.† But from others he hears only what he has already discovered; that Varuṇa does not refuse his pity to him who in dire need calls upon him.[263]

This thing by day, the same by night they tell me,
And this my own heart's voice is ever saying:
He, to whom cried the fettered Çunaḥçepa,
Great Varuṇa the king shall give us freedom.

For Çunaḥçepa once, bound to three pillars,
Called in his chains on Âditya for succor.
Let Varuṇa the monarch free me also,
He can, — and may the true one loose the fetters.

We turn aside thy anger with our offerings,
O King, by our libations and devotion.
Do thou, who hast the power, wise king eternal,
Release us from the sins we have committed.
1. 24. 12–14.

And so the oppressed man calls and cries to him, the pitiful, in mercy to release him from all the guilt of sin;[264]

* *Cf.* Ps. 77. 6–10, and Note 262.

† Ps. 22. 2: O my God, I cry in the daytime, but thou hearest not; and in the night season, and am not silent. Ps. 88. 2, etc.

upon the heart of the god he presses his song, in which, full of childlike trust, he vows:

> Thee I will follow, jealous god, and serve thee,
> Faithful and true, as slaves a kindly master.
> The god gives light to minds devout though simple,
> The wise a wiser one conducts to blessing. — **7.** 86. 7.

With Varuṇa is connected also the belief in personal immortality, in the life of the soul after death, "that real *sine qua non* of all true religion."[265] That life is here understood throughout as the free gift of the gods,[266] which they grant to every upright adorer. The dead body was either consigned to the flames or laid away to gentle rest in the mother earth.[267] The earth-born shell is given back; it takes possession of its home in the broad bosom of the earth; but the soul of the pious man, which springs from above, cannot remain in the grave;[268] another place has been found for it by the righteous forefathers of olden times. Vivasvant's son, Yama, the first man, has gone to the distant heights, and has searched out a way to the 'world of the just' for the multitude after him.[269]

> He went before and found a dwelling for us,
> A place from which no power can ever bar us.
> Whither our fathers all long since have journeyed;
> His path leads every earth-born mortal thither.[270]
>
> **10.** 14. 2.

Therefore, whether the flames devour the body or the earth cover it, the spirit, freed from all needs, moves through the air toward new life;[271] led by Pûṣan,[272] it crosses the stream[273] and passes by Yama's watchful dogs[274] to the world of spirits from which it came.[275] "Go forth, go forth," — so one hymn cries to the soul of the departed at the funeral ceremony:

> Go forth, go forth upon the path so ancient,
> By which our fathers reached their home in heaven.
> There Varuna shalt thou behold, and Yama,
> The princes both, in blessedness eternal.[276]

The spotted dogs of Saramâ, the four-eyed,
Pass calmly by and hold thy way straight onward;
Enter the band of the propitious fathers,*
Dwelling in blest abodes in bliss with Yama.[277]

Join thou thyself to Yama and the fathers;
Meet there with thy reward in highest heaven;
Return to home, free from all imperfection;
In radiant power gain union with thy body.[278]
10. 14. 7. 10. 8.

In the highest heaven, therefore, is the place, in Yama's bright realm,

Where men devout in blessedness are dwelling,
Where life to life succeeds for righteous spirits,
And each is fuller than the last in beauty.[279] —**1.** 154. 5.

There in the inmost midst of the highest heaven beams unfading light, and those eternal waters spring; there wish and desire and yearning are stilled; there dwell bliss, delight, joy and happiness. This life of bliss is not pictured more clearly in the hymns of the Rig;[280] it is not asked how the new body will be endowed in that spirit-world, and whether new tasks await it there;[281] the man strives only, living according to the commands of Varuṇa, to be guiltless before him and Aditi, and hopes in childlike confiding trust that he shall at some time live above in eternal light, united with his ancestors, with his father and mother,[282] as a divine spirit among the blessed gods;[283] that, like them in appearance and might, he may be their companion and helper in their works.

As to the eternal gods, so also reverence is shown to all who have passed away, the earlier, middle and last. When a man dies, or when the anniversary of a relative's death is celebrated, then with Yama and Agni all the fathers

* "Fathers" is here the standing epithet for the 'blessed'; the souls of the departed pious ones; *cf.* Note 270 and the following.

who are known and who are not known are summoned to the funeral feast, to the food on the sacrificial straw and to the prized Soma.[284] And these who have become immortal look down upon mortals; these spirits of the dead care faithfully for their children here on earth. They move through the circle of the earth's atmosphere, through all the space of the air, among the races that dwell in beautiful villages, where men prepare the sacrifice and call them, there the holy, true, wise fathers come, full of gifts, with succor rich in blessing, with prosperity and blessing to the mortal adorer. They bring their sons might and wealth and posterity; they hear, help, comfort; they fight boldly like heroes in battle, they give a thousandfold reward for the offerings and punishment for wrong, if ever in human fashion mortals sin against them; for, themselves just, they rejoice in the right and preserve right[285] and the divine ordinances of the Eternals. They lead the dawn across the sky, and with a thousand means and ways guard the sun; they deck the heavens with stars, as a dark steed with pearls, and lay darkness in the night, and in the day the light's radiance.[286]

But to the wicked, lying evil-doers, to perverse, godless men, who violate the firm decrees of Varuṇa and Mitra, the ever watchful, to lustful, wicked women who hate their husbands, to all these that highest gift of the gods is denied; they remain shut out from the companionship of the immortals and the spirit-life in eternal light. As their bodies are sunk in the tomb, so their souls are cast into the pit, into deepest, hopeless darkness.[287] Of the descriptions of the place of torment, as the phantasy of the later Indians and other peoples evolved them, the Rigveda knows as little as of the gloomy doctrine of metempsychosis, which afterwards fettered the spirits of India in chains.

Two gods yet remain to be mentioned, to each of whom in time the qualities and deeds of the other gods collectively were ascribed.

Soma was originally the sap pressed out from the swelling fibres of a plant.[288] This herb, itself called Soma, was once brought by a fair-winged falcon from afar, from the highest heaven, or from the mountains, where Varuṇa had placed it, the world's governor.[289] Its sap, purified, mixed with milk or a decoction of barley, and left for some time for fermentation,[290] showed intoxicating effects, and was the favorite drink of the Aryans, the soul and adornment of the sacrifice, the joy of men.[291] It is drunk by the sick man as medicine at sunrise; partaking of it strengthens the limbs, preserves the legs from breaking, wards off all disease and lengthens life. Then need and trouble vanish away, pinching want is driven off and flees when the inspiring one lays hold of the mortal; the poor man, in the intoxication of the Soma, feels himself rich; the draught impels the singer to lift his voice and inspires him for song; it gives the poet supernatural power, so that he feels himself immortal.[292] On account of this inspiring power of the drink, there arose even in the Indo-Iranian period[293] a personification of the sap as the god **Soma,** and ascription to him of almost all the deeds of other gods,[294] the strength of the gods even being increased by this draught.[295] Like Agni, Soma causes his radiance to shine cheeringly in the waters; like Vâyu, he drives on with his steeds; like the Açvins, he comes in haste with aid when summoned; like Pûṣan, he excites reverence, watches over the herds, and leads by the shortest roads to success.[296] Like Indra, as the sought-for ally, he overcomes all enemies, near and far,[297] frees from the evil intentions of the envious, from danger and want,[298] brings goodly riches from heaven, from earth and the air.[299] Soma, too, makes the sun rise in the heavens, restores what has long been lost, has a thousand ways and means of help, heals all, blind and lame,[300] chases away the black skin (the aborigines), and gives everything into the possession of the pious Ârya.[301] In his, the world-ruler's, ordinance these lands stand; he, the bearer of heaven and the prop of earth, holds all peoples in his hand.[302] Bright-shining as Mitra, awe-compelling as Aryaman, he exults and gleams like Sûrya;[303] Varuṇa's commands are his commands; he, too, measures the earth's spaces, and built the vault of the heavens; like him, he, too, full of wisdom, guards the community, watches over men even in hidden places, knows the most secret things.[304] By Soma's side also, as by Varuṇa's, stand ready, never-sleeping scouts, his binding fetters follow at every step; he, too, is zealous to punish untruth and guilt.[305] Therefore, to him, also, men pray to take away the wrath of the gods, to approach with good will and without anger, and mercifully to forgive every error of his adorer, as a father pardons his son.[306]

King Soma, be thou gracious, make us prosper;
We are thy people only; know this surely.
Now rage and cunning lift their heads, O Soma;
Give us not over to our foes' desires.

Thou, Soma, guardian of our bodies, madest
Thy dwelling in each member, lord of heroes.
Though we transgress thy firm decree so often,
Be merciful to us, and kind and gracious.[307]—8. 48. 8. 9.

He will lengthen the life of the devout endlessly, and after death make him immortal in the place of the blessed, in the highest heaven.[308]

It has already been remarked above (p. 32), that **Bṛhaspati** or **Brahmaṇaspati,** the 'lord of prayer,' was 'a creation, and at the same time a personification of the priestly activity, to which later priestly poets ascribed the deeds of might for which formerly other gods, notably Indra, were praised.'[309] Thus it is said of Bṛhaspati, that his prayer upheld the ends of the earth, he embraces the All; he split the rocks, took the strongholds, opened the cow-stalls and caused the floods to flow freely.[310] All haters of devotion, despisers of the gods and enemies he exterminates, the stern avenger of crime;[311] but on the man who believingly trusts in him he bestows victory and freedom, security and plentiful riches, youthful strength and a numerous family.[312] He brings joy to the gods as well as to men; for only through his wisdom have the first obtained a share in the sacrifice[313]; for the latter he created all prayers and makes them availing; he is their rightful, skilled priest[314] and the Pontifex, the preparer of the way to the heights of heaven.[315]

We must finally call attention to the fact that a not inconsiderable number of hymns is directed to "all gods" (p. 34). These are either each one in succession called by name and entreated, or the petitions are presented to them in a body; the adorer assures them that he neither secretly is guilty of many errors nor openly provokes their wrath, and entreats of them imperishable prosperity.[316]

We will here close our survey of the religious songs, and it remains to cast a glance at the not too numerous examples of

SECULAR POETRY,

if we may embrace under this title the songs not specially directed to divinities. We can naturally not look for a sharp division of the two chief groups; the transition from the first to the second is, perhaps, best formed by two hymns, which, belonging half to the religious, half to the secular poetry, are of the greatest interest for the history of civilization.

The **Wedding-hymn,** which, in the existing form is not a unit but a collection of marriage verses,[317] relates first the wedding of the moon and sun, 'this prototype and ideal of all human weddings and marriages.' The two Açvins present the suit of Soma to Savitar for the hand of his daughter, Sûryâ, and he causes the bride heartily agreeing to be led to her husband's house. This wedding of Soma and Sûryâ (*i.e.*, of **moon** and **sun**[318]) is pointed to as the pattern of married union in general to be followed.[319] "As sun and moon ever support each other and alternate in their office, on the constant fulfillment of which depend not only the prosperity of all inanimate nature, but also the possibility of intercourse between men and the ordering of civil relations, even so man and wife must work together in harmony and with united powers untiringly fulfil the duties laid upon them in their vocation for the advancement of the family."[320] The following quotations throw important light on the rites of marriage, which in the most essential traits agree with those of related peoples.[321] When the relatives and acquaintances of the affianced pair are gathered in the house of the bride's parents (p. 15), the fire is kindled on the house-altar and the bride is given over to the bridegroom by her father or his representative (p. 15). With the formula

> By thy right hand for happiness I take thee,
> That thou mayst reach old age with me, thy husband.
> Aryaman, Bhaga, Savitar, Puraṁdhi,
> Gave thee to me to rule our home together.—**10**. 85. 36.

the bridegroom with his right hand takes the right hand of the bride.[322] He murmurs a number of traditional verses, as, *e.g.*, "I am he, thou art she; thou art she, I am he.[323] Come, we two will go forth, we will beget us posterity, many sons will we get for us, they shall reach great age. In love united, strong, cheerful, may we see a hundred years, live a hundred years, hear a hundred years." Then he leads the bride solemnly three times from left to right around the altar. With this,—by the taking of the right hand and the leading about the altar,—the bride becomes legally a wife, the bridegroom her husband. After the wedding feast is finished, the wife, in her festal adornment, is transported to the new home on a wagon decked with flowers and drawn by two white steers.[324] Here the newly-married couple are greeted with admonitions and good-wishes:

Here now remain, nor ever part;
Enjoy the whole expanse of life,
With son and grandson joyous sport,
Be glad in heart within your house.

Children and children's children grant, Prajâpati,*
Till hoary age may Aryaman preserve the bond.
From evil free enter thy husband's house and thine,
Within the home may man and beast increase and thrive.

Be free from evil looks and lack not wedded love,
Gentle in mind and face, bring e'en the beasts good luck;
Fearing the gods, do thou a race of heroes bear;
Within the home may man and beast increase and thrive.

In sons, O Indra, make her rich,
Give her a life of happiness;
Ten children grant, and spare to her
As an eleventh her dear spouse.

So rule and govern in thy home
Over thy husband's parents both;
His brother and his sister, too,
Are subject likewise there to thee.[325]—**10.** 85. 42–46.

Another solemn occasion in the life of the Vedic people is presented in a **Funeral-hymn.**[326] The relatives and friends of the dead man, about to be buried, are assembled about the corpse which has been brought to the grave. By it the widow sits; the liturgy adjures death to depart, and summons those present to devotion.

Depart, O Death, and go thy way far from us,
Far from the path which by the gods is trodden.
Thou seest and hear'st the words to thee I utter;
Harm not our children, harm not thou our heroes.

Ye who have come here, blotting out Death's footprints,
And in your yet extended life rejoicing,

* Prajâpati, '*lord of descendants,*' a genius presiding over birth, then in general protector of the living, and afterward '*lord of creatures, creator,*' as highest god over the mentioned gods of the Vedic period.

In wealth and children's blessing still increasing,
O righteous men, your minds be pure and spotless.
10. 18. 1. 2.

It then gives expression to the feeling of joy that the death-lot has not fallen to any of the assembly and urges all gladly to enjoy life in the future. A stone laid between those present and the dead typifies the separation of the realms of life and death; and in connection with it the wish is expressed that for all there a long life may be decreed.

The living from the dead are separated,
The sacred rite to-day has prospered for us,
And we are here, prepared for mirth and dancing,
Prolonging still the span of our existence.

This boundary I place here for the living,
That to this goal no one of them may hurry.
May they live on through full a thousand harvests,
And through this rock keep death away far from them.
10. 18. 3. 4.

Now women with ointments enter the circle and approach the dead lying on the bier, to deck the widow, in token of her re-entrance into intercourse with the living. The priest summons her to separate herself from the corpse and himself takes the bow out of the hand of the dead man as the symbol of his ability, which they hope will remain in the community. The interment[327] proceeds in fitting words and closes with the wish that the departed may find a place in the other world.

The women here, still happy wives, not widowed,
Shall come and bring rich oil and precious ointment;
And tearless, blooming, rich adorned, may they first
Approach the resting-place of the departed.[328]

Raise to the living world thy mind, O woman;
His breath is fled and gone by whom thou sittest;
Who took thee by the hand once and espoused thee,
With him thy plighted troth is now accomplished.

From out his lifeless hand his bow I've taken,
A pledge to us of power, strength and honor.
Thou yonder, and we here below as brave men,
Shall overcome the force of every onslaught.

Return once more unto the earth, thy mother,
Her arms she opens kindly to receive thee.
To good men kind and tender as a maiden,
May she henceforth preserve thee from destruction.

Firm may his spacious earthly home continue,
Beneath supported by a thousand pillars,
Let it henceforward be his house and riches,
A sure protecting refuge for him ever.[329]

I settle firmly now the earth about thee;
I cast the clods on thee, — let this not harm me.[330]
The Fathers shall uphold these columns for thee,
But yonder Yama shall prepare a dwelling. — **10**. 18. 7–13.

If we may not altogether look for **historical poems** among the ancestors of the Indian race, yet a number of songs of victory and triumph, most of them indeed only fragmentary, have been preserved to us.[331] Although the really historical gain is not very rich and the statements are exceedingly deficient, these fragments still give us a glance into the active, war-disturbed life of the Vedic period. The individual clans, Aryan and non-Aryan, or even Aryans among themselves, oppress and drive each other from the homes just conquered; individual pretenders to a throne seek with armed hand to make their claims good or even dare to offer violence to a whole assembly with their band. Princes and clans form alliances to offer resistance to a too powerful ruler or, in later times, to throw off the yoke of the priest-class, ever becoming more oppressive.[332]

The victorious princes love to hear their achievements praised in the loud song, and the singers soon know how to make their services indispensable; Indra, the ruler of battles, takes no pleasure in the Soma offered without prayer; he scorns the sacrificial food prepared without a song, and no mean song of praise finds favor with the divine dispensers of riches.[333] Therefore the king who cannot himself prepare a proper song of praise is forced to seek the skill of others, and so we find, among the more important princes, singers and families of singers who first through their prayers make great deeds possible for the rulers and afterwards celebrate them. In the foreground of these families of singers stand those of Viçvâmitra and Vasiṣṭha. The former had caused the rushing stream to stand still for the renowned Tṛtsu King Sudâs, made the crossing possible for his patron and sent his steed forward to victory and spoils; but in course of time, pushed forward by the rising influence of his rival Vasiṣṭha, Viçvâmitra went over to the gens of the Bharatas. With them he sets forth and comes to the junction of the rivers Vipâç and Çutudrî (Ὕφασις and Ζαδάδρης), which stream lustily forth from the bosom of the mountains, racing, like two mares let loose. At the call and loud entreaty of the singer the waves yield, they make the passage easy and do not even moisten the axles with their billows. The host proceeds confidently to battle; then the singer, sprung from Kuçika, proudly proclaims: "My prayer, the prayer of Viçvâmitra, protects the race of the Bharatas." But Indra prefers Vasiṣṭha; like ox-goads the haughty Bharatas are broken and the territory of the Tṛtsus is extended.[334] And many other exploits Sudâs accomplished with Vasiṣṭha's help; the wide-pouring river becomes a passable ford for Sudâs, while the (pursuing?) insolent Çimyu becomes the sport of the waves.

> The evil minded fools in other pathways
> Turned from its course the rushing great Paruṣṇî.*
> The lord of earth with mighty power seized them,
> And prone upon the earth lay herd and shepherd.

* Name of a river: v. p. 12* and Note 39.

At once the stream, their aim, was their destruction,
The swiftest even found rest beneath the waters.
There Indra into Sudâs' hand gave over
His flying foes, the boasters to the strong man.[335]

7. 18. 8. 9.

The defiant Bheda is overcome, the Ajas and Çigrus and Yakṣus bring the heads of the horses as tribute; Sudâs conquers the challenging Pûrus in even fight, then takes the possessions of the Anus and from them and the people of the Druhyus sinks in sleep sixty hundred, six times a thousand spoilers, and sixty-six heroes in requital; ten kings had allied themselves and surrounded Sudâs on all sides, but the adoring hymn of the guests (*i.e.*, the royal singers) was effectual; for the sake of the prayers of the Vasiṣṭhids Indra rescued the prince.[336] And many other fights are mentioned; Divodâsa quarrels with Çambara, and the Vetasu Daçadyu with the Tugras;[337] the Bharatas war with the Pûrus, and on the Harîyûpîya the rearguard of the Vṛcîvants was scattered in fear when the van had been overcome: thirty hundred mailed Vṛcîvants, united at the Yavyâvatî full of ambition, fell by the arrow and sank into destruction,[338] etc.

As sources of history may be mentioned also the so-called Dânastutis, *i.e.*, 'praise of gifts.'[339] These are portions, not of the very highest poetical order, interpolated among or added to the real hymns, in which singers of an earlier period praise the generosity of the princes who bestowed presents on them. From these we not only see that these gifts were often considerable, but also discover the names of tribes and kings, together with indications of their homes; and some light is thrown on the families of singers and their genealogies.[340] An example may be quoted here:

In this the Ruçamas did well, O Agni,
In that they gave me forty hundred cattle;
The freely offered gift of Rinamcaya,
Of heroes most heroic, we have taken.

The Ruçamas let me depart, O Agni,
Rewarded richly with a thousand cattle.
The sharp and gladdening juice made Indra merry,
When darkness lightened at the dawn of morning.

When darkness lightened at the dawn of morning,
From Rinamcaya, king of the Ruçamas,
Like speedy coursers, harnessed for the races,
Babhru received four times a thousand cattle.

Yea, forty hundred from the herds of cattle,
Did we, O Agni, get from the Ruçamas,
And, ready heated for our use in cooking,
A brazen pot did we receive, the singers.[341] — 5.30.12–15.

Among the few **humorous** pieces we find the jest of a poet, who banteringly likens the awakening of the frogs at the beginning of the rainy season, their merry croaking, and their jollity to the songs of priests intoxicated with soma, and to the noise of a school of priests.[342]

The frogs were silent all the year,
Like Brâhmans fettered by a vow.
But now Parjanya calls them forth,
And loud their voices they uplift.

Soon as the rain from heaven has fallen on them,
Like shrivelled skins within the dry pool lying,
From all at once comes up a noisy croaking,
As when the cow calls to her calf with lowings.

When the first shower of the rainy season
Has fallen on them, parched with thirst and longing,
Then each with merry croak and loudly calling
Salutes the other, as a son his father.

One seizes and congratulates the other,
Delighted at the falling of the water.
In glee each wet and dripping frog jumps upward,
The green one and the speckled join their voices.

What one calls out, another quickly answers,
Like boys at school their teacher's words repeating.
Ye seem but many members of one body,
When in the pool ye lift your varied voices.

Some low like cattle, some like goats are bleating,
And one is yellow, and another speckled.
Alike in name, but various in appearance,
In many tones they modulate their voices.

Like priests attending at the Soma-offering,
Who sit around the full bowl, loudly singing,
Ye frogs around the pond hail the recurring
Of autumn when the rain-fall first commences.

They shout aloud like Brâhmans drunk with Soma,
When they perform their annual devotions.
Like the Adhvaryu, sweating o'er the kettle,*
They issue forth, — not one remains in hiding.

The sacred order of the year observing,
These creatures never disregard the seasons;
When autumn comes and brings the time of showers,
They find release from heat and summer's scorching.

The frogs that bleat like goats, and low like cattle,
The green one and the speckled, give us riches.
Whole herds of cows may they bestow upon us,
And grant us length of days through sacrificing.† — 7. 103.

In other places we meet with reflections upon the fact, that different as are the minds of men and various as their callings, yet all run after gain; for example, continues the author, he himself is a poet, papa a physician, and mama

[* The priest who offers the prayers and praises (ṛcas) at the sacrifice is the hotar, the speaking priest; the adhvaryu, the acting priest *κατ' ἐξοχήν, performs* the sacrifice.

† This verse appears to have been added in order to give the hymn the appearance of a prayer. — GKR.]

a miller; so in the most varied ways men chase after money.[343] Another song makes us acquainted with a poet, who as poet, physician and apothecary in one person journeys about the country, carrying with him in a wooden box all sorts of healing herbs, and plying his vocation not without humor; especially with a frankness that merits recognition he makes no secret of the fact that it is not altogether philanthropy which urges him to practice, but that gain is his leading motive.[344]

Two short hymns of the tenth book display fine perception and an intelligent interpretation of nature; one, to Râtrî, the Goddess of Night, describes how she, looking out from a thousand eyes, comes forth adorned with all the glory of the stars, fills heights and depths, and puts all, even the greedy bird of prey, to rest.[345] The other sings of Araṇyâni, the mocking genius of the forest, and the solitude of the woods.[346]

As an example of the secular poetry of that ancient time a few strophes of the well-known Dice-song follows, the contents of which are indeed more tragic than humorous.[347] A passionate player describes his propensity for the brown nuts;* he cannot free himself from them, though he sees well how much misery they produce for him and his.

The nuts that once swayed on the lofty branches
Intoxicate me, rolling on the dice-board.
The fruit of the Vibhîdaka can charm me,
As 'twere the Soma of the Mûjantavas.†

My wife has never angered me nor striven,
Was ever kind to me and my companions;
Though she was faithful to me, I have spurned her,
For love of dice, the only thing I value.

* For dice the brown nuts of the Terminalia bellerica were used, the taste of which intoxicates, just as their use as dice enthrals the gambler's senses.

† A tribe living on the mountain Mûjavant in the western Himâlayas.

My wife rejects me and her mother hates me;
The gamester finds no pity for his troubles.
No better use can I see for a gambler,
Than for a costly horse worn out and aged.

Upon his wife are laid the hands of others,
While his possessions by the dice are wasted.
His father, mother, brothers, — all deny him:
"We know him not, — away with him in fetters."

The gambler's wife deserted mourns; his mother
Laments her son, she knows not where he wanders.
And he, in debt and trouble, seeking money,
Remains at night beneath the roof of strangers.

It grieves the gambler when he sees another
With wife and happy home untouched by trouble.
He yokes the brown steeds in the early morning,
And when the fire goes out he sinks degraded.

And when I say that I will play no longer,
My friends abandon me and all desert me;
Yet when again I hear the brown dice rattling,
I hasten, like a wanton to her lover.

The gambler hurries to the gaming table,
"To-day I'll win," he thinks in his excitement.
The dice inflame his greed, his hopes mount higher;
He leaves his winnings all with his opponent.

10. 34. 1–6. 10. 11.

Of **didactic-gnomic** poetry we find not a few products in the Rigveda. Experience repeatedly introduced is brought together in verse and lives as a 'winged word' in the mouths of all.[348] It seems only a variation of the proverbs of our day when we read:

The plough brings plenty when the soil it furrows;
Who moves his feet accomplishes his journey;
Speech benefits a Brâhman more than silence;
A friend who gives is better than a niggard.[349]—**10**. 117. 7.

The truth of the proposition: *Si duo faciunt idem, non est idem*, is confirmed in various directions, and it is commended as the "blessing of instruction," that "the straight path to the goal is found."[350]

To Indra himself is ascribed the saying, "Woman's mind is hard to direct aright and her judgment too is small"; while another has better words for women, and finds that many a man is better than his reputation.[351] "How many a maiden," reasons a singer, "is wooed only for her rich possessions," while another testifies "that even an ugly man is found beautiful, if only he is rich."[352] "Prudent and stupid, every one tries to extort," seeks the greatest possible gain, without being fastidious in his methods,—this seems even at that time to have been the result of experience, as well as that "many a one brings gifts of sacrifice only through fear of blame."[353] But in other passages the duty and the blessing of good deeds are loudly proclaimed:

> Let him who can give succor to the needy,
> And well his future path of life consider.
> For fortune like the wheels of chariots rolling,
> Now, shifting, comes to one, now to another.[354]—**10. 117. 5.**

By sharing with others one's own store is never decreased, and through beneficence a man gains to himself good friends for the changeful future.[355] The so-called Song of Wisdom among other matters, reflects how many see without perceiving, how many hear without understanding, while for others all difficulties disappear of their own accord.[356] The saying of Vâmadeva, "Not without pains are the gods made friends" could serve as admonition and encouragement, and on the other hand as recognition that "the rule of the gods is too high for man's wisdom; we men, all, are companions in death; speedily life runs away," and each one in death must abandon his wealth and become a solemn memento to some one.[357]

The **Formulas** of **Incantation** and **Exorcism** may also be regarded as a kind of didactic poetry, although their proper department is really the Atharvaveda (above, p. 4); but a number of such formulas are to be found in the Rig, *e.g.* for healing the most various diseases. Such a '*mantra*' is repeated, and the healing of the sick person accomplished by the laying on of hands[358] or some other ceremony;[359] one who is near to death is recalled to life,[360] an evil intention, a hostile demon, may be made harmless, a bad omen averted,[361] a fortunate rival in love driven off,[362] a herd gathered together again, etc.

As a second branch of didactic composition we must mention the **Poetical Riddles.** The simplest form is shown in a short hymn of the eighth book;[363] from the very short descriptions the gods meant can be guessed, thus:

> One in his mighty hand holds fast the thunderbolt,
> With it his enemies he smites.
>
> And one bears in his mighty hand a weapon sharp,
> Yet kind withal, he seeks to heal.
>
> Through empty space another made three mighty strides
> Where the gods dwell in blessedness.
>
> And two, with but one bride, on winged steeds go forth,
> They journey onward far away. — **8.** 29. 4. 5. 7. 8.

Much more intricate and difficult, however, were the riddles and enigmas (*brahmodya*), which in later Vedic time came into use at the great sacrifices of the kings, and at contests of various kinds. The priests propounded all sorts of questions from the whole circle of priestly knowledge, not only to the princes offering the sacrifice, but also to their companions in office, with whom they strove for pre-eminence. In these questions "the matters in discussion are usually not called by their ordinary, commonly understood names, but are indicated by symbolical expressions, or even only by mystical references, in which numbers play an important part. They are taken now from nature, now from the spiritual life. Heaven and earth, sun and moon, the atmosphere, the clouds, rain and its production by evaporation of the mists by means of the sun's rays, the sun's course, the year, the seasons, months, days and nights, are here favorite subjects of symbolic clothing; their interpretation is regarded as the highest wisdom."[364]

With this enigmatical poetry the last group of hymns which have still to be mentioned, the **Philosophical Poetry**, stands in the closest connection.[365] With few exceptions[366] the compositions of this class are occupied with questions concerning the beginning and origin of all things, such queries occurring also here and there in the enigmatical hymns. A system of cosmogony is naturally not yet found here; they are throughout only first questions and attempts, the most primitive beginnings of natural philosophy and theories of creation. The poets like infants in their ignorance search with their intellect for the hidden traces of the invisible, unseen gods, for their origin and deeds.[367] They are no longer satisfied with hearing that this or that god has created heaven and earth and fire and sun and dawn; in all seriousness "in order to know it, not for pastime alone," one asks, how many fires and how many suns, how many dawns and waters there are; whether day was created before night, or night before day, while another desires to know what tree it was, what kind of wood,* of which heaven and earth once were built, eternally firm, while days, many mornings, vanish; upon what the creator stood, when he upheld the worlds; what then was his standing-ground, what was the order of events, having made the earth out of w h a t he enclosed the heavens with might.[368] The question repeatedly appears, how and when from not-being the way was found to being, while others exert themselves to establish the

* *i.e.*, the ὕλη, the material, the original matter.

beginning of all existent things, the original matter.[369] The solution of these problems is naturally, where not evidently from the first shown to lie outside of human wisdom, very varied in result,[370] and even the lines of development, if we may use the term, differ greatly.[371] Sometimes fire, sometimes the all-nourishing water is named as the original matter, as among the Greek philosophers;[372] in other passages an original germ is spoken of, which, on the other side of heaven and this earth and the living gods, the waters received into themselves, in which the gods all met.

Far out beyond this earth, beyond the heavens,
Far, too, beyond the living gods and spirits,
What earliest germ was hidden in the waters,
In which the gods were all beheld together?

The waters held that earliest germ within them
In which the living gods were all united.
That One lay in the bosom of the unborn,
And all created beings rested in it.

Him ye can never know who formed these creatures,
Between yourselves and him lies yet another.
With stammering tongue and all in mist enveloped,
The singers go about in life rejoicing.[373]—**10.** 82. 5–7.

Another prominent hymn praises Hiraṇyagarbha, the 'gold-germ,' as the kindly origin of all being, who existed even before the first breath of the gods, who alone is god among all the gods.

In the beginning rose Hiraṇyagarbha,
Born as the only lord of all existence.
This earth he settled firm and heaven established:
What god shall we adore with our oblations?

Who gives us breath, who gives us strength, whose bidding
All creatures must obey, the bright gods even;

Whose shade is death, whose shadow life immortal:
What god shall we adore with our oblations?

Who by his might alone became the monarch
Of all that breathes, of all that wakes or slumbers,
Of all, both man and beast, the lord eternal:
What god shall we adore with our oblations?

Whose might and majesty these snowy mountains,
The ocean and the distant stream exhibit;
Whose arms extended are these spreading regions:
What god shall we adore with our oblations?

Who made the heavens bright, the earth enduring,
Who fixed the firmament, the heaven of heavens;
Who measured out the air's extended spaces:
What god shall we adore with our oblations?

To whom with trembling mind the two great armies
Look up, by his eternal will supported;
On whom the sun sheds brightness in its rising:
What god shall we adore with our oblations?

10. 121. 1–6.

The monotheistic conception lying at the foundation of this hymn (above, p. 34) appears more prominently, with the exception of some single verses in two hymns directed to Viçvakarman, *i.e.*, the 'All-creator' of unrivalled power of mind and body, to him

Who is our father, our creator, maker,
Who every place doth know and every creature,
By whom alone to gods their names were given,
To him all other creatures go, to ask him.[374] — **10**. 82. 3.

By far the most important composition of this class in the whole Veda is the 'Song of Creation,' recognized even by Colebrooke.[375] In the beginning, when the contrasts of being and not-being, of death and immortality, of day and night, did not yet exist, only one thing hovered over the empty waste, and this one came into life through the force of heat; there the first germ of mind showed itself; then the wise ones, the cosmogonic gods, were able to call forth being out of not-being, and to separate and divide the heretofore unordered masses. But in spite of this solution the whole creation and many single things in it remain a riddle to the poet.

Then there was neither being nor not-being.
The atmosphere was not, nor sky above it.
What covered all? and where? by what protected?
Was there the fathomless abyss of waters?

Then neither death nor deathlessness existed;
Of day and night there was yet no distinction.
Alone that One breathed calmly, self-supported,
Other than It was none, nor aught above It.

Darkness there was at first in darkness hidden;
This universe was undistinguished water.
That which in void and emptiness lay hidden
Alone by power of fervor was developed.

Then for the first time there arose desire,
Which was the primal germ of mind, within it.
And sages, searching in their heart, discovered
In Nothing the connecting bond of Being.

And straight across their cord was then extended:
What then was there above? or what beneath it?
Life giving principles and powers existed;
Below the origin, — the striving upward.

Who is it knows? Who here can tell us surely
From what and how this universe has risen?
And whether not till *after* it the gods lived?
Who then can know from what it has arisen?

The source from which this universe has risen
And whether it was made, or uncreated,

He only knows, who from the highest heaven
Rules, the all-seeing lord, — or does not He know?

10. 129.

We stand at the end of our survey. From it we ought to recognize that we have in the Rigveda a literature which well deserves 'at least in extracts to be known to every student and lover of antiquity,' to every one who would have the poet's words, *Homo sum; humanum nihil a me alienum puto*, applied to himself. The chief importance of the Veda is not indeed for the history of literature, but it lies elsewhere; it lies, as the following commentary seeks to show, in the very extraordinary fullness of disclosures which this unique book gives to the student of philology and the history of civilization. In this, no other literature is to be compared with it, and though the aesthetic value of this relic of long-vanished times has sometimes been exaggerated, yet its historical importance, its value for the history of mankind, cannot easily be overrated.

ABBREVIATIONS.

AfKM.: Abhandlungen für die Kunde des Morgenlandes, published by the German Oriental Society. Leipzig 1857 ff.

BI.: Bibliotheca Indica, a collection of oriental works, published under the superintendence of the Asiatic Society of Bengal. Calcutta 1849 ff.

BR.: Sanskrit Wörterbuch, by Otto Böhtlingk and Rudolph Roth: Note 30.

GKR.: Siebenzig Lieder des Rigveda, übersetzt von K. Geldner und A. Kaegi mit Beiträgen von R. Roth: see p. 34 and Note 116. For the sake of brevity quotations are given in large italics, so that *e.g.* ***4, 33, 4*** (121) means 4, 33, 4, translated in GKR. page 121.

ISt.: Indische Studien, edited by A. Weber. Vol. 1–17. Berlin and Leipzig 1849–1885.

JAOS.: Journal of the American Oriental Society.

JLZ.: Jenaer Literatur-Zeitung von A. Klette.

JRAS.: Journal of the Royal Asiatic Society of Great Britain and Ireland (NS.: New Series).

Jbb.: Fleckeisen's Jahrbücher für classische Philologie. Vol. 121 (1880).

KZ.: Kuhn's Zeitschrift für vergleichende Sprachforschung. Vol. 1–28.

OO.: Orient and Occident, insbesondere in ihren gegenseitigen Beziehungen, Forschungen und Mittheilungen. Quarterly, edited by Theo. Benfey.

SBE.: The Sacred Books of the East, Translated by various Oriental Scholars and edited by F. Max Müller. Oxford 1879 ff.

Benfey, GdSpr.: Geschichte der Sprachwissenschaft und orientalischen Philologie in Deutschland, München 1869.

Lassen, IA.: Indische Alterthumskunde. Vol. 1 and 2 quoted in the second ed. (Leipzig 1867, 1874), vol. 3 and 4 in the first ed. (Bonn 1858, 1861).

M. Müller, ASL.: A History of Ancient Sanskrit Literature. London 1859.

M. Müller, LSL.: Lectures on the Science of Language. First and Second Series. New York (Scribners) 1872. (Quotations refer to the American edition; the paging of the English edition is given on p. 180.)

M. Müller, OGR.: Lectures on the Origin and Growth of Religion as illustrated by the religions of India. London 1882.

J. Muir, MTr.: Metrical Translations from Sanskrit writers. London 1879.

J. Muir, OST.: Original Sanskrit Texts: see Note 115.

Roth, ZLGW.: Zur Litteratur und Geschichte des Weda: see p. 2 and Note 7.

A. Weber, HIL.: History of Indian Literature. Translated from the second German edition. Boston 1878. (Reprint of the English edition.)

A. Weber, IStr.: Indische Streifen. Berlin and Leipzig 1868–1879.

W. D. Whitney, OLSt.: Oriental and Linguistic Studies. 2 volumes. New York 1873, 1874.

ZDMG.: Zeitschrift der Deutschen Morgenländischen Gesellschaft. Leipzig, vols. 1–39, 1847–1885.

H. Zimmer, AIL.: Altindisches Leben. Berlin 1879: see p. 11 and Note 35.

Beside the works already mentioned the following treat of the Veda: Müller in the Chips from a German Workshop, especially vol. 1.— Whitney in the treatises, The Vedas; The Vedic Doctrine of a Future Life; Müller's History of Vedic Literature; The Translation of the Veda in vol. 1 of his Oriental and Linguistic Studies, and in his notes to Colebrooke's Misc. Essays (see Note 5). — Westergaard, Ueber den ältesten Zeitraum der indischen Geschichte mit Rücksicht auf die Literatur. Aus dem Dänischen übersetzt. Breslau 1862. — P. Wurm, Geschichte der Indischen Religion. Basel 1874, pp. 21–62. — A. Ludwig, Die Nachrichten des Rig und Atharvaveda über Geographie, Geschichte, Verfassung des alten Indien. Prag 1875. Die Philosophischen und Religiösen Anschauungen des Veda in ihrer Entwickelung. Prag 1875. Der Rigveda oder die heiligen Hymnen der Brâhmana. Vol. 3: Die Mantraliteratur und das alte Indien als Einleitung zur Uebersetzung des Rigveda (*cf.* Note 116). Prag 1878. — [A. Bergaigne, La Religion Védique d'après les Hymnes du Rig-Veda. Paris 1878. — Barth, The Religions of India. Translated by Rev. J. Wood, London 1882.]

NOTES.

1. Essai, etc.: Introd. § 10 and 1ère partie, chap. 4 (vol. 1, 77 and 2, 57 ff. of the edition of an XIII = 1805, or Œuvres, t. 14, p. 79 ff. and 290 ff. of the ed. of 1785); *cf.* Barthélemy-Saint-Hilaire, Des Védas, 1854, p. 15 ff.

2. The *Ezour-(= Yajur) Vedam* (Ith.: see Gildemeister, Bibl. Sanscr. 28, 103–106), presented by Voltaire to the Royal Library in Paris in 1761, published in 1778 by Sainte-Croix, and also translated into German, is a forgery made in the 17th century by a Jesuit missionary, perhaps Robertus de Nobilibus (*cf.* Müller, LSL. 1, 155 and 156 note); see Fr. Ellis, Asiat. Res., vol. 14, Calcutta 1822, pp. 1–59; A. Schlegel, Indische Bibliothek, vol. 2 (1824), 50 ff.

3. Ed. of Julian Schmidt, Leipzig 1869, vol. 2, 148 ff.

4. In the same year (1784) the "Asiatic Society" was founded in Calcutta, for the investigation of Asiatic antiquity in its widest extent. In 1785, Wilkins' translation of the *Bhagavad-gîtâ* appeared in London; 1789, the celebrated translation of *Çakuntalâ*, by W. Jones, in Calcutta (German by G. Forster, Mainz and Leipzig 1791; 2d ed. Frankfurt 1803); 1792, the first printed Sanskrit text (*Ritusanhâra:* The Seasons, a Descriptive Poem by Cálidás, in the Original Sanscrit, Calcutta), etc. See Gildemeister, Bibl. Sanscr., p. 173 ff.

5. Asiat. Res. vol. 8, Calc. 1805, pp. 369–476; newly edited, with valuable notes by Whitney, in Colebrooke's Miscellaneous Essays, edited by Cowell, 1873, vol. 1, pp. 8–132.

6. Rigvedae Specimen, ed. F. Rosen, London 1830; then Rigveda Sanhita, liber primus, sanskrite et latine, ed. F. Rosen, London 1838. (R. died Sept. 12, 1837.)

7. The enormous progress in knowledge of the Veda shown in this work of Roth can to-day only be appreciated if we compare with it what Benfey was able to give a few years before in his article *India* in Ersch and Gruber's Allgem. Encycl., 2 sect. vol. 17, p. 161 f. Müller's *History* appeared 1860; Weber's *Vorlesungen* in a second, much enlarged edition, Berlin 1875 (additions to it 1878).

8. The first complete edition of the text was that of Aufrecht, 2 vols., Berlin 1861, 1863 (= ISt. vol. 6. 7), in Latin transliteration;

2d ed., Bonn 1877, with valuable additions (among others, an index of first lines and quotations, when the verses are cited in other Vedic literature; reprint of the *Khila*, *i.e.* the 'supplements' found in the manuscripts, but not counted with the hymns). The text in Sanskrit characters is given by M. Müller, The Hymns of the Rigveda, London 1873. 2 vols. (Sanhitâ- and Pada-Text: *cf.* note 77); 2d ed., London 1877. With the commentary of Sâyaṇa, complete index of words and first lines, in 6 vols., edited by M. Müller, London 1849–75.

The first alphabetical index of first lines was given by W. Pertsch, ISt. 3, 1–118 (additions by Aufrecht, ISt. 4, 434 f.); a tabulated synopsis of the four Sanhitâs: Whitney, ISt. 2, 321–368; a very valuable dictionary, H. Grassmann, Leipzig 1873–75.

9. *Sâman*, according to Burnell (Introd. to the Ârṣeya-Brâhmaṇa, Mangalore and Basle 1876) and Barth (Rev. Crit. 1877, II, p. 21), means only "*melody*," independent of the text (Rig-verse) connected with it, which may be changed at will. The edition *Sâmavedârcikam*, Die Hymnen des Sâmaveda, herausgegeben, übersetzt und mit Glossar versehen von Th. Benfey, Leipzig 1848, gives the *Rânîyanîya*çâkhâ; elsewhere, the *Kauthuma*çâkhâ, of which the *Naigeya* is a sub-division (see S. Goldschmidt, Berl. Monatsber. 1868, p. 228 f.). A. Weber's assertion, HIL. 9. 64 ff., that the variants of the Sâmasanhitâ are older and more original than those of the Rigsanhitâ (*cf.* Ludw. Rv. 3, 83-95; 91: "Thus it is evident that the Sâmaveda has an older form than the Rigveda") is opposed by Burnell, Ârṣeyabrâhmaṇa, p. xvi f., and Aufrecht, Rigveda, 2d ed., vol. 2, pref. p. xxxvii to xlv. The latter gives p. xlv–xlvii an alphabetical index of the 75 verses peculiar to the Sâmaveda, not contained in our Rigveda [Hillebrandt, Spuren einer älteren Rigveda Recension, Beiträge zur Kunde der Indo-Germ. Spr. vol. 8, 195 ff.], which are translated by Ludw. Rv. 3, 419–426.

10. The two principal groups of these prayer-books, the *Black* and the *White Yajurveda*, are essentially distinguished by the fact that in the Black the sacrificial verses are followed immediately by their dogmatic interpretation, description of the accompanying ritual, etc., and the Brâhmaṇa belonging to it is to be considered as an addition differing only in time; while in the White the verses for the sacrifices are contained in the Sanhitâ, the interpretation and ritual in the Brâhmaṇa, and thus are separated throughout.

1. Of the Black Yajurveda two recensions have been known for some time: the *Taittirîya-sanhitâ* (text of the school of Âpastamba: ed. by A. Weber, Leipzig 1871–72 = ISt. vol. 11, 12), and the *Kâṭhaka* (text of the *Kaṭha* school, v. Weber ISt. 3, 451–479, HIL. 88 ff., L. v. Schroeder, Berl. Monatsber. July 1879, p. 675–704). The first inform-

ation of a new recension, the *Maitrâyaṇî-sanhitâ*, was given by Haug (ISt. 9, 174 f., Brahma und die Brahmanen, München 1871, pp. 31–34); then Bühler, ISt. 13, 117–128, and lately L. v. Schroeder, ZDMG. 33 (1879), 177–207 [Ueber die Mâitrayaṇî Sanhitâ, Dorpat 1879; ed. by Schroeder, Leipzig 1881], and Berl. Monatsber. 1879, pp. 675–704. The latter makes it very probable that this Çâkhâ is to be put at the head of the whole Yajus period, and is identical with the famous text of the *Kalâpins*.

2. Of the White Yajurveda both the known recensions of *Mâdhyandina* and *Kâṇva* are contained in Weber's edition, *The Vâjasaneyi-Sanhitâ*, Berlin 1852. The last, fortieth, book of this Sanhitâ is the Îçâ-, or Îçâvâsya-Upaniṣad, translated *e.g.* by Röer in BI. Ludw. Rv. 3, 34 f. M. Müller, see Note 16.

11. *Cf.* RV. 10, 90, 9; AV. 7, 54, 2; 12, 1, 38; Ait. Br. 5, 32, 4. — AV. 10, 7, 20, with the Rig, Yajus and Sâman mentions also the Atharvângiras, *i.e.* a fourth collection in the style of our Atharvaveda. According to Burnell (Vançabrâhmaṇa of the Sâmaveda, p. xxi) the most influential scholars of Southern India still obstinately deny the genuineness of this Veda.

12. *E.g.* Ad. Kuhn, KZ. 13, 48–74 and 113–157, places side by side a number of Indian formulas (especially those contained in the Atharva) for banishing sickness, and similar Germanic ones, "which in both peoples correspond so remarkably, not only in purpose and contents, but also partially in form, that we must fully recognize in them the remains of a kind of poetry, which, even in the old Indo-Germanic period, had developed the contents of incantations designed for certain uses into a fixed form, preserved up to the latest times in all the formulas growing out of it." For other traces of Indo-Germanic poetry, *cf.* Note 82.

13. *Atharvaveda-Sanhitâ*, edited by R. Roth and W. D. Whitney, Berlin 1856, contains the "Vulgate" (text of the *Çaunakas?*) in 20 books, the last two of which did not belong to the original collection. Since 1875 the *Paipalâdi*-çâkhâ has become better known through Roth's Der Atharvaveda in Kashmir. Tübingen 1875. (P. 20: "But if all this (*sc.* known in any other place) is taken away, there will remain a mass so large that it may be appraised as the eighth or ninth part of the whole (Atharva).") Sâyaṇa's Commentary to this Sanhitâ was discovered in 1880; *cf.* Academy of June 12, 1880, and Ind. Antiq. Aug. 1880.

Book 1 has been translated by A. Weber, ISt. 4, 393–430; Book 2 by A. Weber, Berl. Monatsber. 1870, June, pp. 462–524 = ISt. 13, 129–216; Book 14 by A. Weber, ISt. 5, 195–217; Book 15 by Aufrecht, ISt. 1, 130–140; besides Hundert Lieder des Atharvaveda von J. Grill,

Tübingen 1879, and many single songs by A. Weber, ISt. 5, 218–266, etc., by Zimmer, AIL. (Index, pp. 453–457), by Ludwig, Rv. vol. 3, especially pp. 428–551, and elsewhere. Whitney, ISt. 4, 9–62, gives an alphabetical index of first lines, and JAOS. 12 (1881) a complete Index Verborum.

14. The name Brâhmaṇa (neut.) is to be derived, not from the masc. *brahmán*, 'chief priest' (Müller, ASL. 172, 342. Haug, Ait. Br. 1, p. 4 f. [Eggeling, SBE. 12. Introd. p. xxii ff.]), but from the neut. *bráhman*, 'formula, ceremony' (Whitney, OLSt. 1, 68, 1. Weber, HIL. 11, ISt. 9, 351 f.). Concerning these books Müller, ASL. 389, says: "The Brâhmanas represent no doubt a most interesting phase in the history of the Indian mind, but judged by themselves as literary productions, they are most disappointing. No one would have supposed that at so early a period, and in so primitive a state of society, there could have risen up a literature which, for pedantry and downright absurdity, can hardly be matched anywhere. There is no lack of striking thoughts, of bold expressions, of sound reasoning, and curious traditions in these collections. But they are only like the fragments of a torso, like precious gems set in brass and lead. The general character of these works is marked by shallow and insipid grandiloquence, by priestly conceit and antiquarian pedantry. It is most important to the historian that he should know how soon the fresh and healthy growth of a nation can be blighted by priestcraft and superstition. . . . These works deserve to be studied as the physician studies the twaddle of idiots and the raving of madmen." Müller places the Brâhmaṇa Period (Chips, 1, 14; *cf.* ASL. 435) between 800 and 600 B.C. (Haug between 1400 and 1200: *cf.* Note 38).

14 *a.* Of the Brâhmaṇas (Roth, Nirukta. Introd. p. xxiv f. A. Weber, HIL. 11 f. M. Müller, ASL. 313 ff. Ludw. Rv. 3, 30 f.; shorter extracts in Monier Williams, Indian Wisdom, London 1875, pp. 27–35) belong

1. To the Rigveda, two (both attaching themselves to recensions of the text differing from that preserved), namely:
   Aitareya-Brâhmaṇa, edited, translated, and explained by M. Haug. Bombay 1863 (with which *cf.* Weber, ISt. 9, 177–380); edited with additions by Th. Aufrecht. Bonn 1879; to this belongs the
   Aitareya-Âraṇyaka in five books, the first three translated by M. Müller, SBE. 1, 155–268 (*cf.* ibid. Introd. pp. xci–xcviii), with the
   Aitareya-Upaniṣad, ed. by Roër in BI., *cf.* Weber, ISt. 1, 387–392;

Kauṣîtaki- or Çânkhâyana-Brâhmaṇa (*cf.* Weber, ISt. 2, 288–315), with the

Kauṣîtaki-Âraṇyaka, the third book of which forms the very valuable

Kauṣîtaki-Upaniṣad; see Weber, ISt. 1, 392–420; ed. and transl. by Cowell in BI.; translated by M. Müller, SBE. 1, 269–308; *cf.* ibid. Introd. pp. xcviii–c.

2. To the Sâmaveda (see the review of the literature by Weber, ISt. 1, 31–67; for the number of the Brâhmaṇas, Weber, HIL. 74; ISt. 4, 375):

Tâṇḍya- or Praudha- or Pancaviñça-Brâhmaṇa, edited in BI.; an addition to it is the

Ṣadviñça-Brâhmaṇa, the last part of which forms the

Adbhuta-Brâhmaṇa; edited, translated, and explained by A. Weber, Zwei vedische Texte über Omina und Portenta. Berlin 1859 (Berl. Akad. Abh. Philol.-Histor. Classe 1858, pp. 313–343).

Chândogya-Brâhmaṇa in ten books, of which, up to the present time, only eight are known in Europe, forming the important Chândogya-Upaniṣad; *cf.* A. Weber, ISt. 1, 254–273; in BI. edit. by Röer, translated by Râjendra Lâla Mitra; translated by M. Müller, SBE. 1, 1–144, Introd. p. lxxxvi f.

Talavakâra- or Jaiminîya-Brâhmaṇa, only lately discovered in Southern India by Burnell [see Whitney, on the Jâiminîya-Brâhmaṇa. Am. Or. Soc. Proc., May 1883], a part of it having already been long known as the

Talavakâra- or Kena-Upaniṣad, see A. Weber, ISt. 2, 181–195; ed. and transl. by Röer in BI; translated by M. Müller, SBE. 1, 147–156, *cf.* Introd. p. lxxxix f. As a part of the same Brâhmaṇa appears now the

Ârṣeya-Brâhmaṇa, edit. by Burnell, Mangalore 1876 (and 1878 in the Jaiminîya text).

The following writings, belonging rather to the Sûtras, are also, but only improperly, called Brâhmaṇa:

Sâmavidhâna-Brâhmaṇa, ed. by Burnell, London 1873.

Vança-Brâhmaṇa, ed. and comment. by A. Weber, ISt. 4, 371–386; ed. by Burnell, Mangalore 1873;

Devatâdhyâya-Brâhmaṇa, ed. by Burnell, Mangalore 1873; the above-mentioned Ârṣeya-Brâhmaṇa and the

Sanhitopaniṣad-Brâhmaṇa (ISt. 4, 375); ed. by Burnell, Mangalore 1877.

3. To the Black Yajurveda (Taittirîya-Sanhitâ):

Taittirîya-Brâhmaṇa (*cf.* Note 10), edit. by Râjendra Lâla

Mitra, in BI. (the legend of Naciketas concerning existence after death, translated by Muir, OST. 5, 329 f., MTr. 54 ff., 252 ff., M. Müller, OGR. 340 ff.); with the
Taittirîya-Âraṇyaka (by the same editor in BI.); with the Taittirîya-Upaniṣad, see A. Weber, ISt. 2, 210–236.

4. To the White Yajurveda (Vâjasaneyi-Sanhitâ), the most important of all Brâhmaṇas, the
Çatapatha-Brâhmaṇa, edited by A. Weber, Berlin 1855 (The White Yajurveda, vol. 2); *cf.* HIL. 116–139. M. Müller, ASL. 349–360; several legends of general interest (story of the flood, the fountain of youth, punishment after death) are translated in Weber's IStr. 1, 9–30. [Transl. by J. Eggeling, SBE., vol. 12; *cf.* Whitney, on Eggeling's Translation of the Çatapatha-Brâhmaṇa, Am. Journ. of Philol. 3, 390–410], and for the whole work Weber, HIL. 116 ff. This Brâhmaṇa contains in the 14th Book the
Bṛhad-Âraṇyaka, edited by Poley (Upaniṣads, Bonn 1844); edited and translated by Röer in BI. (Yâjnavalkya's treatise on immortality is also translated by Müller, ASL. 22 f., OGR. 335 ff.; Muir, MTr. 51 f., 246 f.).

5. To the Atharvaveda:
Gopatha-Brâhmaṇa: Müller, ASL. 445 f., edit. in BI., see Weber, HIL. 150, 151.

15. Magasthenes in Strabo 15, 60, p. 713: Τοὺς δὲ Γαρμᾶνας (leg. Σαρμᾶνας) τοὺς μὲν ἐντιμοτάτους ὑλοβίους φησὶν [ὁ Μεγασθένης] ὀνομάζεσθαι, ζῶντας ἐν ταῖς ὕλαις ἀπὸ φύλλων καὶ καρπῶν ἀγρίων, ἐσθῆτος φλοιῶν δενδρείων, ἀφροδισίων χωρὶς καὶ οἴνου τλ.; *cf.* ibid. ch. 70, p. 719, Weber, HIL. 27 f. — The ὑλόβιοι are the *vânaprasthas* (wood-dwellers). The later development of the ruling priesthood recognizes four stages (*âçrama*) in the life of the Brâhman; first he is a *brahmacârín* (disciple of a Brâhman), then a *gṛhastha* (married, father of a family), then a *vânaprastha*, and finally a *bhikṣu* or *samnyâsin* (a beggar living on alms, who has denied the world); more in full *e.g.* in OGR. 350 ff.

16. "Next follow the Âraṇyakas (*cf.* Müller, ASL. 313–315, 329–339. Ludw. Rv. 3, 33 f.), which, not only by the position which they occupy at the end of the Brâhmanas, but also by their character, seem to be of a later age again. Their object is to show how sacrifices may be performed by people living in the forest, without any of the pomp described in the Brâhmanas and the later Sûtras — by a mere mental effort. The worshipper had only to imagine the sacrifice, to go through it only in his memory, and he thus acquired the same merit as the performer of tedious rites. Lastly come the

Upaniṣads; and what is their object? To show the utter uselessness, nay, the mischievousness, of all ritual performances; to condemn every sacrificial act which has for its motive a desire or hope of reward; to deny, if not the existence, at least, the exceptional and exalted character of the Devas, and to teach that there is no hope of salvation and deliverance, except by the individual Self recognizing the true and universal Self, and finding rest there, where alone rest can be found." M. Müller, OGR. 347 f.

The number of the Upaniṣads is very large; M. Müller's alphabetical index in ZDMG. 19, 137–158, enumerates (1865) 149 of them, while A. Weber, 1875 (HIL. 155, note, *cf.* JLZ. 1878, p. 81 = IStr. 3, 564) counts 235. For this class of writings, consult the review with extracts in English translation, in Monier Williams, Indian Wisdom, pp. 35–47; P. Regnaud, Matériaux pour servir à l'histoire de la philosophie de l'Inde, 2 vols., Paris 1876 and 1878 (*cf.* Weber, JLZ. 1878, pp. 81–84 = IStr. 3, 563–576, concerning vol. 1), Deussen, Vedânta (1883), p. 82 f., and M. Müller, The Upanishads (= SBE. vols. 1 and 15). [For the latter, *cf.* Whitney, Am. Or. Soc. Proc., Oct. 1885.] The first part (1879) contains, besides general and bibliographical introductions, the translation of the above-mentioned

Aitareya-Âraṇyaka and Kauṣîtaki-Upaniṣad of the Rigveda,
Châandogya-Upaniṣad, Kena- or Talavakâra-Upaniṣad of the Sâmaveda,
and the Vâjasaneyi-Sanhitâ-Upaniṣad or Îçâ- (Îçâvâsya-) Upaniṣad (*cf.* Note 10, 2), pp. 311–320, Introd. pp. c. ci.

17. Müller, ASL. 72, OGR. 150. — Müller places the Sûtra period between 600 and 200 B.C. (ASL. 244).

18. A well-known mnemonic verse gives the order (*e.g.* in Müller, ASL. 111):

çikṣâ kalpo vyâkaraṇam niruktam chando jyotiṣam.

Of these names for classes of writings some were applied specially to individual treatises of relatively late origin; thus Çikṣâ (edited and translated by Weber, ISt. 4, 375–371), Jyotiṣa (ed., transl., and comment. by A. Weber, Berl. Akad. Abh. Philol.-Hist. Cl. 1862, pp. 1–130: Ueber den Vedakalender Jyotiṣam) and Chandas (ed., transl., and comment. by Weber, ISt. 8, 209 f.). — More recently other Çikṣâs have been discovered; Kielhorn, ISt. 14, 160.

19. Yâska's Nirukta sammt den Nighantavas, herausgegeben und erläutert von R. Roth. Göttingen 1852. [Ed. also in BI.] The *Nighaṇṭavas* (sing. *Nighaṇṭu*) are collections of words placed together (γλῶσσαι). Yâska's book is founded on five of these collections (1–3 put synonyms together, 4 contains specially difficult words, and 5 gives a classification of the Vedic divinities), to which Yâska's *explanation* (nirukti) in 12 books is added (Books 13 and 14 are later). Yâska is himself commentated by Durga (13th cent.).

20. The first account of the Prâtiçâkhyas was given by Roth, ZLGW. 53 f. Nirukta, Introd. p. xlii f. Their real purpose is shown by Note 78. Of these specially important and interesting works the following have been edited and translated:

The Rig-Prâtiçâkhya of Çaunaka, German by M. Müller. Leipzig 1856–1869. French by Ad. Regnier. Paris 1857–1858.

The Taittirîya-Prâtiçâkhya, English by Whitney, JAOS. 9, 1–469 (1871).

The Vâjasaneyi-Prâtiçâkhya of Kâtyâyana, German by A. Weber, ISt. 4, 65–171, and ibid. 177–331.

The Atharva-Prâtiçâkhya of Çaunaka, English by Whitney, JAOS. 7, 333–615 (1862), addenda ibid. 10, 156–171.

21. The date of Pâṇini is a matter of much dispute; *cf.* Lassen, IA. 1, 864 ff. M. Müller, ASL. 304–310. Whitney, OLSt. 1, 75 f. Benfey, GdSpr. p. 48, 1. A. Weber, *e.g.* ISt. 1, 141 f., 4, 87 f., 5, 172. HIL. 217 ff. IStr. 3, 408.

According to G. Bühler, OO. 2, 703, Pâṇini's work is an "improved, completed, and partially rewritten edition" of Çâkaṭâyana; *cf.* Burnell, On the Aindra School of Sanskrit Grammarians. London 1875. p. 97 ff. A. Weber, IStr. 3, 414 f. [Pâṇini's Eight Books of Grammatical Sûtras. Ed. with an Eng. transl. and commentary by W. Goontilleke. Bombay 1882 ff.]

22. Benfey, GdSpr. p. 35, 36 (*cf.* Gött. Gel. Anz. 1860, 279 f.), where, pp. 35–100, an excellent survey of Indian grammar is given. [Whitney, The Study of Sanskrit and the Hindu Grammarians. Am. Journ. Philol. 5, 279–297.]

23. Certain of the Vedic teachers and schools did not occupy themselves with the 'revealed texts,' Sanhitâ and Brâhmaṇa, but only with the Sûtras (*Sûtracaraṇa*): they created a new systematic presentation of all the requirements of the ritual, a compendium of the whole Kalpa. *E.g.* the Kalpa of Âpastamba (belonging to the Black Yajus), consisting of 30 praçnas, contains in praçna 1–24 the çrauta-regulations, praçna 25 the general regulations of the sacrifice (applying both to public and family sacrifice), praçna 26 and 27 the gṛhya-regulations, praçna 28 and 29 the dharma-regulations, and praçna 30 the Çulva-sûtras (see Note 26). — "Pâraskara's Gṛhya-sûtra is closely connected with Kâtyâyana's Çrauta-sûtra, and is considered a mere component part of the latter to such an extent that it is often quoted directly under Kâtyâyana's name." (Stenzler.)

23 *a*. Of the Çrauta-sûtras we may mention

1. Belonging to the Rigveda: those of
   Âçvalâyana: edit. in BI.
   Çânkhâyana.
2. Belonging to the Sâmaveda: those of
   Mâçaka.
   Lâtyâyana, edit. in BI (Kauthuma school).
   Drâhyâyana (belonging to the Râṇâyanîya-school).
3. Belonging to the Black Yajurveda (Taitt.-Sanh.): those of
   Baudhâyana, Lit. in Weber, HIL. 100 ff.
   Âpastamba: Weber, HIL. 100 ff. Bühler, SBE. 2, Introd. p. xi f., xviii; portions translated by M. Müller, ZDMG. 9, Supplement, p. xliii f. and R. Garbe, ZDMG. 34 (1880), 319–370; ed. by Garbe, Calcutta 1881 f.
   Hiraṇyakeçi, the Mânavas, the Bhâradvâjas, } which have now all been brought to light.
4. Belonging to the White Yajurveda (Vâj.-Sanh.): those of
   Kâtyâyana, edit. by A. Weber. Berlin 1859. (The White Yajurveda, vol. 3.)
5. Belonging to the Atharvaveda:
   the Kauçika-sûtra,
   the Vaitâna-sûtra, edit. by R. Garbe. London 1878, transl. and comment. by the same, Strassburg 1878. [Bloomfield, On the position of the Vaitâna Sûtra. JAOS. 11, 375 ff.]

24. The Gṛhyasûtras, of which only a few have been published, will have the greatest importance for the comparative study of customs: with their aid it will be possible to show that many customs, whether in the life of the classic nations, in the ritual of the Catholic church, or in the common life of the present day, come from primeval times; *cf.* Stenzler's excellent discussion, "Ueber die Sitte", AfKM. 1865, vol. 4, 147 f. — Some individual points have already been treated, such as

the Birth-ritual by Speijer, De ceremonia apud Indos quae vocatur jâtakarma. Lugd. Bat. 1872;
the Marriage-ritual by Haas and Weber in ISt. 5; *cf.* Note 317;
the Burial-ritual by M. Müller, ZDMG. 9, Sup.; *cf.* Roth, ZDMG. 8, 467 f. (above p. 76 f. and Note 326).

Of such Gṛhyasûtras the following are in existence:

1. Belonging to the Rigveda: those of
   Âçvalâyana, edit. by Stenzler, Leipzig 1864; transl. by the same, 1865 (AfKM. vol. 3, part 4, and vol. 4, part 1); *cf.* A.

Kuhn, KZ. 15, 224 f. and the review of the contents by Mon. Williams in Ind. Wisdom, p. 197–209.

Çânkhâyana; edit. and transl. by H. Oldenberg, ISt. 15, 1–166.

2. Belonging to the Sâmaveda: those of

Gobhila: edit. in BI. (a late addition edit. and transl. by Bloomfield, ZDMG. 35, 533–537).

3. Belonging to the Black Yajurveda: those of

Baudhâyana,

Âpastamba (*cf.* Note 23 and 23 *a*, 3).

Laugakṣi (Bühler, ISt. 14, 403),

the Mânavas, etc.: Note 23 and 23 *a*, 3 (J. v. Bradke, ZDMG. 36, 417–477).

4. Belonging to the White Yajurveda: those of

Pâraskara, edit. by Stenzler. Leipzig 1876, transl. by the same. Leipzig 1878 (AfKM. vol. 6, part 2 and 4).

5. Belonging to the Atharvaveda:

the Kauçika-sûtra (two chapters on expiatory ceremonies have been edited, translated, and commentated by A. Weber: Zwei ved. Texte über Omina und Portenta, Berl. Akad. Abh. Philos.-Hist. Cl. 1858, pp. 344–413). [Bloomfield, on a proposed edition of the Kauçika-Sûtra. Am. Or. Soc. Proc. Oct. 1883.]

25. The Dharma- or Sâmayâcârika-sûtras were first distinguished as a special group by Müller, ASL. 206 f.; more detailed information was given by Bühler in the Introd. to West and Bühler, A Digest of Hindu Law, Bombay 1867. Of these Sûtras, I mention those of

Âpastamba, ed. and transl. by Bühler, Bombay 1868 f., translation in SBE. 2, 1–170; Introd. pp. ix–xliv;

Gautama, ed. by Stenzler, London 1876, transl. by Bühler in SBE. 2, 173–307; Introd. pp. xlv–lvii;

Vâsiṣṭha, Baudhâyana, } translated by Bühler in SBE.;

Viṣṇu, transl. by J. Jolly in SBE. 7, 1–302 (1880) [BI. (NS.) 458 ff.]; Introd. pp. ix–xxxvii; Jolly, Das Dharmasûtra des Vishnu und das Kâthakagṛhya. Münch. Sitzgsber. 1879. II. 1, 22–82.

25 *a*. The metrical law-book of the 'father of mankind,' Manu (ed. and transl. *e.g.* by Loiseleur-Deslongchamps, Paris 1830, 1833; new ed. of the text, with Indian commentary, Calcutta 1874). [Translated from the Sanskrit, with an Introduction, by the late A. C. Burnell. Completed and edited by E. W. Hopkins. London (Trübners) 1884. — Whitney, On the origin of the laws of Manu, Am. Or. Soc. Proc. May 1885], is proved to be relatively young by the fact that it rests on the Sûtras of the Mânava school (*cf.* note 23*a*, 3; 24, 3), but its period cannot be more definitely decided. Yâjnavalkya's Dharmaçâstra (ed. in Sanskrit and German, by Stenzler, Berlin 1849) must, at the earliest, have been composed in the third century A.D. (H. Jacobi, ZDMG. 30, 306). Of Nârada's law-book (not edited) an English translation has been given by J. Jolly, London 1876.

A whole collection of such texts is presented in the Dharmashastrasangraha, ed. by Pandit Jîbânanda Vidyâsâgara, 2 parts, Calc. 1876; *cf.* besides Burnell, The Law of Partition and Succession, Mangalore and Basle 1872; Aurel Mayr, Das indische Erbrecht, Wien 1873 (resting on the work of West and Bühler, Note 25); and Jolly's works: Ueber die rechtliche Stellung der Frauen bei den alten Indern, München 1876 (Sitzungsber. der Akad.). Ueber das indische Schuldrecht, München 1877 (Sitzungsber. der Akad.). Ueber die Systematik des indischen Rechts, 1878 (Extract from the Zeitschrift für vgl. Rechtswissenschaft, vol. 1, 234–260; also Bernhöft, Ueber Zweck und Mittel der vergleich. Rechtswissenschaft, ibid. vol. 1, 1–38).

26. Purâṇas (like Itihâsa; saying, legend; *iti ha âsa; so it was*) are often mentioned in the Brâhmaṇas, but in their present shape — eighteen in number — are all young, and almost all serve sectarian ends in Indian popular religion, since Brahma, Viṣṇu, and Çiva are each extolled in six of them. I mention the

Mârkaṇḍeya-P., ed. and transl. by Banerjea, Calc. 1851 f.; Books 7 and 8 translated by Wortham in JRAS. NS. 13 (1881), 355–379; [Books 81–93 in JRAS. 17 (1885), 221 ff.];

Bhâgavata-P., traduit et publié par Eug. Burnouf, Paris 1840 f.;

Viṣṇu-P., ed. Bombay 1867, transl. by H. H. Wilson, London 1840; newly edited by F. E. Hall, 1864–77 [also Madras and Calcutta 1882];

Agni-P., appearing since 1870 in BI.

Portions translated in Muir's MTr. — Weber, HIL. 190 f. Mon. Williams, Ind. Wisdom, pp. 489–501. — Of other Pariçiṣṭas, two only need be mentioned:

The Anukramaṇîs: tables of contents which give in order the divinity, composer, and metre of the individual hymns in the Sanhitâ; the contents of the Anukramaṇi of Kâtyâyana for the Rig is edited in the editions of the text by Aufrecht (1st ed., vol. 2, 458 f.; 2d ed., vol. 2, 463 f.), and in Müller's large edition, vol. VI. pp. 621–671. An extensive Anukramaṇî is the Bṛhaddevatâ of Çaunaka, intended to assign the divinities to their hymns, with strict regard to the order of the Rig-Sanhitâ, but at the same time giving an extraordinarily rich store of legends; see A. Kuhn, in ISt. 1, 101–120.

The Caraṇavyûha: a (modern) statement of the schools belonging to each of the four Vedas, ed. by A. Weber, ISt. 3, 247–283.

Here should be mentioned (see Note 23) a class of works which have only recently become known, the

Çulva-sûtras, the last part of the Kalpa system, which contains the geometrical specifications for the proper setting up of the altars (*cf.* Hillebrandt, Das altindsche Neu- und Vollmondsopfer. Jena 1879, p. 187 f.: Versuch einer Construction des Opferplatzes nach Baudhâyana). In these oldest mathematical treatises may already be found, according to Thibaut (Trübner's Amer. and Orient. Lit. Rec., special number, London 1874, p. 27 f.), even attempts at squaring the circle. Thibaut began to publish the texts in the monthly journal, *The Pandit*, Benares, in May 1875; *cf.* his article in the Journ. Asiat. Soc. of Bengal, 1875, pp. 227–275; also, separately, London 1877.

27. For the historical relations see Lassen, IA. 4, 156 f. — All the commentaries bear the names of Mâdhava and Sâyaṇa, according to the custom still existing in India of naming books after those who caused them to be composed and bore the expense. There have been received from that region a number of inscriptions on metal plates, documents relating to royal gifts of villages and lands to learned Brâhmans, who were settled there, most probably, to assist in these and similar works. Roth, ZDMG. 21, 4; *cf.* A. Weber, IStr. 3, 190 f.

According to Burnell (Introd. to the edition of the Vançabrâhmaṇa), Mâdhava and Sâyaṇa are only different names of the same person, a Telugu Brâhman, who in A.D. 1331 became head of the monastery at Çṛngerî, died while holding that position in 1386, and wrote all the commentaries himself; *cf.* Weber, l.c.

28. So H. H. Wilson in his Translation of the Rigveda Sanhitâ. London 1850. 4 vols. edit. by Cowell 1866 (5th and 6th vols. still wanting). 2d ed. 1 vol. 1866.

29. See especially the clear exposition in the preface to vol. 1 of the Lexicon (Note 30), pp. iv–vi (1855), and the masterly treatise: Ueber gelehrte Tradition im Alterthum, besonders in Indien. ZDMG. 21, 1–9 (1865). *Cf.* Benfey's deductions, GdSpr. p. 46 f. and Gött. Gel. Anz. 1858, p. 1608 f., with which latter A. Weber agrees, ISt. 5, 174 f. "Such passages, and others of similar character, — and there is a number of them, — should be noticed by those who still consider that Vedic interpretation according to the Indian method is preferable to our own, freeing itself in essentials from the native method. Whoever has carefully studied the Indian interpretations knows that absolutely no continuity of tradition can be assumed between the production of the Vedas and their interpretation by Indian scholars; that on the contrary between the genuine poetical remains of Vedic antiquity and their interpretation a long break must have occurred in the tradition, out of which, at the most, the understanding of a few details may have been preserved up to later times, through liturgical uses and words, passages, and perhaps also hymns connected with it. Beyond these remains of the tradition, which must be estimated at a very small value, the interpreters of the Veda had almost no other aids than those which are in great part at our own disposal, the usage of the classical language and the grammatical, etymological, lexical investigations. At most they found assistance in matter preserved in dialects; but this advantage is almost entirely outweighed by that which we have at command, the comparison with Zend and with the other languages related to the Sanskrit, which, while it must of course be applied with care and discrimination, has already afforded so much help to a clearer understanding of the Vedas. But independently of all aids in particular cases, through the confusion with which it seeks to comprehend from its own religious standpoint, so many centuries later, the ancient conditions and conceptions completely foreign to it, the Indian interpretation comes to be false throughout its whole spirit; while we, through our knowledge, drawn from analogous conditions, of the life, conceptions, and needs of ancient peoples and of popular poetry, are better equipped for an understanding of the whole; and this superiority, even if the Indians owed much more in details to tradition than they really do, would not be dimmed by their interpretation."

Foot-note on p. 10: Yâska Nir. 1, 15: *cf.* Note 373.

30. Laid down principally in the Sanskrit Lexicon published by the Petersburg Academy of Sciences, produced by the labors of Otto Böhtlingk and Rudolph Roth (with the assistance of A. Weber, H. Kern, A. F. Stenzler, W. D. Whitney, A. Schiefner, and A. Kuhn). 7 vols. large quarto. 1852–1875. At the end of vols. 5 and 7 are additions, which are now included, with later additions and corrections in the "Sanskritwörterbuch in Kürzerer Fassung bearbeitet von Otto Böhtlingk," now publishing (1879 f.), of which Parts 1–5 and 6,[1] (*a – vedha*), have already appeared.

31. Especially John Muir in his article: On the Interpretation of the Veda, extr. from JRAS. NS. vol. 2 (1866), pp. 303–402; *cf.* Whitney, On the Translation of the Veda. OLSt. 1, 100–132.

32. In opposition to Goldstücker's polemic it may suffice at present to refer to Whitney's Essay mentioned above, and to A. Weber, IStr. 2, 106 f. (*cf.* ISt. 14, 414 f.); in opposition to Haug (Transactions of the London Oriental Congress. 1877. pp. 213–226 and often; *cf.* N. 116, foot-note), to Delbrück, JLZ. 1875. p. 152 f., and E. Kuhn, Wissensch. Jahresber. 1877. 1, 92 f. (Leipzig 1880). ["The principles of the 'German school' are the only ones which can ever guide us to a true understanding of the Veda." Whitney, Am. Or. Soc. Proc. Oct. 1867.]

33. *Vedârthayatna*, or an attempt to interpret the Vedas. Bombay 1876 f. The publisher, Shankar Pandurang Pandit, beside the complete Sanhitâ- and Pada- text (Note 77), gives three translations, in Sanskrit, in Mahrâthî, and in English (*imgrajî*). Similar undertakings in Hindi and Bengâli, without an English translation, are to appear in Benares and Calcutta (E. Kuhn, Wissensch. Jahresber. 1877. 1, 94).

34. Lit. Centralbl. 1873, Col. 84; *cf.* E. Kuhn, l.c. p. 92 f.: "that we have learned to place ourselves on the standpoint of free criticism in opposition to native tradition will always be an undeniable service of the Petersburg Lexicon. But just as certainly that native tradition will continue to be an element which we must regard in our interpretation, and which under some circumstances deserves the same attention as the opinion of a European scholar."

35. I have given a detailed review of the contents of this excellent work in Jbb. 121, 433–469, and in connection have referred occasionally to related characteristics among the Greeks and Romans.

36. Whereas formerly Asia, especially the highland of Central Asia, the region of the sources of the Oxus and Yaxartes was in general held to be the original as well as the last home of the Indogermanic people while they were still living together (see the rich literature in Muir, OST. 2, 306 f., besides *e.g.* Justi in Raumer's Histor. Taschenbuch 1862. p. 333 and 339 f., Höfer in KZ. 20, 382–85, etc.), other investigators in later times thought they had grounds for seeking it in Europe,* while others again spoke out decidedly in favor of Asia,† so that the question must still be considered an open one; so now (opposed to his former championship of Asia) Spiegel, Eran. Alterthumskunde 1, 428. Ausland 1871, p. 553 f.; 1872, p. 961 f. JLZ. 1878, p. 286; Whitney, Language and the Study of Language

* Latham in L. Geiger, Zur Entwickelungsgeschichte der Menschheit, p. 119. Benfey, Introd. to Fick's Indogerm. Wörterb.[1] p. ix, and GdSpr. 600; the following localities are specially mentioned:

Germany, particularly the middle and west: L. Geiger, l.c. p. 118. Th. Poesche, die Arier. Jena 1878. pp. 58–74.

Northern Germany and the northwest of France; J. G. Cuno, Forschungen, vol. i. (1871) p. 21: *cf.* A. v. Gutschmied in the Lit. Centralbl. 1871. p. 1025.

Southeastern Europe (to which the Indog. tribes came from Armenia): F. Müller, Allg. Ethnographie.[2] 1879. p. 86 f.

† Pauli, Die Benennung des Löwen bei den Indogermanen. München 1873; Gerland, JLZ. 1875. pp. 738, 740;

V. Hehn, Kulturpflanzen und Hausthiere.[3] Introd. viii, and: Das Salz. p. 16 (Bolur-Tagh);

O. Peschel, Völkerkunde.[2] p. 544 f. (both slopes of the Caucasus);

The geologist Désor, Les pierres à écuelles. Genève, Carey 1878. pp. 33-43, etc.

(N. Y., Scribner 1874), p. 200 f.; Whitney, Life and Growth of Language (N. Y., Appleton 1883), p. 194: "Evidences of real weight bearing on the question may possibly yet be found; but certainly none such have been hitherto brought to light"; *cf.* Hübschmann, JLZ. 1876, p. 250, etc.; now especially O. Schrader, Sprachvergleichung und Urgeschichte. Jena 1883. pp. 117–149. [Brunnhofer, Ueber den Ursitz der Indogermanen. Basle 1884.]

37. Skt. *aryà, árya;* old Bactrian (East Iranian, e language of the Avesta), *airya;* old Persian (West Iranian, the language of the inscriptions of Darius and Xerxes), *ariya,* properly, *the truly devoted,* designates in the first place the *people of (their) own race;* then the governing classes, the *rulers; cf.* Hdt. 7, 62: οἱ δὲ Μῆδοι . . . ἐκαλέοντο πάλαι πρὸς πάντων Ἄριοι. The word is also found as Ἀρια- Ἀριο- in Graecized Iranian proper names, *e.g.*, Ἀριαράμνης = old Pers. Ariyaramna. Moreover, that the Celts (the Irish) in olden times also called themselves Arya, that this group of words still exists in the Celtic (Airem = Aryaman, Erin [gen. Erenn] = Aryana, aire [gen. airech] = âryaka: princeps, primus, airechas: principatus), and that 'Aryan' is a thoroughly justifiable designation for 'Indogermanic,' is proved minutely by H. Zimmer, in Bezzenberger's Beiträge, 3, 137–151. [See now especially A. F. Pott on the word in the Internationale Zeitsch. fur Allgemeine Sprachwissenschaft, vol. 2, p. 105 ff., Leipzig 1885.]

38. The older Indian chronology presents great difficulties. The determination of the Vedic period must be deduced from the histories of the various literatures which lie between the hymns and the fixed dates of Buddhism, from the difference in language and in the religious and social views between the former and latter, and can therefore approximate the true period only by centuries.

The estimates in Bunsen, Aegypten's Stellung in der Weltgeschichte, V, 4, 5, 211. 225 f., are too high; N. L. Westergaard refrains from any chronological determinations, Ueber den ältesten Zeitraum der indischen Geschichte mit Rücksicht auf die Literatur, Breslau 1862, pp. 14, 93; *cf.* Ludw. Rv. 3, 183 f.

Müller, ASL. 572, hesitatingly placed the beginning of Vedic literature at 1200 B.C. ("We can do so only under the supposition that during the early periods of the history the growth of the human mind was more luxuriant than in later times, and that the layers of thought were formed less slowly in the primary than in the tertiary ages of the world"), and Whitney, OLSt. 1, 78, says concerning this: "To this date no one will deny, at least, the merit of extreme modesty and caution"; similar judgments were expressed by Wilson and Barthélemy St. Hilaire; *cf.* Lassen, IA. 1, 862–874. Müller himself afterward called this estimate too low (*cf.* Rigveda Sanhitâ, vol. IV., Preface, p. viii f.; according to p. lxxviii, Sâyaṇa lived [about 1350 A.D.: see Note 27] "thirty centuries after the rishis"), and then (Chips, 1, 11) named the period from

1500–1200 B.C. as the period of composition of the Vedic hymns; similarly A. Weber, who has repeatedly (*e.g.* IStr. 1, 6; Ind. Skizzen, pp. 14, 46, 43) placed the migration into the Indus-land in the 16th century B.C., but *cf.* HIL. p. 2, note 2; Spiegel (*e.g.* Ausland 1874, p. 31), Duncker, Geschichte des Altert. 3, 24. 5, etc.—The period from

2400–1400 B.C. is considered by Haug as the period of the production of the Vedic hymns (Introd. to the Ait. Brâhm. 1, 47 f.; *cf.* Die fünf Gâthâ's Zarathustra's, vol. 2, 244).

An estimate which, if we take everything into account, is certainly not too high, and which has the greatest claims to probability, is that of Whitney, OLSt. 1, 21, and elsewhere, of

2000–1500 B.C., the first half of the second thousand years B.C.; *cf.* his note on Colebrooke's Misc. Essays, ed. Cowell, 1, 124 ("somewhere between 2000 and 1000 B.C."; and his Life and Growth of Lang. p. 186: "The period of the oldest hymns . . . was probably nearly, or quite, 2000 B.C."); and in his Sanskrit Gram. 1879, Introd. p. xiii: "It may have been as early as 2000 B.C." So Benfey (GdSpr. 600: "It can hardly be doubted that the most eastern branch had their abode on the Indus as early as 2000 years before our era"); F. Müller (Allg. Ethnogr.[2] 1879, p. 512: "Between 2000 and 1500"; cf. p. 88 *** and p. 509), etc.

39. [Geographical location: Vivien de St. Martin, Études sur la géographie du Veda; Ludw. Rv. 3, 197 ff. Zimmer believes the eastern sea was not known (AIL. 27), but we have a trace of it in RV. 10, 136, a late hymn.]

Rivers: after Zimmer, AIL. 32, with p. 16. 6 (RV. 7, 95, 1. 2), and p. 27. Thomas, The Rivers of the Veda, and how the Aryans entered India, JRAS. 14, 4.

Sindhu: the 'stream' *κατ' ἐξοχήν*. The Greek form Ἰνδός is derived through the Iranian *Hindu;* Pliny, Nat. Hist. 6, 20, 71, knows that *Indus incolis Sindus appellatus.* To the Indus also belongs, for the most part, the designation *sam-udra*, 'gathering of waters' (not to the *ocean*); and in the same way it is the much-praised Sarasvatî ('rich in water'), not the small, in later times most sacred, stream in Madhyadeça: see Zimmer, pp. 5–10.

Kubhâ: 'bending,' Κωφήν or Κωφής among the Greeks.

Suvâstu: 'having beautiful places,' Σόαστος.

Krumu and Gomatî: 'rich in cattle,' not mentioned by the ancients.

Vitastâ: 'stretched out,' Ὑδάσπης (Ptolemy, Βιδάσπης), now *Bihat* or *Jihlam.*

Asiknî: 'black,' called by the natives at the time of Alexander's arrival *Candrabhâga* ('moon portion'), which name in Greek dress had to assume the ominous form Σανδαροφάγος. It was, therefore, natural that the Macedonian conqueror should re-christen the 'Alexander-devourer,' and he named it, evidently with an intelligent use of the older name, Asiknî, the 'Healing': Σανδαροφάγος ὑπὸ Ἀλεξάνδρου ποταμὸς μετωνομάσθη καὶ ἐκλήθη Ἀκεσίνης (Hesychius. Roth, ZLGW. 139). Alexander's innovation obtained a foothold so that the name displaced by it is known, among all the ancient writers, by Ptolemy alone, 7, 1, 23: Σανδάβάγα (the Mss. wrongly Σανδαβάλ; Pliny, Nat. Hist. 6, 20, 71, *Cantabas?*): the river is now called *Cinâb:* 'gathered water' (*cf.* Arr. An. 6, 15, 4. Ind. 4, 20).

Paruṣṇî: 'arundinosa,' the later

Irâvatî: 'giving drink,' in Arrian (with distinct reference to ὕδωρ), Ὑδραώτης; in Strabo, Ὑαρώτης; in Ptolemy, Ῥουάδις, now *Rawi.*

Vipâc, later, Vipâçâ: 'fetterless,' in Arrian, Ὕφασις; in Pliny, *Hypasis;* in Ptolemy, Βίπασις, now *Beyah* or *Bias;* the variant Ὕπανις in Strabo, Diod. and others is wrong, and undoubtedly to be changed.

Çutudrî, changed later by popular etymology into Çatadru, 'Hundred-course'; in Ptol., Ζαδάδρης (var. Ζάραδρος), in Pliny, 6, 17, 63, *Sydrus;* Megasthenes must also have mentioned it, for the most complete description of the river-system of those regions, originating with that author, in Arr. Ind. 4, 8 f., comes into proper order only if Ὑδραώτης μὲν ἐν Καμβισθόλοισι καὶ ὁ Ζαδάδρης παρειληφώς κτλ. is read in that passage, as Lassen, IA. 1², 57 f., observes.

Yamunâ: Διάμουνα in Ptol. 7, 1, 29, *Jomanes* in Pliny, corrupted to Ἰωβάρης in Arr. Ind. 8, 5, and elsewhere.

[The Ganges, which in later times became the backbone of India, is not mentioned in the Rig, except 10, 75, 5.]

40. Climate, soil and products of the mineral, vegetable and animal kingdoms: Zimmer, AIL. 40–99; *cf.* Jbb. 121, 436–442.

41. Dwelling: Zimmer, AIL. 148–156; quotation from p. 153 f.

42. Settlement: Zimmer, AIL. 145–148; certainly correct as opposed to the acceptation, resting upon an etymological anachronism, of "cities" (*pur* is radically identical with πόλι-ς) among Aryans and aborigines.

43. Cattle-raising: Zimmer, AIL. 221–225; 'all good,' etc., RV. 3, 30, 14.

44. Agriculture, chase: Zimmer, AIL. 235–245.

45. Food: Zimmer, AIL. 275–282; quotation from p. 272.

46. Occupations: Zimmer, AIL. 245–260. — The cow as monetary unit (*cf.* τεσσαράβοιος, ἐννεάβοιος): Weber, IStr. 1, 101. — 'Active tradesmen' (*vaníj vankú:* 5, 45, 6), in Ludw. Rv. 3, 213 f., 'wandering tradesmen.' — Usurers: 8, 55, 10. — Mina: *manâ*, with the Greeks μνᾶ, μνέα: 8, 67, 2. — Trade with the west: see Weber, HIL. p. 2 f., Note 2. Ophir also was in India, whence King Solomon got "many hundredweight of gold and silver, sandalwood, precious stones, as well as apes and peacocks"; *cf.* Jbb. 121, 440 f.

47. Family: Zimmer, AIL. 305–318. Wedding, induction of the wife into the new house, above p. 75 f. 'Home, darling abode, bliss' (*ásta yóni suráṇa*): 3, 53, 4, 6. — Morning prayers (*pûrváhûti*): 1, 122, 2; 10, 86, 10: "From former times the wife comes to the common sacrifice and to the assembly of the feast, she the cherisher of the rite."

48. Monogamy, Polygamy: Zimmer, AIL. 323–326. — Marriage of blood relations is considered immoral and reprehensible: see *10, 10* (142 ff.). — Adopted children: 7, 4, 7: "That is not (real) posterity which is begotten by another." — Birth of a girl: AV. 6, 11, 3: "The birth of a girl, grant it elsewhere; here grant a boy."

49. The right to expose new-born children was possessed by the father among the Indians (exposure is evidenced in the Yajus texts, though not indeed in the RV. and AV.: Weber, ISt. 5, 54. 260. Zimmer, AIL. 319 f.) as well as among the Greeks (Schömann, Griech. Altert. 1³, 531. 113. Becker, Charikles 2³, 22 ff.), Romans (Marquardt, Privatleben der Römer, 1, p. 3, Note 1, p. 81), and Germans, among which last people, after the birth of a child, the father decided on its life by raising it up from the place where the mother had given birth to it (Grimm, Deutsche Rechtsalt. p. 455 f.; Weinhold, Deutsche Frauen, p. 75 f.; Altnord. Leben, p. 260 ff.).

50. Treatment of the Aged: "Among the Germans, when the master of the house was over sixty years old, if the signs of the weakness of age were of such a character that he 'no longer had the power to walk or stand, and to ride unassisted and unsupported, with collected mind, free will and good sense,' he was obliged to give over his authority to his son, and to perform menial service; then old men might be made by hard sons and cruel grandsons to expiate painfully the love and gentleness they had neglected in their more powerful days; those who had grown useless and burdensome were even either killed outright, or exposed and abandoned to death by starvation (Grimm, Deutsche Rechtsalt. p. 487 ff.; Haupt's Zeitschrift für Deutsch. Altert. 5, 72; W. Wackernagel, Kleine Schriften,

1, 15–17; Weinhold, Altnord. Leben, p. 473 f.). We have to imagine exactly similar conditions among the Indians, when the texts speak of 'the divided possessions of an old father,' and of 'old men exposed' (Zimmer, AIL. 326–328), and this the more, because exactly similar things are told by the attendants of Alexander the Great of Iranian tribes,* and even among the Romans there was a period when old men over sixty were thrown down from the bridge into the Tiber." † Jbb. 121, 459.

51. Burning of Widows: Zimmer, AIL. 328–331; Fleckeisen's Jbb. 121, 460; RV. ***10, 18, 7*** (above p. 77) with Note 328. — AV. 18, 3, 1 proves the death of the wife with her departed husband as an old custom (*dharma purâṇa*). — But that this custom was not general, other passages beside RV. 10, 18, 7 show, which prove the re-marriage of the widow (AV. 9, 5, 27, — with her brother-in-law: RV. 10, 40, 2: levirate marriage), and that the usage only received decided sanction in late times, is evident from the fact that "the Indian law literature, from the oldest times up to the late period, treats fully of the widow's right of inheritance, and that the isolated references to the burning of widows in some of the law-books endorse it only as a matter of choice." J. Jolly, Augsb. Allg. Ztg. 1879, Supplement 199, p. 2914; *cf.* the same in the Münchener Sitzungsber. 1876, p. 447 f. [See Colebrooke, On the Duties of a Faithful Hindu Widow, Misc. Essays, 1, p. 133 ff.]

52. Hehn, Kulturpflanzen und Hausthiere,[3] p. 473.

53. Zimmer, AIL. 331–336. — Fickleness, etc.: above, p. 85, with Note 351. — Sons of unmarried women: cf. ***4, 19, 9*** (67) and ***4, 30, 16*** (74). — Fallen women: 2, 29, 1: "Put guilt away far from me, as a woman secretly giving birth" (puts away the child). [Roth, The Morality of the Veda, JAOS. 3, 331–347.]

54. State: Zimmer, AIL. 158–162. Ludw. Rv. 3, 248 f. — The Aryan tribes: Zimmer, AIL. 119–138. 430 f.; Ludw. Rv. 3, 167 f. 204

* Hehn, Kulturpflanzen, p. 472 ff. Strabo 11, 11, 3, p. 517, says of the Bactrians: *λέγουσιν οἱ περὶ Ὀνησίκριτον, τοὺς ἀπειρηκότας διὰ γῆρας ἢ νόσον ζῶντας περιβάλλεσθαι τρεφομένοις κυσὶν ἐπίτηδες πρὸς τοῦτο, οὓς ἐνταφιαστὰς καλεῖσθαι ἐν τῇ πατρῴᾳ γλώττῃ . . . καταλῦσαι δὲ τὸν νόμον Ἀλέξανδρον.* — ibid. 11, 11, 8, p. 520, of the Caspians: *τοὺς ὑπὲρ ἑβδομήκοντα ἔτη λιμοκτονήσαντες εἰς τὴν ἐρημίαν ἐκτιθέασιν,* ibid. 11, 8, 6, p. 513 of the Massagetes.

† Festus (*cf.* Grimm, Deutsche Rechtsalt. p. 489, 8; W. Wackernagel, Kleine Schriften, 1, 17; Hehn, Kulturpflanzen, above): *depontani* appellabantur qui sexagenarii de ponte deiciebantur, and *sexagenarios de ponte* olim deiciebant, etc.: Cic. pro S. Roscio 35, 100: habeo etiam dicere quem contra morem maiorum minorem LX annis de ponte in Tiberim deiecerit. The matter was repellant to the patriotism of Varro and others, and they tried to argue it away; see Ossenbrüggen, Introd. to the oration, pp. 45–58.

f. — Order of battle: Tac. Germ. 7: quodque praecipuum fortitudinis incitamentum est, non casus nec fortuita conglobatio turmam aut cuneum facit, sed familiae et propinquitates. Nestor in Hom. Il. 2, 362 f.: κρῖν' ἄνδρας κατὰ φῦλα, κατὰ φρήτρας, Ἀγάμεμνον, ὡς φρήτρη φρήτρηφιν ἀρήγῃ, φῦλα δὲ φύλοις.

55. Government: Zimmer, AIL. 162–177. Ludw. Rv. 3, 249–256.

56. Origin of the Castes: Zimmer, AIL. 185–192, *cf.* Ludw. Rv. 3, 216–247. Zimmer graphically describes, p. 193–204, the gradual transition to the new hierarchical order, and pp. 204–220 this new form of the state itself. — The four castes are mentioned only in the late verse 10, 90, 12 (Note 375 *d*). [Muir and Zimmer deny the existence of the caste system in the Veda, while Ludwig asserts it (Rv. 3, 216 ff.). The questions of name and fact should be kept separate. The system is distinctly enunciated only as stated above, but many passages seem to point clearly to its existence, as *e.g.* 8, 35, 16, 17, 18, where the classes are designated almost certainly: "May the Brahma (potentiality of holiness) prosper . . . may the kṣatra (quality of warrior) prosper . . . may the cows (special possession of the Vaiçya) prosper," etc. Zimmer, treating the subject of caste in connection with the purohitâ (AIL. 195 f.), evidences later conditions as proof of its non-existence in the Vedic period.]

57. Law and administration of justice: Zimmer, AIL. 177–185. — Ordeal (in exactly the same form as among the Greeks): Jbb. 121, 449; *cf.* E. Schlagintweit, Die Gottesurtheile der Juden. München 1866. — Banishment: *parâ-vṛj*, radically identical with Old Sax. *wrekkio*, Old High Germ. *reccho*, New High Germ. *Recke*.

58. After ***10, 117*** (155 f.) and ***10, 71, 6*** (163).

59. Village assembly (*sabhâ:* related to Germ. *Sippe*): Zimmer, AIL. 172 f. 'Sift their words': ***10, 71, 2*** (162). Dice: 2, 29, 5; ***5, 85, 8*** (5); ***7, 86, 6*** (7); ***10, 34*** (158), above p. 83 f.; Zimmer, AIL. 283 f. (quotation from p. 283), where the little that is known about the arrangement of the game is adduced; *cf.* Jolly, Augsb. Allg. Ztg. 1879, Supplement 199, p. 2914.

60. Zimmer, AIL. 287 f.

61. Zimmer, AIL. 289 f. The hymn 8, 69 is the prayer of a charioteer for victory before the race.

62. The *Dasyus:* Zimmer, AIL. 101 f.; Ludw. Rv. 3, 207 f.; their tribes: Zimmer, AIL. 118 f. They seem to have been designated *Phallus-worshippers* (*çiçnadeva*): Ludw. Rv. 3, 212; for the ἄστομοι and ἄρρινες in Megasthenes: Jbb. 121, 443 f.

63. War, weapons: Zimmer, AIL. 293–301. — In the so-called "Weapon song," 6, 75, a number of verses in praise of weapons (coat of mail, bow, bowstring, arrow, etc.) are put together; freely imitated by Muir, OST. 5, 469 f., MTr. p. 195 f.

64. Writing, its use: For the (not consistent) statements of Strabo (after Nearchus and Megasthenes) concerning the use of writing, see A. Weber, Indische Skizzen, p. 131 f.—It may now be considered as proved that the Vedic texts were for a long time transmitted orally, and were only at a comparatively late date fixed in a written form (*cf.* Note 76), that the Indian alphabets are of Semitic origin, and that the application of writing to literary uses arose chiefly with Buddhism; *cf.* Benfey, Indien. p. 240, Einleit. in die Gram. der ved. Sprache. p. 31 (Gött. Abhandl. vol. 19. 1874); A. Weber, ISt. 5, 18 f., IStr. 2, 339 f.; 3, 342. 349 f.; Haug, Wesen und Wert des ved. Accents, p. 16 f.; Zimmer, AIL. 347 f.

65. Numbers, measures: The highest number fixed is a hundred thousand (*çatâ sahasrâ*); as a common miracle of Indra's and Viṣṇu's the division of the number 1000 by three is praised (6, 69, 8). See Zimmer, AIL. 348; for later Vedic time, A. Weber, ZDMG. 15, 135 f. = IStr. 1, 95.

The term *sâmi*, half (*sâmi-ἡμι-semi:* Curtius, Grdz. n. 453), as well as the numbers up to 100 (*çatam* = *ἑ-κατόν* = *centum* = *hund-ert:* Curtius, Grdz. n. 18), are known to have belonged to the original tongue, while for 1000 Asiatics and Greeks on the one hand (Skt. *sahasria*, East Iran. ha-*zanr*-a, Aeol. χέλλιοι from χέσλιοι, Attic χίλιοι), and the Northern Europeans on the other (Lith. *túkstantis*, old Prussian *tusimtons*, old Slav. *tysąšta*, Goth. *thusandi:* J. Schmidt, Verwandt schaftsverhältnisse der Idg. Sprachen. 1872, pp. 40, 52), had a common term, while the Italians and Celts stand alone (*mille*, *mile*).

66. Zimmer, AIL. 357 f.; *cf.* above p. 27 f. with Note 91.—The childish conceptions of the Brâhmaṇas: A. Weber, ISt. 9, 358 f.

67. Zimmer, AIL. 349–357.—Pleiades: 1, 24, 10 (above pp. 27. 64) and 10, 82, 2. See the explanation of the statement of Dio Chrysostomos 2, 363 Emp. (τὰς ἄρκτους οὔ φασι φαίνεσθαι παρ' αὐτοῖς (*sc.* τοῖς Ἰνδοῖς) by Weber, ISt. 2, 165.—Sirius: Skt. tiṣya = old Bact. tistrya.—The five planets, Mercury, Venus, Mars, Jupiter, Saturn, and the frequently mentioned Nakṣatras or lunar stations, are known to the youngest portions of the Veda, their names only to the Taitt. Sanh. and the Atharvaveda (Zimmer, AIL. 353–356, with M. Müller and Ludwig, Nachrichten, p. 4 = Rv. 3, 183 f. in opposition to Weber). The knowledge of the planets as well as of the Nakṣatras is (with Weber and Zimmer) not to be held as indigenous in India but as imported from Babylonia. [Whitney, JAOS. 8, 72 ff. 382 ff.; OLSt. 2, 341–421; note on Colebrooke, Misc. Essays, p. 126 ff.]

—Eclipse of the Sun: 10, 27, 20; *cf.* 5, 40, 5–9 [see Whitney, Am. Or. Soc. Proc. Oct. 1885].—Lunar Phases mentioned in 2, 42.

68. Intercalary days, month: Zimmer, AIL. 366 f. The year was regulated, even in the Indo-Germanic period, by the insertion of the "twelve days," or according to the older expression "twelve nights."* (A. Weber, Omina und Portenta, Berlin Akad. Abhdl. 1858, p. 388 = ISt. 10, 242); mentioned in the Rigveda: ***4, 33, 7*** (122) and ***1, 161, 11. 13*** (119), *cf.* above p. 37.* The intercalary month "born after" is mentioned in 1, 25, 8, above p. 64 and Note 250.—Division of the year: Zimmer, AIL. 371 f. (Jbb. 121, 464). In the Vedic period the threefold division predominates; in later times (*i.e.* in dwelling-places situated more to the southeast) five, six, or seven seasons were distinguished.

69. Medical art: Zimmer, AIL. 374–399.—1, 116, 15 (above p. 50 with Note 180) seems to point to a knowledge of the first elements of surgery.

70. Above p. 66 f.

71. In the manuscripts a purely external, uniform division, originating in the practical necessities of the school, is presented, by which the whole is divided into eighths (*aṣṭaka*), each of these into eight subdivisions (*adhyâya*, lessons), these into sections of about five verses each (*varga*).—This division, formerly used in quoting, has been generally abandoned since Roth, ZLGW. p. 5 f. brought to light the original division into books (chapters) and hymns (*maṇḍala* [*anuvâka*], *sûkta*).

72. After 8, 48 the Mss. present eleven hymns from another recension (the *Vâlakhilya*), which by Müller and in Aufrecht's second edition are numbered with the others, in Aufrecht's first edition are consigned to the end; there are, besides, a number of scattered "supplements" (*khila*), which are now collected in Aufrecht's second edition of the text, vol. 2, 672–688.

The Vâṣkala-çâkhâ mentioned beside the Çâkala-çâkhâ contained further hymns, and seems to stand in closer relations to the Çâukhâyana texts (note 14*a*, 1; 23*a*, 1; 24, 1) and to the Bṛhaddevata (Note 26): see Weber, HIL. 314 f.

73. Relative age of the separate books: H. Brunnhofer, Ueber Dialektspuren im vedischen Gebrauche der Infinitivformen, KZ. 25, 329–377, publishes the first very valuable attempt to collect the indications of the Vedic language (especially the uses of the various infinitival formations) in a methodical manner for the determination

* The Indians, like the Germans and other related tribes (*cf. e.g.* Tac. Germ. 11 and Caes. B. G. 6, 18), in the oldest times reckoned not by days, but by nights: Zimmer, AIL. 360 (Jbb. 121, 463).

of the relative age of the various collections of hymns (family books, etc.). He gets the following chronological order of the families of singers:

1. Gautamas: Maṇḍ. 4 (principal poet Vâmadeva).
2. Bhâradvâjas: Maṇḍ. 6.
3. Vâsiṣṭhas: Maṇḍ. 7.
4. Âtreyas: Maṇḍ. 5.
5. Vaiçvâmitras: Maṇḍ. 3.
6. Bhârgavas: Maṇḍ. 2 (principal poet Gṛtsamada).
7. Ângirasas: portions of Maṇḍ. 1. 8. 9. 10.
8. Kâṇvas: portions of Maṇḍ. 1. 8. 9.

[Lanman, Noun-Inflection, p. 580 (the relative frequency of ancient and modern equivalent grammatical forms as a criterion of the age of different Vedic texts), reaches a different result for Book 8: ". . . The result is, that the family books 2–7 are, in general, of about the same age. . . . As between Books 8, 9, 7, and 10, a rude chronological arrangement may be made. . . . Our result indicates that the eighth is older than the other family Books."]

The poet's names handed down for books 2–8 may, in general, be correct; yet even here, but especially in the later books, it is evident that many of them have simply been got out of the hymns by ingenuity, of which we have examples enough in other literatures. [*E.g.* 5, 1 the real author is *Gaviṣṭira*, as appears from v. 12; and the Anukramaṇî gives this name, but also gives *Buddha* from *abodhi* v. 1.] — As yet the only copious collections and investigations in Ludw. Rv. 3, 100 f.

74. Arrangement of the hymns in the family books: Müller, ASL. 461 f. — To the critique of the composition after Delbrück, JLZ. 1875, p. 867, Grassman has given the most careful attention in his Translation. In the case of many hymns, whose position indicates their origin from a number of separate, originally independent pieces, this supposition is proved by the variety of metre, or by the occurrence of the separate pieces in the Sâmaveda.

[Diminishing order of verses: violations of the law. Examining the exceptions to the rule in *e.g.* Book 7, we find

In order.	Hys.	Exceptions.
Agni-group	1–14	15–17
Indra	18–30	31–33
Viçve devâs	34–54	55
Maruts	56–58	59
Sûrya, Maruts, and Varuṇa	60–65	66
Açvins	67–73	74
Uṣas	75–80	81

i.e. all violations of the law occurring at the *end* of the group. If we assume that the hymns are in their proper places, having originally had a different number of verses, why should these violations not be found in other parts of the groups? The probable explanation is, that the shortest hymns, which stand at the end of each group, were at some time, through whim or misunderstanding, combined. So Grassmann, Delbrück and Oldenberg (Rigveda Sanhitâ and Sâmaveda-dârcikam. ZDMG. 38, 439–480)].

75. M. Müller, Chips 1, 13: "And thus we are brought to 1100 or 1200 B.C. as the earliest time when we may suppose the collection of the Vedic hymns to have been finished"; ibid. p. 15: "If, therefore, the years from about 1000 to 800 B.C. are assigned to this collecting age," so ASL. 497, *cf.* Whitney, OLSt. 1, 78 f.; on the other hand, Müller, OGR. 210. [347: "If we put that collection at about 1000 B.C., we shall not, I believe, expose ourselves to any damaging criticism."]

The sage Vyâsa ('separating, dividing'), whom the Indian tradition names as the collector, is the personification of the whole period and activity of collection.

76. Transmission of the text: *cf.* Whitney, On the History of the Vedic Texts, JAOS. 4, 245–261; Ludw. Rv. 3, 70–99. That the written fixation could not have taken place until a much later period (*cf.* A. Weber, HIL. 22, 10) from what has been said, p. 20 and Note 64, is self-evident, *cf.* Roth, KZ. 26, 53 f.

Concerning the oral transmission, *cf.* Müller, ASL. 503 f., Westergaard, Ueber den ältesten Zeitraum ind. Gesch. pp. 30–51. The method of instruction in the schools is treated (according to the Prâtiçâkhyas and Gṛhyasûtras) by Weber, ISt. 10, 128–135; the statements of the Rig Prâtiç. concerning the memorizing method are given by Weber, l.c. p. 129, Zimmer, AIL. 210 (Jbb. 121, 451), and Müller, OGR. 160 ff. [see Whitney, OLSt. 1, 82–88]. OGR. 163–172, is given an interesting account of the present method of Vedic study; *cf.* also Haug's account of the enormous memory of the Brâhmans to-day, in his essay, Brahma und die Brahmanen, Münich 1871, p. 21, and 47, 17.

The only possible alterations are interpolations; *cf.* Note 79 *b*.

77. It is a peculiarity of the Sanskrit that adjoining words in a sentence are united with each other according to certain laws, by which their initial and final portions are subjected to various changes through assimilation, elision, etc., which naturally cause difficulties in understanding; these it was sought to obviate by fixing the text, not only in the ordinary *connected form* (*Sanhitâ-pâṭha*), but also in an *unconnected* (*Pada-pâṭha, word-text*), which gave the separate words as each originally appeared, independently; thus we have presented to us in the Pada-pâṭha one of the first exegetical works. [Roth, Von Pada und Samhitâ, KZ. NS. 6 (26), pp. 45–62.] But soon the two pâṭhas named appeared no longer sufficient; new ones were made, in part very complicated, in order to make every alteration of the sacred text absolutely impossible. Three of these forms of the text may be mentioned:

The *Kramapâṭha* ('step-text') puts each word of the Padapâṭha twice: first, in connection with the preceding words; next, with the succeeding, so that the order *a b c d* gives the Krama members *ab. bc. cd;* the Krama is treated by the Upalekha (ed. Pertsch, Berlin 1854); Roth, ZLGW. 83 f.; Thibaut, Das Jaṭâpaṭala, Leipzig 1870, p. 36 f.

The *Jaṭâpâṭha* ('the woven text') exhibits each Krama member three times, the second time in reversed order: *ab. ba. ab* | *bc. cb. bc* | *cd. dc. cd* | ; the Jaṭâ is treated in the Jaṭâpaṭala, herausgegeben, übersetzt und mit Aumerkungen versehen von G. Thibaut, Leipzig 1870.

The *Ghanapâṭha* shows the order: *ab. ba. abc. cba. abc* | *bc. cb. bcd. dcb. bc* | *bc. cb. bcd. dcb. bcd* |, etc.; for the Ghana, see Haug, Wesen und Werth des vedischen Accents, Munich 1874, p. 58; Bhandarkar in Müller, OGR. 169 f.

Senseless as such endless repetitions are in themselves, they still have this value for us, that they fix absolutely the wording of the text, and in that, indeed, their purpose is accomplished.

78. It is the Prâtiçâkayas mentioned above, p. 7 and Note 20, the real purpose of which is to exhibit exactly all alterations, which make a retroversion of the Padapâṭha to the Sanhitâpâṭha necessary. Whitney, JAOS. 4, 259.

79*a*. Erratic portions are often placed in their connection through conjecture, on account of external accordance of individual similar words, etc.; sometimes a number of other verses of related contents attach themselves to an old hymn as a centre; as examples, with many of which every one familiar with the text is acquainted, *cf.* ***1, 161*** (117); ***4, 18*** (62); ***4, 24*** (69).— ***4, 18, 13,*** from a totally different connection is attached, on account of line *b* (*ná* devéṣu *vivide* marditâram), to stanza ***12,*** line *c*: *Kás te* devó *ádhi* mârḍîká *âsîd*. In the same manner to ***4, 24, 9*** (with *avi*krî*to*) is joined ***4, 24, 10*** (with krî*ṇâti*), which, by the metre alone, is proved to be foreign: "Who offers me ten cows for this Indra of mine? When he has overcome the enemy he will return him to me." Since this offer — recalling 8, 1, 5: "Not even for a high price would I exchange thee, thou that art armed with sling-stones; not for thousands, not for myriads (of cows), not for a hundredfold price, thou with hundredfold riches," and Arist. Pax. 848: οὐχ ἂν ἔτι δοίην τῶν θεῶν τριώβολον — is hardly conceivable without an image or some symbol of the god, the verse shows itself to be very young; for images of the gods are foreign to the old Vedic period, as Müller rightly declares (Chips, 1, 37; the inferences of Bollensen, ZDMG. 22, 587 f., are incorrect; *cf.* Muir, OST. 5, 453 f.); they first appear here and there in the Sûtras (*e.g.* Pârask. gṛhya 3, 14, 8, and in the Kauçikasûtra, § 105), or in secondary additions to the Brâhmaṇas, as in the Adbhuta-Br. (Note 14*a*, 2), while at the time of Pâṇini (p. 4), Manu and Yâjnavalkya they are very frequent. Weber, Omina und Portenta, 337, 367 f., ISt. 5, 149.

b. Interpolations: to support doctrine, *e.g.* vs. *7–9* of the hymn *4, 50* (108). *10, 97, 22* (175). 10, 107 (Note 349), and the like; the Puruṣasûkta 10, 90 (Note 375*d*), which alone in the Rigveda mentions the four castes.

The six verses, 7, 59, 12; 10, 20, 1; 10, 121, 10 (Note 373), and 10, 191, 1–3, appeared to have forced themselves into the Rig-text only after the introduction of the Padapâṭha, and show the Sanhitâ form even in the Pada manuscripts.

80. Benfey, GdSpr. 53, finds it "probable, on many grounds, that among the Vedic tribes the tribe of the Bharatas (*cf. 3, 33, 11, 12* (134); above p. 79 and Note 334) was, or became, the most important; that there even was a time when the predominant language of the Vedic hymns was called after them Bhâratî."

81. Up to a recent time, the most convenient treatment of Vedic forms was afforded by Th. Benfey, in his Practical Grammar of the Sanskrit Language, 2d ed., London 1868; now W. D. Whitney's Sanskrit Grammar, London 1879 (German by H. Zimmer, Leipzig 1879), treats the language of the Sanhitâs and Brâhmaṇas, as well as the Sanskrit, on the foundation of the texts themselves.

With a view to a Vedic grammar on a large scale, Benfey published a number of preliminary labors (especially in the Göttinger Abhandlungen, Anzeigen und Nachrichten); in addition, the following monographs, relating to Vedic morphology, may be mentioned:

a. The Accentuation first really became known through the Veda, since the post-Vedic texts (above p. 5) are not accented, and the meagre grammatical remains were for a long time the sources of information. "Das Accentuationssystem des altindischen Nominalcompositums" is treated by R. Garbe, KZ. 23, 470–518; the "Accentsgesetze der Homerischen Nominalcomposita" are described and compared with those of the Veda by Leopold Schröder, KZ. 24, 101–128; Haskell, On the Accentuation of the Vocative case in the Rig- and

Atharva-Vedas, JAOS. 11, 57 ff.; for the verbal accent, *cf.* Note 84. [Whitney, On the Nature and Designation of the Accent, Am. Phil. Ass. Trans., vol. 1, p. 20; Bollensen, Die Betonungssysteme des Rig- und Sâmaveda, ZDMG, 35, 456 ff.]

b. Word-formation: See the valuable survey of the vocabulary of the Rigveda, arranged according to the ending, the suffixes, in Grassmann's Wörterbuch zum Rigveda, Leipzig 1873, column 1687–1740, and B. Lindner's Altindische Nominalbildung, Jena 1878. Whitney, The Roots, Verb-forms and Primary Derivatives of the Sanskrit Language (supplement to his grammar), Leipzig 1885.

c. Declension: On Noun-Inflection in the Veda. By Ch. Lanman, New Haven 1880 (JAOS. 10, 325–601).

d. Conjugation: Das altindische Verbum aus den Hymnen des Rigveda seinem Bau nach dargestellt von B. Delbrück, Halle 1874 (*cf.* Avery in JAOS. 10, 219–324). Avery, The Unaugmented Verb-forms of the Rig and Atharva-vedas. JAOS. 11 (1885), 326–361. [Whitney, Numerical Results from Indexes of Skt. Tense and Conj.-stems. Am. Or. Soc. Proc. May 1885; The system of the Skt. verb. Am. Phil. Ass. Proc. July 1876; Bloomfield, on Differences of use in Present systems from the same Root in the Veda. Am. Or. Soc. Proc. Oct. 1882; Whitney, Derivative Conjugations, Am. Or. Soc. Proc. May 1878; Lanman, on Multiform Presents, Am. Or. Soc. Proc. May 1885, etc.].

To indicate the great wealth of Forms the following fact from the verbal inflection will suffice: While Greek, admittedly the richest in forms of all the European languages, in the finite verb shows 68 forms from the Present stem (Curtius, Verbum, vol. 1, 4), here the single root *kṛ* (make), which is indeed exceptionally far developed, shows within the same limits no less than 336 forms; to these further belong stems of the Perfect (with an augment-tense, the so-called Pluperfect), of the Aorist with *s*, of the Future with *s*, of the Optative with *s*; further, each a Passive, Causative, Desiderative and Intensive stem; and finally as Infinitive, Verbal noun, ten fully declinable Participles and four Infinitives (Delbrück, l.c. p. 15); the extraordinary wealth of Infinitive forms is now shown (*cf.* Delbrück, pp. 221–228) most clearly by Brunnhofer, KZ. 25, 332 f. (Note 376).

82. Poetry of the old Indo-Germanic period. As was stated in Note 12, A. Kuhn has proved that even the oldest period "had elaborated the contents of charms designed for certain purposes into a settled form and in them possessed a kind of poetry"; concerning the metrical form, the verse of that poetry, Note 85 (after Westphal and Allen) gives fuller information. Further, Heinzel (Ueber den Stil der altgermanischen Poesie. Strassburg 1875) has pointed out that the most essential forms of the poetical style, which are common to the Scandinavian, Anglo-Saxon and Old High German poetry, belong also to the Vedic hymns, and indeed his few examples (as Zimmer, Anzeiger für deutsches Altert. vol. 2 (1876), 296, observes) may be greatly multiplied. Finally it may be mentioned that according to Scherer (Anz. f. d. Alt. vol. 4 (1878), 100) in *brahmán* is contained the common name for poet and priest in the most ancient period: Skt. *brah-mán* = Lat. *flâ-men* (Leo Meyer, Vergleich. Gramm. 2, 275 f.) = old Norse *brag-r*, *Brag-i* (the god of poetry and eloquence: Grimm, Myth. p. 215, 3d ed.); "with the old Norse *brag-na-* in *bragnar* is compared the Greek *βραγ-χο-* for *βραχ-νο-*; the earlier common priest-name was preserved only in the guardians of the oracle at Didyma, the descendants of Βράγκος, the Βραγκίδαι. *Cf.* also Note 95.

83 *a*. Formulaic expressions and verses repeated with small variations: collections in Aufrecht, Rigveda, 2d ed. vol. 2, p. xii–xxxvii, Ludw. Rv. 3, 95–99; *cf. c* of this note.

b. Play on words: *e.g.* 10, 47, 1: "We grasped thy right hand desiring *riches*, O Indra, *riches*-lord of *riches*" (*vasû*yavo, *vasu*pate, *vasûnâm*); 4, 25, 4: "the *manly* (strong) *man*, *manliest* of *men*" (*nare naryâya nṛtamâya nṛṇâm*), and the like very often. Many of these cannot be reproduced in translation; in 6, 24, 4 the poet plays with ambiguous derivatives of the two roots *dâ* give and *dâ* bind (*dắmanvanto, adâmắnah, sudâman* [each word may come from each root]; 7, 41 with the various meanings of the word *bhaga*, which is sometimes an appellative (dispenser; share, lot, fortune), sometimes the proper name of a god granting fortune and riches (Note 227); similarly 3, 44 and 10, 96; 2, 18 is a play with numbers; play on the verbal forms and derivatives of the root *su* (*asavît, âsuvat, prasâva*) and *Savitar:* Note 217. *Cf.* L. Geiger, Ursprung und Entw. der menschl. Sprache und Vernunft, vol. 1, p. 120 with p. 401, 4, and p. 129 with p. 407, 18, etc.). [A. Bergaigne, Les Figures de Rhétorique dans le Rig-Veda. Paris 1880.]

c. Refrain: *cf. e.g.* ***2, 12*** (58 f.), ***1-14*** always *sá janâsa índrah*, "he is, ye peoples, Indra"; besides 2, 15; 3, 55; 5, 6; 5, 79; 8, 41; 8, 62; 10, 133 and others; in 8, 12; 8, 35 (1, 187, 8–10) and others, each set of three verses, *i.e.* each strophe has the same refrain; *cf.* 2, 13. Not seldom such refrains are put by the scholiasts in the wrong place (*e.g.* all the verses of ***9, 112*** (167) and ***9, 113*** (110 f.) have the absolutely foreign refrain, "O Soma, flow forth for Indra"), here and there evidently in order to embrace whole groups of hymns together (especially in Books 2, 7, 8 and 10), by which the original last lines of the hymns may sometimes have been crowded out. The same thing might have happened through the frequent repetition of formulaic endings (*galita*, in the Padapâtha wanting in the second and following positions, not repeated further) and through the solemn end-verses of the families of singers (*e.g.* Bk. 7: *yûyam pâta svastibhih sadâ naḥ*, "Ye gods, protect us in lasting well-being"). — For the literary significance of these repetitions, see M. Müller, Lit. Centralblatt 1876, p. 1700.

84. Directly upon the knowledge of the Vedas rest the investigations in Comparative Syntax, which Schweizer-Sidler opened in Höfer's Zeitschrift für die Wissenschaft der Sprache, vol. 2, 444–456 (1848) with a treatise on the Ablative, and which B. Delbrück especially promoted. The following books may be mentioned here:

a. Case: Delbrück, Ablativ, Localis, Instrumentalis im Altindischen, Griechischen und Deutschen. Berlin 1867. Delbrück, De usu dativi in carminibus Rigvedae. Halle 1867 (rewritten in KZ. 18, 81–106). Siecke, De genetivi in lingua Sanscrita, imprimis Vedica usu. (Dissert.) Berlin 1869. The use of the Ablative in Sanskrit, especially in the Veda, in Kuhn and Schleicher's Beiträge 8, 377–421 (1876). H. Wenzel, Ueber den Instrumentalis im Rigveda. Tübingen 1879. C. Gaedicke, Der Accusativ im Veda. Breslau 1880. — H. Hübschmann, Zur Casuslehre. Münich 1875.

b. Tense and Mode: Delbrück, Altindische Tempuslehre (Syntaktische Forschungen of Delbrück and Windisch. vol. 2). Halle 1877. Delbrück, Der Gebrauch des Conjunctivs und Optativs im Sanskrit und Griechischen (Synt. Forsch. vol. 1). Halle 1871. — L. Meyer, Griech. Aoriste. Berlin 1879. Neisser, Zur vedischen Verballehre. Bezzenb. Beitr. 7, 211–241.

[Whitney, Classification of Aor. Forms, Am. Or. Soc. Proc. Oct. 1884. May 1876; The siṣ and sa Aorists. Am. Journ. Phil. 6, 275 ff.; J. Avery, Modes in Relative Clauses in the Rigveda. Am. Or. Soc. Proc. May 1881. May 1883. Bloomfield, On Certain Irregular Vedic Subjunctives or Imperatives. Am. Journ. Phil. 5, 16–30, etc.]

c. Infinitive: A. Ludwig, Der Infinitiv im Veda. Prag 1871 (in connection Delbrück, KZ. 20, 212–240). Wilhelmi, De infinitivi linguarum sanscritae, bactricae, persicae, graecae, oscae, umbricae, latinae, goticae forma et usu. Isenaci 1873. J. Jolly, Geschichte des Infinitivs im Indogermanischen. München 1873.

Verbal Accent: In the Veda the verb of the principal clause is usually enclitic, while that of the dependent is orthotone (*cf.* Delbrück, Die Altindische Wortfolge, Synt. Forsch. vol. 3, p. 77); the same treatment, according to J. Wackernagel, KZ. 23, 457–470, was originally usual in Greek, therefore even in the Graeco-Aryan or a still earlier period. For Greek, Delbrück's Grundlagen der griechischen Syntax (Synt. Forsch. vol. 4). Halle 1879.

[Whitney, Contributions from the Atharvaveda to the theory of Skt. verbal accent. JAOS. 5, 385–419.]

85. Westphal has shown (Zur Vergleichenden Metrik der indogermanischen Völker, KZ. 9, 436–458) that the Indo-Germanic period possessed a kind of poetry the metrical principle of which was the counting of syllables. This syllabic system is found in pure and unmodified form only in the Iranian people, in the metrical portions of the Avesta (see K. Geldner, Ueber die Metrik des jüngern Avesta. Tübingen 1877. Pref. p. vi f.). The prosody of the Vedas shows the first advance, the transition from metre depending only on the number of syllables to one based on quantity, in which the beginning still shows the stage of mere syllable-counting, while the ending has attained prosodical fixedness. The latter in the case of the Greeks meets us from the commencement of the literature fully developed and as the first principle of metrical composition (as also the metres of later Indian poetry are altogether quantitative). 'But in one point, even with the Greeks, is shown a remnant of that stage, preceding the perfected prosodical metre, upon which they anciently stood together with the Indians. Among the Indians the first half of the Dimeter is prosodically undefined, among the Greeks the first half of the Dipody, where the trochee may interchange with spondee. The "free base" of the Aeolians may also be referred to this stage' (Westphal). In correction of Westphal, Allen has shown (KZ. 24, 556–592: Ueber den Ursprung des Homerischen Versmasses) that "the common ancestors of Germans, Indians and Iranians sang their ballads in a verse which consisted of two sharply separated members, of which each had four ictus and four light syllables; and each member began with a light syllable and closed with an ictus" (p. 567). To this verse Allen further refers the Homeric hexameter and the Italic Saturnian verse.

The Vedic metres are described in the Anukramaṇî (Note 26); further details in Westphal, l.c., and Ludw. Rv. 3, 47–69 [Weber, Metrik der Inder. ISt. vol. 8. Kuhn, Aufträge, vols. 3 and 4. Benfey, Introd. to the Sâmaveda and Quantitâtsverschiedenheiten in Sanh. und Pada Text. der Veden. Abhandl. Gött. Gesellschaft der Wissenschaften, 1875 ff. Bollensen, ZDMG. 22, 569 ff.; 35, 448 ff. Oldenberg, Altind. Âkhyâna, ZDMG. 37, 54 ff.; Rigveda Sanhitâ und Sâmavedarcikam, ZDMG. 38, 439 ff.; Âkhyâna-Hymnen im Rigveda, ZDMG. 39, 52 ff. Haskell, On the Metres of the Rigveda, Am. Or. Soc. Proc. May 1881 and May 1882; Lanman, Catalectic verses of seven syllables, Am. Or. Soc. Proc. May 1880. — Brunnhofer, Ueber den Geist der Ind. Lyrik. Leipzig 1882].

86. Formation of the Strophe: Shown in GKR. (see Introd. p. viii), and in great numbers by Grassmann in his Translation (Note 116); *cf.* ibid. vol. 1, p. 3.

Lyrical Dialogue: See the hymns translated in GKR. ***1, 165*** (84); ***3, 33*** (132); ***4, 42*** (26); ***10, 10*** (142); ***10, 51*** (104); ***10, 108*** (78). [Oldenberg, Âkhyâna-Hymnen im Rigveda, ZDMG. 39, 52–90, discusses a number of hymns of this class.]

87. Though the later time regarded the hymns as 'revealed' (above p. 5), the poets themselves say nothing different on the point than as is said elsewhere: "To him Apollo granted the gift of singing, the sweet mouth of songs, etc. (Hom. Od. 8, 44 f., 63 f., 480 f.; 22, 347 f.). Agni is called 'god-given devotion,' 'inventor' (1, 37, 4.—2, 9, 4; 6, 1, 1; 9, 91, 1); from him, who enchains the singer's mind, come gifts of prophecy, prayers and spells: 4, 11, 2. 3. Indra gives the singer songs of devotion: 3, 34, 5; *cf.* 6, 34, 1. From Varuṇa: 1, 105, 15 in Note 253; 8, 42, 3 in Note 244. Bṛhaspati gives the poet the song heard by the gods: 10, 98, 7. The intoxicated Soma lifts his voice and awakens yearning devotion: 6, 47, 3 (*cf.* Eur. Bacch. 300 f.); see in general the theory of revelation in Muir, OST. 3, 252 f.

"Giving expression to the emotions of the heart," ***10, 71, 8*** (163). Chariots, clothing; 5, 29, 15; 10, 39, 14; 4, 16, 20; 1, 61, 4, and often.—6, 21 6 (*yâd evá vidmá*); 1, 31, 18 (*çákti vâ vidâ vâ*); *cf.* 6, 47, 10: "Whatever I speak here, in reverence toward thee, receive it graciously."—P. 25, foot-note: Müller, OGR. p. 157.

88. After Grassman, Transl. vol. 1, p. v f. and M. Müller, Chips, 1, 3. [Otherwise Barth, Religions of India, Pref. p. xiii f.: "In it (the Veda) I recognize a literature that is pre-eminently sacerdotal, and in no sense a popular one. Neither in the language nor in the thought of the Rigveda have I been able to discover that quality of primitive, natural simplicity which so many are fain to see in it," etc.]

89. L. Geiger, Ursprung und Entwickelung der menschlichen Sprache und Vernunft. Stuttgart 1868, vol. 1, 119 f.; *cf.* vol. 2, 339: "The Indians developed their religion to a kind of old-world classicity, which makes it for all time the key of the religious beliefs of all mankind"; and Müller's Origin and Growth of Religion.

90. Aufrecht, Rigveda, 2d ed., vol. 2, Pref. p. xvii f.: 1, 62, 9; 1, 180, 3; 2, 40, 2; 4, 3, 9; 6, 17, 6; 6, 44, 24; 6, 72, 4; 8, 78 (89), 7; 32, 25; 3, 30, 14 is added by A. Bergaigne, Observations sur les Figures de Rhétorique dans le Rigveda. Paris 1880, p. 21, 5.

91. 4, 13, 5: *cf.* James Darmesteter, Ormazd et Ahriman . . . Paris 1877, p. 51: "Les deux peuples sont frappés avant tout de la fixité de ce ciel et de cette terre dont un si merveilleux équilibre arrête la chûte toujours imminente: 'Qui a fixé, s'écrie le poète iranien, qui a fixé la terre et les astres immobiles pour empêcher qu'ils ne croulent?' (Jaçna 43, 4.) Et de l'autre versant de l'Himâlaja répond le cri du Rishi védique: 'Oh! puisse, à bas du ciel, ne jamais crouler ce soleil' (RV. 1, 105, 3)"; then 1, 24, 10 und ***5, 85, 6*** (5)."

92. M. Müller, OGR. 198 ff.—*Ṛta*, the '*world-ordinance*,' means first the '*course*,' and designates "the *course* of the stars eternally the same," etc. (*cf.* Skt. *ṛtu*, season, and the Latin *rătus* in passages like Cic. Tusc. 5, 24, 69: quorum (siderum sc.) *vagi motus rata tamen* et certa sui cursus *spatia definiant*, and Nat. Deor. 2, 20, 51: maxume vero sunt admirabiles motus earum quinque stellarum quae falso vocantur errantes; nihil enim errat *quod in omni aeternitate conservat* progressus et regressus reliquosque *motus constantis et ratos*, so ibid. 2, 37, 95: in omni aeternitate *ratos immutabilisque cursus*); then "the eternally unchanging *order*, the *law* in nature as in human life" (*cf.* Cic. De Sen. 21, 77: sed credo deos immortalis *sparsisse animos* in copora humana, ut essent qui terras tuerentur *qui*que *caelestium ordinem* contemplantes *imitarentur* eum *vitae modo atque constantia*, similarly Nat. Deor. 2, 14, 37).—For *ṛta*, Müller, OGR. 243 ff.; Ludw. Rv. 3, 284 f.

93. *Mensch*, O.H.G. *mannisco*, root *man*, *think*.—10, 68, 10 (*cf.* 2, 24, 5); 1, 24, 8. 10;—10, 55, 5 *cf.* 10, 85, 18 f. in Note 319.—1, 62, 8; 1, 113, 2. 3 (p. 52 ff.).

94. 8, 75, 5; "The horn of ṛta is stretched out far and near; ṛta conquers even the mighty fighters."—8, 28, 4: "As the gods will, so it will happen; this no one can take from them." In 10, 33, 7 ff. the singer speaks consolingly to Upamaçravas, the son of Kurnçravana: "Mark this, my son Upamaçravas, I am the singer of thy father; if I were lord of the immortals, or even of mortals, he who rewards me (*i.e.* thy father Kuruçravana) should live; but no one lives beyond the will of the gods (ὑπερ αἶσαν), not even if he had a hundred lives; still he would be separated from his companions."

95. Even the Graeco-Aryan period praised the "givers of good things," *dâtaras vasuâm* = δωτῆρες ἑάων; see Benfey, Enstehung des Vocativ. Götting. Abhandh. 1872, vol. 17, 57, n. 58. Fick, Spracheinheit der Indogermanen Europas, p. 276. As other liturgical formulas, which even at so early a period were peculiar to the poetry (*cf.* Note 82), we find: *vā́râ bhar*, ἦρα φέρειν, show love ('bring the wishes'); *vásu mánas*, μένος ἠΰ, good courage; *çrávas ákṣitam*, κλέος ἄφθιτον, imperishable renown, etc.

96. 1, 109, 1: "I looked forth in spirit, seeking good, o Indra and Agni, to relations and kinsmen; but I have no other helper than you; therefore I have made you a powerful song." 1, 71, 7: "No sustaining aid was visible for us among kinsmen; do thou, O Agni, find assistance for us among the gods."—10, 64, 1. 2 (should *âdíçaḥ* "projects," be read instead of *â díçaḥ*, "into the worlds"?).

97. ***6, 9, 3*** (102) and 10, 55, 5: "Look on the wisdom and greatness of the god (*mahitvâdyā́ = mahitvám adyá* with Zimmer, AIL. 349); to-day he dies who breathed yesterday" (p. 28), etc. 1, 103, 5: "Behold this his miracle, and believe in Indra's power." 1, 102, 2 (p. 32, Note 110): "Sun and moon move on, that we may look and believe."

98. ***4, 33, 11*** (122); 1, 53, 1; 8, 2, 18; 2, 20, 3.—10, 42, 4 f.; ***4, 24, 2–5*** (69; above p. 43 f.); 10, 49, 1; 10, 160, 4 and often; *cf.* p. 47 f. and 79 with Note 333.

99. 2, 35, 2 (*kuvid asya védat*), 7, 15, 4 (*cf.* 8, 43, 24; 8, 44, 6: *agnim iḷe sá u çravat*).—3, 53, 2.—8, 6, 34; 6, 47, 14.—5, 42, 2.—7, 72, 1; 6, 49, 12.—4, 32, 16; 3, 62, 8.

100. ***10, 71, 7*** (163)–7, 32, 18. 19; 8, 19, 25. 26; 8, 44, 23 *cf.* 8, 14, 1. 2 and 1, 38, 4–6.

101. 1, 30, 9; 8, 69, 2. 3; 6, 21, 8; 3, 49, 3; 7, 29, 4.—10, 74, 6 (*vâvâna; required,* 1st sing. in spite of Delbrück, Altind. Verb. p. 116).

102. 6, 46, 17; 8, 19, 5 (instead of *védena* with Roth, BR. 6, 1357, and Grassman, Dict. and Transl.; with M. Müller, ASL. p. 205, 1 and p. 28, note, and Ludw. Rv. 1, 424 and 3, 18 f.: *vedéna*); 8, 24, 20.

103. 1, 27, 13; 5, 69, 3; 8, 1, 29, etc.—1, 71, 10; 1, 89, 9: "When our sons become fathers,—break not off our life in the midst of its course."—3, 36, 10; ***2, 27, 10*** (22) and often.—1, 179, 1 *cf.* 1, 116, 25: "May I, seeing, attaining to long life, enter old age as into my home." (*Cf.* p. 66 with Note 254.)

104. 10, 63, 16; 6, 51, 15; 6, 24, 10; 7, 1, 19, etc.—6, 22, 10; 6, 33, 3; 10, 69, 6, etc.

105. With this passage 2, 21, 6 used in the house ritual (Pârask. Gṛhyas. 1, 18, 6) *cf.* the wish of the Greeks in the scholium (Bergk, Poet. Gr. Lyr.[3] 3, 1289, 8):

> *Ὑγιαίνειν μὲν ἄριστον ἀνδρὶ θνατῷ,*
> *δεύτερον δὲ φυὰν καλὸν γενέσθαι,*
> *τὸ τρίτον δὲ πλουτεῖν ἀδόλως,*
> *καὶ τὸ τέταρτον ἡβᾶν μετὰ τῶν φίλων.*

106. 8, 56, 18; 8, 18, 12; 8, 56, 17 (*pratiyántam énasaḥ*: "turning about, returning from sin," repenting and expiating it; *cf.* Geldner, KZ. 1877, NS. 4 (24), 141 f. for the analogy of this conception in the Avesta.

107. 10, 63, 8; 8, 47, 8.—1, 24, 1; 10, 14, 2; more in detail, p. 68 f. and Note 265–286.

108. *Cf.* Hom. Il. 1, 37–42 (εἴ ποτέ τοι . . . ἢ εἰ δή ποτέ τοι—τὸ δέ μοι κρήηνον ἐέλδωρ), Od. 4, 762–765 (εἴ ποτέ τοι — τῶν νῦν μοι μνῆσαι καί μοι φίλον υἷα σάωσον), Virg. Aen. 9, 403 ff., and in general, Peschel, Völkerkunde, p. 281 f., 2d ed.

109. *Cf.* Weber, HIL. 17 f. and Zimmer, AIL. 191 f.

110. Bṛhaspati: p. 73 f. with Notes 309–315; Note 79 has already referred to the characteristic composition ***4, 50, 7-9*** (108) and ***10, 97, 22*** (175); Weber gives the passages of the Brâhmaṇas in ISt. 10, 35 f. ("Whatever Brâhmaṇa knows, he has the gods in his power," Vâj.-San. 31, 22); more from the Sanhitâs: Zimmer, AIL. 205 f.

111. 1, 102, 2 (Note 97); 8, 21, 14; 1, 55, 5; Hor. Ode 1, 34, 1 f.; *cf.* p. 46 f. with Note 163 f.

112 *a.* Dyaus (from *diu*, *div*, "to shine," p. 28, genet. Divás: Ζευς: ΔιϜός, Dyaùs-pitar (voc. 6, 51, 5): Ζεῦ πάτερ: Diespiter etc.), named in many single verses, but without appearing in life or playing an important part in hymn or cult. According to Bréal and Benfey this highest god of the ancient period in India especially was displaced by Indra; *cf.* Muir, OST. 5, 118 f. and Ludw. Rv. 3, 310 f. *Cf.* now J. v. Bradke, Dyaûs Asura, Ahura Mazda und die Asuras, Halle 1885. [Mehliss, Ueber die Bedeutung des homerischen Epitheton's διος, Eisleben 1883.]

b. With Dyaus as Father of Heaven, the Mother Earth Pṛthivi is mentioned in many single verses, and a few later hymns are addressed to the divine pair Dyâvâpṛthivî, in which some of the questions mentioned on p. 87 f. concerning their origin, etc., appear. On Dyâvâprthivî, *cf.* Muir, OST. 5, 20–34 = 00. 3, 450 f.

c. **5, 84** only is addressed to Pṛthivî (GKR. 124; *cf.* AV. 12, 1, translated by Bruce, JRAS. 1862, vol. 19, 321–337).

d. Of Trita with the appellative Âptya (from *ap*, water: "dwelling in the water") it is said in one passage that he carried on the fight with the demons Vṛtra, Vala, and others, independently, or as comrade of the Maruts and of Vâta; in other passages he is incited to it or assisted by Indra (*e.g.* 1, 187, 1; 1, 52, 5; 5, 86, 1; 10, 99, 6; 5, 54, 2; 8, 7, 24; 10, 64, 3.—10, 8, 8; 10, 48, 2; 2, 11, 19); see Roth in BR. and Grassmann in the Translation *s.v.*—For the relation of Trita (RV. 1, 158, 5: Traitana) Âptya to the Iranian Thraêtana

Athwya, Ferîdun, and further to Τριτωνίδ-'Αθάνα, see A. Kuhn in Höfer's Zeitschrift für Wiss. der Sprache 1, 276–291; Benfey, Sâmaveda-Gloss. *s.v.* *âptya* and *trita;* Roth, ZDMG. 2, 216–230 (Die Sage von Feridun in Indien und Iran); Spiegel, Avesta-Uebersetzung, vol. 1, 7; vol. 2, 71; Pott, KZ. 4, 429; and especially Benfey, Götting. Nachricht. 1868, pp. 36–60; also Myriantheus, Die Acvin 1876, Introd. p. xvii f.

113. M. Müller, ASL. 532, 546; Chips, 1, 28 (where 'Kathenotheism' is proposed); G. Bühler, OO, 1, 227; Muir, OST. 5, 6 f. and 12 f. and OO. 3, 449; Zimmer, in ZfDA. NS. 7 (19), 175; *cf.* Hillebrandt, Varuna und Mitra, Breslau 1877, p. 105, and Müller, OGR. 266, 285, 298 f. — Müller's term, *Henotheism*, has been adopted for the sake of its brevity, though C. P. Tiele (in the notice of the first edition of the present work in the Theol. Tijdschrift 1880. Letterkundig overzicht. Geschiedenis der Indische godsdiensten, p. 9), "deze geleerde daarme toch mit geheel hetzelfde bedoelt;" *cf.* Ludw. Rv. 3, Introd. p. xxvii f., and Muir, OST. 5, 412–420. [Barth, Religions of India, p. 26. See Whitney, On the so-called Henotheism of the Veda, Ind. Antiq. May 1881 = Am. Or. Soc. Proc. Oct. 1881; his note on Colebrooke's Misc. Essays, p. 110.]

114. Dual Divinities: A. Kuhn, Herabkunft des Feuers, Berlin 1859, p. 161 f.; Hillebrandt, Varuna und Mitra, p. 98; Müller, OGR. 297 f. — The most important are:

Agni-Soma.	Indra-Pûṣan (Note 211).
Indra-Vâyu.	Indra-Viṣṇu (Note 214).
Indra-Agni.	Dyaus and Pṛthivî (Note 112).
Indra-Bṛhaspati.	Soma-Rudra: ***6, 74*** (116 f.).
Indra-Soma.	Indra-Varuṇa: ***7, 82; 7, 83*** (29 f.).

Mitra-Varuṇa: ***1, 152; 7, 61*** (13 f.); Note 226 f., 241.
Viçve devâs: p. 74, with Note 316.

Older and newer gods: 10, 72, 3, in Note 371. Muir, OST. 5, 16 f.

Systematizing: *e.g.* according to the three regions; see 1, 139, 11; 3, 9, 9 in Note 117.

Classes of gods: The *Angiras*, above p. 42*; the *Rudriyas*, belonging to Rudra; the *Vasus*, the light, good ones; the *Âdityas*, p. 58 ff.; the *Tritas*, *cf.* Note 112*d*; the *Âptyas*, the dwellers in the water, etc.

Several gods identical: 1, 164, 46, and 10, 114, 5 in Note 374.

Monotheistic conception: p. 89 f. (pantheistic: Aditi 1, 89, 10 in Note 225).

115. Such a presentation of the Vedic mythology, after de Gubernatis' Letture sopra la Mitologia vedica. Firenze 1874, is greatly to be desired, but presupposes a number of special investigations, which have as yet hardly been begun. Abel Bergaigne's work, La Religion Védique d'après les Hymnes du Rigveda, Paris 1878–1883, contains a number of correct remarks and observations on particulars, but, according to our view, is too much dominated by preconceived opinions, and does not even claim to offer such a presentation. The best, most copious and reliable sources are the excellent Original Sanskrit Texts on the Origin and History of the People of India, their Religion and Institutions. Collected, translated, and illustrated by John Muir, especially vols. 4 and 5, from which sketches of various divinities and single hymns are repeated on pages 159–195 of the same editor's Metrical Translations from Sanskrit Writers, London 1879. Monographs will be mentioned in connection with the individual divinities.

116. Concerning the Translation of the Rigveda, it is to be observed: that the '*translation*' of Langlois, Rigveda, ou livre des hymnes, traduit du Sanscrit par Mr. Langlois. Paris 1848–1859, does not in any manner whatever deserve that title, 'that it must be denied all authority,' has long been accepted among scholars; that in the title: *Deuxième édition, revue, corrigée et augmentée d'un Index analytique par Ph. Ed. Foucaux.* Paris 1872, the honored name of Foucaux has been misused in a very strange fashion is shown by the declaration of that scholar to Weber, Lit. Centralb. 1873, 93 f. = IStr. 3, 140 f. ("Je n'ai en aucune manière revu le texte français," etc.).

Concerning Wilson's Translation, which in the five volumes published (1850–1866) reaches to RV. 8, 20, *cf.* p. 9 with Note 28.

Benfey in his periodical *Orient und Occident*, vols. 1–3 (1860–1868) translated RV. 1, 1–118. RV. 1, 119–130 from Benfey's remains in Bezzenb. Btr. 7, 287–309.

Of the Rigveda-Sanhitâ, translated and explained by F. Max Müller, the first (up to the present the only) volume, London 1869, contains twelve hymns of the first book to the Maruts; then followed

Siebenzig Lieder des Rigveda, übersetzt von Karl Geldner und Adolph Kaegi, mit Beiträgen von R. Roth. Tübingen 1875.*

* Detailed reviews are known to me by Delbrück, JLZ. 1875, No. 49, Art. 754, by A. Bergaigne, Rev. crit. 1875, No. 50, 51 (II, p. 369 f., 385 f.) and by A. Weber, JLZ. 1876, Art. 750 = IStr. 3, 440 f. — Haug's polemic (Münchener Sitzungsber, 1875, ii, 457 f.) may be disregarded (*cf.* Note 32): concerning the one single passage really treated, RV. 2, 28, 5 (p. 510 n.) a judge who is certainly competent, A. Weber, expresses himself as follows, JLZ. 1876, p. 653 = IStr. 3, 458: "Bei seiner Polemik gegen die in den *Siebenzig Liedern* vorliegende Uebersetzung von *khâm ritasja* durch 'Quelle des frommen Sinnes,' während er es selbst durch 'Wasserquelle' übersetzt, hat Haug leider die schon von

Der Rigveda, zum ersten Male vollständig ins Deutsche übersetzt von Alfred Ludwig, 2 vols. Prag. 1876; in prose, often incomprehensible for the layman, but valuable to the scholar; vol. 3; Die Mantralitteratur und das alte Indien als Einleitung zur Uebersetzung des Rigveda. 1878. [Vols. 4 (1881) and 5 (1883), Commentary to the Translation.]

Rigveda. Ubersetzt und mit kritischen und erläuternden Anmerkungen versehen von Hermann Grassmann. 2 vols. Leipzig 1876–77; for the most part metrical, somewhat free and occasionally very much modernized, but as a whole successful. In regard to the last two works, see A. Weber, JLZ. 1876, p. 650 ff. = IStr. 3, 447 ff., and E. Kuhn, Wissensch. Jahresber. 1877, 1, p. 93 f. (Leipzig 1880).

Single hymns, as mentioned in the following notes, have been translated in various places, a great number of course by Muir in the OST.

117. On this threefold division (see Note 118) rest the statements concerning the number of the gods, which say that there are thirty-three of them, eleven in the heavens, eleven on the earth, and eleven in the waters (*i.e.* the air, in the clouds): 1, 139, 11; further details in OST. 5, 9 f. and Haug, Ait. Brâhm. 2, 212, n. 21. At the same time, 'three hundred, three thousand and thirty and nine' gods are also mentioned (3, 9, 9 = 10, 52, 6). "These combinations of three must, even in the most ancient times, have been used of the gods and things relating to them, since we find them also among the Romans, who clung closely to such forms; Livy, 22, 10, where it is reported concerning the expiatory sacrifices instituted after the battle of Trasimenus: Eius causa ludi magni voti aeris trecentis triginta tribus millibus trecentis triginta tribus triente; praeterea bubus Jovis trecentis, multis aliis divis bubus albis atque ceteris hostiis." A. Kuhn, KZ. 13, 135; *cf.* ibid. 15, 223. Wölfflin on this passage of Livy compares the prophecy in Virg. Aen. 1, 265 ff., by which Aeneas is to rule 3 years, Iulus 33 years, and the dominion is to remain in Alba Longa for 300 years, together 333 years to the founding of Rome; *cf.* Wölfflin on Livy 22, 1, 15. The sacredness of the trinity and its frequent occurrence in popular superstitions up to the present day are well known.

Benfey aufgewiesene Parallele mit dem zendischen *ashahe khâo* nicht im Gedächtnis gehabt, denn er hätte doch wohl Anstand genommen, die scholastische Erklärung von *rita* durch 'Wasser' uns auch für zend. *asha* aufzudrängen!" — In opposition to the orally expressed opinion of Haug, preserved by W. Christ in JLZ. 1877, p. 472, it may suffice to refer to the preface of the Siebenzig Lieder, p. vi and vii, Delbrück, JLZ. 1875, p. 152 f. (*cf.* E. Kuhn, Wissensch. Jahresber. 1877, 1, p. 92, Leipzig 1880).

118. Roth, ZDMG. 6, 68. This distinction between air and light in Greece, where the poets have however quite remodeled the threefold division of the world (*διὰ τρίχα δασμός*, Hom. Il. 15, 189 f.: *τριχθὰ δὲ πάντα δέδασται κτλ.*) shows itself plainly in the separation of the denser lower stratum of air with clouds and mist from 'that eternally gleaming brightness, which was held to be the source of all light and the substance of all heavenly phenomena.' (Preller.) Hom. Il. 14, 287 f.: *εἰς ἐλάτην ἀναβὰς περιμήκετον, ἣ τότ' ἐν Ἴδῃ μακροτάτη πεφυῖα δι' ἠέρος αἰθέρ' ἵκανεν.* Lehrs, de Arist. Stud. Hom. pp. 167–175.—Benfey, KZ. 8, 187 f.

119. 10, 66, 9; 2, 4, 3.—Next to Indra, most of the hymns, even if not many of very high poetical value, are addressed to **Agni**, the 'Moving' (probably from *aj*: Lat. *ag*-ilis: Slav. *og*-nu: Lith. *ug*-nis; Lat. *ig*-nis); Muir, OST. 5, 199–223; MTr. 183–186; *cf.* Ludw. Rv. 3, 324 f.; GKR. 100 f.; ***1, 143; 6, 9; 10, 51.*** A. Kuhn, in his well-known work: *Herabkunft des Feuers und des Göttertranks*, Berlin 1859, treats of the myths named in the title.

120. 3, 1, 3; 2, 1, 3; 2, 9, 3; 3, 9, 4; 2, 12, 3; 1, 60, 1; 1, 93, 6; 1, 143, 2; 1, 128, 2; 3, 9, 5; 3, 5, 10; 1, 58, 6; 2, 4, 2, etc.—To the Bhṛgus (= *Φλεγύ-αι*: Kuhn, l.c. p. 21 f.) themselves are assigned in 10, 46, 9, the preparation, in 10, 46, 2 the discovery of the fire; *cf.* ***1, 143, 4*** (100).

121. 6, 3, 4; 2, 4, 4, and many others. The technical verb for the act of getting fire (as an act of producing: Kuhn, l.c. p. 69 f.; on 5, 2, 1–6: A. Hillebrandt, ZDMG. 33, 248–251) is *math*, *manth*, whence the word *pra-manth-ana*, which designates the stick by the turning of which fire is rubbed out of the wood; with this *pramanth-ana*, without regard to the suffix, the Greek Προμηθ-εύς (Ζεὺς Προμανθεύς among the Thurians; Lykophr. 537) is identical: Kuhn, l.c. p. 17; J. Schmidt, Vocalismus, 1871, vol. 1, 118.

122. 2, 10, 5; 1, 94, 7; 1, 24, 2; 1, 22, 10; 1, 36, 6. 15, etc.—7, 2, 1, with 6, 2, 6; 7, 3, 3; 6, 9, 4, etc.—7, 4, 1; 1, 128, 6; 5, 9, 1; 7, 1, 18, etc.—1, 74, 6; 2, 36, 4; 5, 4, 4, etc.—1, 36, 3, 4; 3, 11, 4 with 1, 144, 6; 1, 44, 11; 10, 4, 2, etc.

123. ***10. 51*** (104 f.); *cf.* the note GKR. 106 and 10, 52; 3, 9, 4, etc.; ***6, 9, 4;*** 7, 11, 1; ***1, 145, 1–5; 10, 2, 1. 3.***—6, 15, 3 (yajiṣṭha); 4, 3, 4 (ṛtacit, svâdhî); 5, 3, 9; 1, 1, 1 (ṛtvij), etc.

124. 10, 2, 3–5; *cf.* 4, 1, 4; 4, 12, 4, and others below in Notes 259 and 261.—7, 9, 2; 10, 87; *cf.* 7, 104.

125. 6, 1, 5; 1, 189, 2; 10, 87, 22 f.; 3, 18, 1; 7, 5, 6; 1, 59, 1; 1, 69, 4; 4, 4, 4; 3, 1, 18; 7, 5, 3. 6; 1, 59, 2; 7, 6, 5; 10, 69, 6, etc. (*viçâm gopati*).

126. 1, 59, 3; 6, 13, 1; 5, 1, 4; 10, 7, 3; 1, 75, 4; 6, 1, 5; 1, 1, 9; 3, 18, 5, etc. (*vaiçvânara, gṛhapati, damûnas,* etc.).

Among the Agni-hymns, the ten so-called Aprî-sûktas are interpolated in our Rigveda, *i.e.* the songs of invitation (1, 13; 1, 142; 1, 188; 2, 3; 3, 4; 5, 5; 7, 2; 9, 5; 10, 70; 10, 110), which introduce the sacrifices of animals. In these liturgical pieces the fire is invoked under various forms and names; the sacrificial straw, the gates of enclosure of the place of sacrifice, and other personifications of the acts and utensils of the sacrifice, usually to the number of ten, and at the close one or more gods in transmitted order, are called upon; see Roth, Nirukta, Introd. p. xxxvi f.; explanations p. 117 f. 121–124; Müller, ASL. 463–466; Weber, ISt. 10, 89–95; Grassmann, Transl. vol. 1, p. 6.

The hymn 3, 8 is addressed to the sacrificial posts (*yûpa*); to the stones used in the pressing of the Soma (*grâvan*), the hymns 10, 76; 10, 94 and ***10, 175*** (154), and others.

127. The **Ṛbhus**: Nève, Essai sur le mythe des Ribhavas, Paris 1847; *cf.* A. Kuhn, KZ. 4, 103 ff., and Mannhardt, Germanische Mythen. Forschungen, Berlin 1858.—GKR. 117 f.: ***1, 161*** and ***4, 33.***

Three names are mentioned: *Ṛbhu*, the "*adroit, skillful*" (from the root *ṛbh*, German *Arb*-eit); *Vâja*, the "*stirring*"; and *Vibhvan*, the "*capable*," the *artist;* three seasons; above Note 68. This construction by Ludwig, Nachrichten, p. 5 = Rv. 3, 187 f.; Zimmer, AIL. 366.

128. 3, 60, 2; 1, 20, 8; ***1, 161, 6;*** 3, 60, 1; 4, 36, 4; 1, 110, 4.—4, 36, 1 f.; 1, 20, 3; 1, 111, 1.—***4, 33, 8; 1, 161, 6.***—1, 20, 4; ***1, 161, 9; 4, 33, 10;*** 1, 20, 2; 3, 60, 2; 4, 35, 5.

129. 4, 36, 3; ***4, 33, 2*** f.; 1, 111, 1.—1, 20, 4; 1, 110, 8; ***1, 161, 7;*** 4, 35, 5.

130. 1, 110, 2; ***4, 33, 7*** with ***1, 161, 10. 13.***

131. ***1, 161, 1-5; 4, 33, 5. 6*** (*cf.* 1, 20, 6; 1, 110, 3; 3, 60, 2; 1, 110, 5); ***4, 33, 9; 1, 161, 14. 6; 4, 33, 2.***—The custom of offering to the Ṛbhus at evening (***4, 33, 11;*** 4, 35, 6. 7. 9) the composer of ***1, 161, 8*** tries to explain by telling that the Ṛbhus had neglected the Soma libations at morning and noon, on which account it was preserved for them for the "third libation."

Tvaṣṭar, the 'Artist' not only made the cup of the gods and Indra's thunderbolt (p. 41 and Note 144), but especially he forms the offspring in the womb of men and beasts (*e.g.* ***10, 10, 5*** (143); 10, 184, 1.—1, 142, 10; 2, 3, 9.—7, 34, 20, etc.); so he (as the gods have their hosts, Indra the Vasus, Rudra the Rudriyas, Varuṇa and Aditi the Âdityas) has the wives of the gods (*gnâs, janayas, devânâm* *patnîs*) for his surroundings (7, 35, 6; 10, 66, 3; ***1, 161, 4*** (118); 2, 31, 4; ***6, 50, 13*** (128); 10, 64, 10; *cf.* Note 148). — Tvaṣṭar also, like Dyaus, Trita and others (Note 112. 142), appears to belong to an earlier race of gods and to have been pushed aside by the later gods.

132. Vata (identical with the Germanic Wuotan: Zimmer, ZfDA. NS. 7 (19), 172, 179 f. Mannhardt, ibid. 10 (22), 4) or Vâyu: few hymns; Muir, OST. 5, 143–146, in GKR. 95: ***10, 168.***

"First . . . to drink the Soma": *pûrvapâ.* With the foot-note St. John 3, 8, *cf.* Xen. Mem. 4, 3, 14: *καὶ ἄνεμοι αὐτοι μὲν οὐχ ὁρῶνται, ἃ δὲ ποιοῦσι φανερὰ ἡμῖν ἐστι καὶ προσιόντων αὐτῶν αἰσθανόμεθα.*

133. Rudra. The name is obscure even to the commentaries, and also to modern scholars (*cf.* BR. and Grassmann, *s.v.*). Müller, OGR. 216, interprets the 'Howler,' the Thunderer; Muir, OST. 4, 299–320 (420); *cf.* Ludw. Rv. 3, 320 f.; GKR. 90 f.: ***2, 33*** and ***7, 46*** (***6, 74*** to Rudra-Soma). For the identification of Rudra with Agni the hymns give no foundation, but A. Kuhn first recognized, and has frequently insisted on the fact, that Rudra is essentially identical with the Greek Apollo; see J. V. Grohmann, Apollo Smintheus und die Bedeutung der Mäuse in der Mythologie der Indogermanen, Prag 1862, p. 4, 45 f. — Rudra still lives, in part, in the present Hindu Triad of gods as Çiva, *cf.* Muir, OST. vol. 4.

134. ***2, 33, 3;*** 1, 43, 5; ***7, 46, 2; 2, 33, 14, 11*** (AV. 11, 2, 19; VS. 16, 9. 52); ***7, 46, 1,*** etc. (Apollo ἑκηβόλος: Grohmann, KZ. 12, 70).

135. ***2, 33, 5. 12. 3.*** Protector of herds: ***2, 33, 1;*** 1, 43, 6. — ***2, 33, 13;*** 1, 114, 2; ***7, 46, 3;*** 1, 114, 5; 1, 43, 4, and ***8, 29, 5*** (129); ***2, 33, 4.***

136. The **Maruts** are at all events no Death-gods; perhaps the 'Shining' (*μαρ-μαίρω, μαρ-μαρυγή, Mars*); see Grassman, KZ. 16, 161 f.; Muir, OST. 5, 147–154; twelve hymns from the first book in Müller's Translation, vol. 1 (Note 116); in GKR. 84 f.: ***1, 165,*** and ***7, 57.*** — *Divó arkâs:* 5, 57, 5; *cf.* 5, 30, 6; 1, 19, 4; 1, 85, 2; 1, 166, 7.

137. 1, 166, 11; 2, 34, 2; 5, 60, 4. — 1, 166, 9. 10; 5, 54, 3. 11; 5, 57, 6, and others.

138. See the beautiful hymn ***1, 165*** in Roth's translation, GKR. 84 f. — 5, 57, 1; 8, 7, 27; 5, 55, 6; 5, 57, 3; 2, 34, 3; 1, 87, 4, etc. — 5, 54, 10; 8, 7, 7. 8; 1, 39, 1; 1, 168, 8. — 5, 60, 3; 8, 20, 5; 1, 64, 7; 8, 7, 5; 1, 38, 9; 3, 32, 4; 1, 64, 5, and others.

139. Parjanya: G. Bühler, OO. 1, 214 ff.; Zimmer, ZfDA. NS. 7 (19), 164 f. (*cf.* AIL. 42 f.), who has proved the identity of the name with Goth. *faírguni,* Norse *Fiörgyn,* and Lith. *Perkuna* (still the name of the thunder); Muir, OST. 5, 140; GKR. 96 f.: ***5, 83*** and ***7, 102.***—Parjanya (a great choice of etymologies in Nir. 10, 10) probably stands for Parcanya, from the root *pṛ-c, fill*, and is the designation for the filled rain-cloud" (Grassman, Zimmer).

140. ***5, 83, 3. 4. 2.***—On ***7, 103,*** which, according to the tradition, is addressed to Parjanya, see p. 81, with Note 342.

141. To **Indra** are addressed by far most hymns; Muir, OST. 5, 77–139 and MTr. 164–177, *cf.* 318 ff.; Ludw. Rv. 3, 317 f.; Perry, Indra in the Rigveda, JAOS. 11, 117–208. GKR. 58 f.; ***2, 12; 4, 18. 19. 24. 30; 7, 28; 10, 108. 119*** and ***10, 27, 1–4*** (p. 71).—The etymology of the name is still obscure; Nir. 10, 8 and Sâyaṇa on 1, 3, 1 (vol. 1, p. 68), guess like modern scholars; Benfey, Sâma Vedagloss. 25, the 'Raining one, Pluvius' (from the root *ind, sind, syand:* "a name dialectically originated somewhere, and afterward extended with the cult," Benfey, OO. 1, 49); so M. Müller, LSL. 2, 449; OGR. 218.—Grassman, *s.v.* the 'Shining One' (from *indh*), as formerly Roth (Theol. Jahrbücher 1846. 5, 352*), who, however, in BR. *s. v.* translates 'Bezwinger, Bewältiger, der Vermögende' (from the root *in, inv* with suffix *-ra* and epenthetic *d*).

142. Whether the Iranic demon Indra, Añdra, coincides with Indra, must appear very questionable; it is certain that Indra represents a new race of gods (*cf.* p. 33), and that in most of the tribes he surpasses even Varuṇa in popularity, as he does Dyaus, Trita, and Tvaṣṭar; *cf.* above p. 62, Note 242, and Muir, OST. 5, 118–126.

143. OST. 5, 98: "The growth of much of the imagery thus described is perfectly natural, and easily intelligible, particularly to persons who have lived in India, and witnessed the phenomena of the seasons in that country. At the close of the long hot weather, when every one is longing for rain to moisten the earth and cool the atmosphere, it is often extremely tantalizing to see the clouds collecting and floating across the sky day after day, without discharging their contents. And in the early ages, when the Vedic hymns were composed, it was an idea quite in consonance with the other general conceptions which their authors entertained, to imagine that some malignant influence was at work in the atmosphere to prevent the fall of the showers, of which their parched fields stood so much in need. It was but a step further to personify both this hostile power and the beneficent agency by which it was at length overcome. Indra is thus at once a terrible warrior and a gracious friend, a god whose shafts deal destruction to his enemies, while they bring deliverance and prosperity to his worshippers. The phenomena of thunder and lightning almost inevitably suggest the idea of a conflict between opposing forces; even we ourselves, in our more prosaic age, often speak of the war or strife of the elements. The other appearances of the sky, too, would afford abundant materials for poetical imagery. The worshipper would at one time transform the fantastic shapes of the clouds into the chariots (*cf.* Psalm 104, 3; Isaiah 19, 1; Daniel 7, 13; Matth. 24, 30; 26, 64. Habakuk 3, 8; Bréal, Hercule et Cacus, 171 f.) and horses of his god, and at another time would seem to perceive in their piled-up masses the cities and castles which he was advancing to overthrow." *Cf.* Zimmer, AIL. 42, also Merk, Acht Vorträge über das Pandschab. Bern 1869, pp. 72–89, etc.

144. 1, 52, 10; 8, 85, 7; ***4, 8, 11.*** — 6, 38, 4; 1, 32, 2; 1, 52, 7; 1, 61, 6, etc. (acc. to 10, 105, 7, Mâtariçvan prepares the thunderbolt); to the Maruts: see above p. 39 and ***1, 165*** (84 f.) The young hero, as soon as he is born, demands the Soma from his mother, and greedily drinks the sap, after outwitting Tvaṣṭar (3, 48, 2–4; 3, 32, 9: ***4, 18, 3*** (64)); or he asks immediately after birth where the renowned champions are, and at once strikes down those that are named to him: 8, 66, 1–3; 8, 45, 4. 5.

145. 3, 34, 3. 6; 6, 22, 6; 1, 32, 7; 3, 30, 8; 1, 52, 15; 1, 80, 5; 3, 32, 4; 5, 32, 5; 5, 30, 6; 1, 32, 5, *cf.* 8, 40, 6; 1, 32, 10. 8 (*mânas* adv., or with BR. "attaining their will"? *Cf.* Grassm. Dict. *s. v. mánas* and Ludw. Rv. 2, 296); 2, 19, 5.

The *Encompasser* is called *âçáyâna* (root *çi*: *κι*: *κεῖσθαι*), a word which, with the Greeks, signifies "the primeval boundary-stream surrounding earth and sea, which, with a deep and mighty flood, like a snake, flows back into itself" (Preller), *âçáyâna* being identical, element for element, with *ὠκεανός* (except the accent; *cf.* Lehrs, De Arist. Stud. Hom. p. 283 f., etc.); Benfey, Gött. Gel. Anz. 1860, p. 222 f.; A. Kuhn, KZ. 9, 247; Leo Meyor, *cf.* Gramm. 1, 334 (in spite of J. Schmidt, Die Wurzel AK in Indogerm. Weimar 1865, p. 40). The word *ὠκεανός* is therefore neither of Semitic origin, nor has it anything at all to do with Ὠγύγης or with *ὠκύς* (in spite of W. H. Roscher, Gorgonen. Leipzig 1879, p. 24, Note 37), or with Skt. *augha.*

146. ***4, 19, 1. 2;*** 6, 17, 8; 1, 80, 15, *cf.* 3, 51, 8; 6, 20, 2; 7, 21, 7; ***1, 165, 6;*** 4, 16, 14: Indra clothes himself in the strength of the elephant, and carries the weapons of the terrible lion.

147. ***4, 18, 9;*** 4, 17, 10; 5, 32, 3; 7, 18, 20; 2, 11, 2; ***2, 12, 10;*** 6, 18, 12; 10, 54, 2; 8, 24, 15; 1, 57, 2; 1, 130, 4; 2, 11, 10; 1, 14, 2; 3, 492 (pṛthujráyâ: Grassm.). — A frequent designation of Indra's weapon, *vadha* or *vadhar* (from root *vadh*), explains the "etymologically obscure" German word *Wetter*, O. H. Germ. wetar, AS. veder. "When the Indo-Germanic languages separated, the root contained only the idea of the lightning-stroke. In the German tongues this was generalized in such a way that the term for the most wonderful and striking atmospheric change was extended to all atmospheric changes." Delbrück, KZ. 16, 266–271. The word is therefore in no way related to ἀήρ or αἰθήρ.

148. 8, 14, 13; ***4, 19, 5;*** 1, 52, 8, with 1, 7, 3.—1, 32, 14 ("Whom sawest thou, Indra, as the avenger of Ahi, after thou hadst killed him, when thou hastenedst through the 99 rivers, like a terrified falcon through the air?"); 6, 18, 14; 1, 61, 8; 8, 21, 5; 8, 12, 22 f.; 4, 22, 5.

Wives of Gods (1, 61, 8; 5, 46, 8) play no part in the Rig; they are only mentioned as the surrounding of Tvaṣṭar (Note 131), and the names appear isolated; *Agnâyî*, *Indrâṇî* (10, 86, 11 in Note 159), *Varuṇânî* in 1, 22, 12; 2, 32, 8; 5, 46, 8; *Rodasî* (the wife of Rudra): ***6, 50, 5;*** 6, 66, 6; 7, 34, 22. Açvinî: 5, 46, 8 (wife of Açvin, as otherwise *Sûryâ* is named; p. 50 and Note 176); for the goddess Aditi, Note 225.

149. After ***10, 108*** (78); then ***2, 12, 1;*** 2, 15, 8; 3, 30, 10; ***2, 12, 3;*** 10, 68, 10; *cf.* 10, 67, 6: "He brought the Paṇis to lamentation." Vala, "the cave," also personified.—In 7, 19, 5, it is told of Indra that in one day he won ninety-nine strongholds, and in the evening the hundredth.

Saramâ (root *sṛ*, 90) is, according to A. Kuhn, ZfDA. 6, 117 f., the storm-cloud (differently Müller, LSL. 2, 481 f.). The regular matronymic of Saramâ is *Sârameya*, in which Kuhn has found the explanation (in no way refuted) of the Greek messenger of the gods Ἑρμείας; on this *cf.* Benfey, Göttinger Abhandlungen, 1877, vol. 22, 1 f.

In the epithets *vîla* and *dṛdha* (from **dardha*), "firm," of these beleaguered strongholds the stems of Ἴλιον (ϝίλιον) and Δαρδανία have been seen: Oscar Meyer, Quaestiones Homericae. Dissert. Bonn, 1867, p. 10 f.

150. GKR. 76; 3, 30, 4; ***2, 12, 4;*** 1, 53, 1.—***4, 19, 4;*** 8, 14, 14 (demons stealthily climbing); ***2, 12, 12.—2, 12, 2;*** 3, 30, 4; 1, 131, 1; 1, 57, 5.

151. 6, 25, 8; *cf.* 2, 20, 8.—7, 32, 14; *cf.* 10, 147, 1; 8, 1, 31.—10, 138, 3; 4, 16, 13.

152. 4, 25, 6. 7; 1, 83, 6; 10, 160, 3; 6, 23, 3; 10, 42, 4; *cf.* 3, 32, 14 (corrupt): "I will praise thee before the day of decision, that, when both the armies call upon thee, thou mayest rescue us from need, as upon a ship."

153. GKR. 69; *cf.* p. 46 f. and Note 164.—6, 18, 3; 4, 26, 2; 2, 11, 18; 1, 103, 3; 5, 54, 6; *cf.* 1, 130, 8; 3, 34, 9; 1, 51, 8, etc.—***4, 19, 6;*** 2, 13, 12; *cf.* 1, 61, 11; 2, 15, 5.

154. GKR. 66 f.; 2, 13, 12; *cf.* 1, 61, 11; 2, 15, 5.—1, 174, 9 = 6, 20, 12; 2, 15, 5; ***4, 30, 17;*** 5, 31, 8; 6, 45, 1.—***4, 30, 3;*** 10, 138, 3.

155. 6, 30, 5; 3, 32, 8; 8, 36, 4; 2, 13, 5; ***2, 12, 2;*** 6, 17, 7 (*cf.* 6, 47, 4: "It is he who measured out the breadths of earth, and formed the heights of heaven; he fixed the sap on the three heights,—Soma fixed the wide air-space"); 10, 89, 4; 10, 138, 6; 3, 32, 8; 10, 89, 2 (read *sûryam* with Grassm.); 4, 17, 14.—2, 13, 7; 8, 67, 10.

156. 6, 34, 1; 3, 30, 1; 8, 87, 2; 8, 37, 3; 8, 67, 5; 3, 34, 2; 4, 30, 1; *cf.* 8, 21, 13.

157. 10, 54, 3; *cf.* 5, 42, 6; 6, 27, 3. 4.—6, 30, 1; 1, 61, 8. 9; 10, 89, 11; *cf.* further 1, 52, 14. 11; 2, 16, 3; 3, 32, 11; 3, 36, 4; 7, 23, 3; 8, 6, 15; 8, 59, 5; 8, 83, 12; 1, 81, 5; 8, 77, 5; 1, 55, 1; 1, 81, 5 etc.; 8, 59, 5: "If, Indra, a hundred skies and a hundred earths were thine, a thousand suns could not equal thee, thunderer, nor could anything created [nor], the two worlds [even then], when thou wert born."

158. 3, 32, 7 [with Aufrecht in Muir, OST. 4, 102, n. 82, and Benfey, Gött. Abhandl. vol. 19, p. 238]; 6, 30, 1; 3, 30, 5 (*cf.* 1, 33, 9; Isaiah 40, 12); 8, 6, 5; (*cf.* ***10, 119, 6-8,*** 81 f.); 1, 53, 1; 8, 6, 38; *cf.* ***4, 30, 2:*** "The races of men, all things, roll after thee like wheels."

159. 1, 51, 1; 6, 24, 7; 8, 82, 5; *cf.* 10, 48, 5 (Indra speaks): "Never shall I fall into the hands of Death." 10, 86, 11: "I have heard that among all these females Indrâṇî is the most fortunate; for her husband shall never at any future time die of old age."

160. 3, 32, 9; 7, 20, 1; ***4, 30, 23;*** *cf.* 1, 165, 9; 6, 24, 5 [otherwise BR. vol. 7, column 1707]; 7, 18, 17 ("He slays the lioness by a ram, and tears the spears? [Ludw.] with a needle;" similar paradoxes 10, 28, 4, 9); *cf.* 8, 52, 6: "In Indra abide all heroic deeds, the accomplished and that are to be done." 10, 49, 3, Indra says: "They praise me for that which is and that which is to be done."

161. 6, 31, 1; 1, 176, 3, *cf.* 6, 45, 8; 3, 46, 2 (8, 1, 2: "Indra, who does both, who puts at enmity and reconciles"); 10, 22, 10.

162. 10, 28, 9; 7, 98, 4; 3, 34, 10; 2, 30, 10; then 5, 34, 3 [quite differently Haug, Die Gâthâ's 2, 239]; 7, 98, 4.—4, 17, 13; 6, 47, 15.
"Now to the front brings one, and now another:" Hes. Op. 6: *ῥεῖα δ' ἀρίζηλον μινύθει καὶ ἄδηλον ἀέξει, ‖ ῥεῖα δέ τ' ἰθύνει σκολιὸν καὶ ἀγήνορα κάρφει ‖ Ζεὺς ὑψιβρεμέτης* (Arist. Lys. 772: *τὰ δ' ὑπέρτερα νέρτερα θήσει Ζεὺς ὑψιβρεμέτης*). Hom. Od. 16, 211: *ῥηΐδιον δὲ θεοῖσι, τοι οὐρανὸν εὐρὺν ἔχουσι ‖ ἠμὲν κυδῆναι θνητὸν βροτὸν ἠ δὲ κακῶσαι.* *Cf.* besides the beautiful Fragm. 56 of Archilochos (Bgk.) and Hor. Od. 1, 34, 12: Valet ima summis mutare et insignem attenuat deus obscura promens.

"The lord of both the worlds hates all the haughty" (restrainer of the proud: 3, 34, 10): *cf.* Aesch. Pers. 827: Ζεύς τοι κολάστης τῶν ὑπερκόπων ἄγαν ‖ φρονημάτων ἔπεστιν εὔθυνος βαρύς, the fate of Kapaneus: Aesch. Sept. 427 f.; Soph. Ant. 127 f.; — the μηδὲν ἀσεπτεῖν and the μεγάλοι λόγοι in Soph. Ant., the θεῖον φθονερόν of Hdt. 1, 32; 3, 40; 7, 10, the *dis te minorem*, etc., of Hor. Od. 3, 6, 5, etc.

163. ***2, 12, 10; 10, 27, 1*** (71) (10, 27, 6: the wheels shall roll over the mockers who have fallen by his arrow), *cf.* 10, 89, 8; 1, 131, 4. — 10, 160, 4; 8, 14, 15; 5, 34, 7; 10, 48, 7, Indra says: "I alone vanquish this one enemy; I vanquish two; what can even three do? I destroy many [of them] like sheaves of corn on the threshing-floor. Why do the enemies who regard not Indra revile me?" 4, 25, 6: "The unfriendly he hurls down into the deep" (p. 71 with Note 287).

164. GKR. 71; 1, 84, 8: "He thrusts aside the men who offer no gifts with his foot, like bushes"; 8, 53, 2.

"Turn to the god in day of need": *cf.* above p. 32, with Note 111, and p. 44 (with ***4, 24, 5***); Hor. Od. 1, 34, 1 f.

"When they see how fierce the battle rages": Aesch. Pers. 498 f.: Θεοὺς δέ τις ‖ τὸ πρὶν νομίζων οὐδαμοῦ, τότ᾽ εὔχετο ‖ λιταῖσι, γαῖαν οὐρανόν τε προσκυνῶν, etc.

165. 7, 31, 5; 2, 30, 7: "Let me never grow weary, nor lame, nor give over; we will never say, 'Press no Soma.'" 5, 37, 1; 7, 22, 5; 5, 32, 11. 12.

166. 5, 36, 4; 7, 37, 3; ***10, 27, 1*** (71); 8, 87, 11; 8, 50, 17; 8, 45, 17: "We call thee from afar to help, for thou art not deaf, but of listening ear"; — 7, 20, 1. — *Cf.* 3, 53, 5; 10, 23, 7; 6, 21, 8; 10, 47, 1; 10, 42, 3; 1, 104, 7; 6, 45, 1. 7, and many others. 10, 48, 1, Indra says: "Men call me as a father." 8, 87, 11: "Thou, o good one, art our father; thou, o mighty one, our mother." 4, 17, 17:

> "Appearing as our friend, do thou defend us, —
> The Soma-presser's comforter and safeguard;
> Friend, father thou, most fatherly of fathers,
> Who gives the suppliant life, and grants him freedom."

167. ***7, 28, 5;*** 4, 17, 19; 3, 32, 16; 8, 70, 3; 8, 77 3; 8, 14, 4; *cf.* 5, 34, 5; 8, 82, 11. — 7, 37, 6 (*vāsáyasi*).

168. (*Cf.* 4, 23, 1. 2, 5. 6); ***2, 12, 5*** ("Of whom the doubter asks, 'where then is Indra?' and denies that he exists, although so awful"); 6, 18, 3 ("Hast thou now conquered the enemies? Hast thou alone won the land for the Aryan? Is this really thy deed? or is it not? Tell me truly").

169. 10, 22, 1; *cf.* 8, 50, 9: "Whether a poet or one who is not a poet sing thy praise."

170. 8, 6, 44; 10, 89, 10: "In labor and pleasure Indra is to be called on."

171. The **Açvins**, as is at once evident, are gods of the breaking day, perhaps of twilight, and, at all events, originally identical with the Greek Dioskuroi; but a satisfactory solution of their original signification in all points has not yet been given. See Muir, OST. 5, 234–257, and the monograph, Die Açvin oder arischen Dioskuren, by Dr. L. Myriantheus, Münich 1876, well worthy of notice for the significance of the myths. — GKR. 40 f.; *7, 69; 10, 39.*

172. In the Rigveda the Açvins are always adored together (*cf.* 2, 39, 1–7); their later names, *Dasra* and *Nâsatya*, are here (as adj.) always in the dual; I can recall only one passage where the heroes are thought of as separated, 1, 181, 4: "The one a prince, victorious over heroes; the other, the blessed son of heaven." *Cf.* Nir. 12, 1 f.; Müller, LSL. 2, 507 ff. — 3, 58, 4; *7, 69, 5;* 5, 77, 1. 2.

173. 6, 63, 3 [*uttânáhasta*: χεῖρας ἀνασχών: palmas tendens]; 6, 63, 1; 3, 39, 3; 7, 67, 1; *cf.* *10, 39, 1:* "Like a father's name men love to call their names."

174. *7, 69, 2. 1. 3;* *cf.* 1, 30, 19. — 4, 36, 1 (with golden bridles: 8, 5, 28; 8, 22, 5); 4, 36, 2; 1, 183, 1; *cf.* 1, 46, 3.

175. 1, 118, 4; 4, 45, 4; 1, 118, 1; 5, 77, 3; 4, 45, 7; *cf.* 1, 180, 1; 7, 70, 2; 5, 77, 3; 6, 63, 7; 7, 68, 3; 1, 117, 2; *10, 39, 12;* 1, 118, 1; 8, 62, 2.

176. 7, 69, 4 [*páritakmyâyâm* with Grassmann; *cf.* especially *aktór vyùṣṭan páritakmyâyâm*]; 1, 119, 5; 1, 116, 17; 1, 117, 13; 4, 43, 6; 5, 73, 5; 8, 22, 1; *10, 39, 12* (instead of Sûryâ Açvinî; 5, 46, 8. Note 148); 7, 67, 2; 7, 73, 1; 8, 8, 12; *cf.* 1, 112, 2: "For your favor weighty, unexhausted acts of help have mounted your chariot, so that it almost seems to give way."

177. 8, 18, 8; Medicines 1, 157, 6. — 1, 112, 8; 8, 5, 23: "To Kâṇva, blinded in his house, ye gave sight in delight at his song"; 1, 118, 7; *10, 39, 3;* *cf.* 10, 40, 8. — 1, 180, 5; *10, 39, 4;* *cf.* 1, 118, 3 = 3, 58, 3: "Why else do the old sages call you the speediest helpers in need?"

178. GKR. 43. — Vimada: 1, 116, 1 ("on chariot swift as the arrow"); 1, 117, 20; 10, 65, 12. Puraṁdhi: 1, 116, 13: "Puraṁdhi called you helpers at the great sacrifice; ye listened to the eunuch's wife as though it were a command, and gave her Hiraṇyahasta"

("Goldhand"); 10, 65, 12, he is called Çyâva ("Brown"); *cf.* 1, 117, 24: "Ye, favoring, gave Hiraṇyahasta as son to the eunuch's wife; Çyâva, though twice cut apart, ye raised up to life."

179. Kali is also (1, 112, 15) mentioned as the protegé of the Açvins. — Vandana, according to this passage, is drawn out of an antelope-pit, into which he had fallen; so 1, 118, 6; according to 1, 116, 11 [where with BR. 3, 539 *riçyadâd* is to be read], and 1, 117, 5, the Açvins bring forth to light for Vandana that which was buried, like him who slumbered in the bosom of Death, and like the sun, which rests in darkness, like beautiful ornaments of gold, *cf.* 1, 117, 12; according to 1, 119, 7, like artists they fashioned a car for the old and feeble Vandana, and miraculously brought forth the singer from the earth.

180. In the contest of Khela the foot of Viçpalâ had been cut off like a wing from a bird; at once the Açvins furnished her an iron leg, so that she could run for the offered prize; 1, 116, 15; 117, 11; 112, 10. Myriantheus, pp. 100–112.

181. 1, 116, 6 ("Pedu with evil steed"); 117, 9; 118, 9; 119, 10; 7, 71, 5. — 9, 88, 42.

182. 1, 117, 3; 5, 78, 4; 1, 116, 8; 1, 180, 4; 8, 62, 8; 7, 71, 5: "From the calamity of darkness ye seized Atri"; 6, 50, 10: "As ye released Atri out of great darkness"; 10, 143, 1. 2: "Ye raised the hoary Atri up to walk . . ., ye released Atri . . . in full youthful strength"; for *10, 39, 9*, *cf.* Gkr. p. 45, n. 13. — A sunset, under the keeping of the Açvins, the Dioskuroi, who, as mediators between darkness and light, protected Helios. They guarded the evening sky, the glowing fire which surrounds the sun, with refreshing coolness (of evening), with a draught, which seems to point to the evening dew. Sonne, KZ. 10, 331. At morning they overpower the demon of darkness, and lead back the sun to heaven in full beauty.

183. 1, 116, 10; 7, 68, 6; *10, 39, 4*: "Cyavâna, who lay like an old cart, ye made young again to walk"; 5, 74, 5: "And made young again, he raised the maiden's love." The Sun, gone down and thought to be dead, is brought up by the Açvins in the full vigor of youth and beauty; and becomes the companion, wins the love, of the Dawn. Benfey, OO. 3, 160; Myriantheus, p. 93 f.

184. 1, 112, 5; 1, 116, 24; 1, 117, 4; *10, 39, 9*. — For the signification, Benfey, OO. 3, 162. 164; differently Myriantheus, p. 174.

185. 1, 116, 7; 1, 117, 6. The horse's hoof, as spring or opener of springs, recalls the Ἵππου κρήνη, opened by Pegasus, on Helicon (Strabo, 8, 21, p. 379: τὸν δ' αὐτόν φασι καὶ τὴν Ἵππου κρήνην ἀναβαλεῖν ἐν τῷ Ἑλικῶνι πλήξαντα τῷ ὄνυχι τὴν ὑποῦσαν πετραν; *cf.* Ov. Met. 5, 256: fama novi fontis . . . dura Medusaei quem praepetis ungula rupit); and in Troezene (Paus. 2, 31, 9), Paus. 2, 3, 5, tells of a spring specially worth seeing in Corinth: Καὶ ὁ Βελλεροφόντης ἔπεστι, καὶ τὸ ὕδωρ οἱ δ' ὁπλῆς ἵππου ῥεῖ τοῦ Πηγάσου. Myriantheus, p. 149 f.

186. 1, 117, 7; *cf. 10, 39, 3:* "For ye bring happiness in love to the old unmarried maid."—Myriantheus, p. 95.

187. 1, 116, 14; 1, 117, 16; 1, 112, 8; 1, 118, 8; *10, 39, 13* [in 7, 68, 8, I consider *vṛka* corrupt]. *Vṛka* = wolf = λύκο-ς is the Demon of Darkness; here the Açvins destroy him, elsewhere the Sun-god, Apollo λυκοκτόνος. *Cf.* Myriantheus, pp. 78–81, and for the quail (*vartikâ*, Ortygia), Müller, LSL. 2, 525 f.

188. 1, 112, 21.—The Açvins put a horse's head upon Dadhyanc, with whose bones Indra slew the enemies; thereupon he showed them where they could find the sweetness, *i.e.*, the Soma-draught with Tvaṣṭar: 1, 84, 13; 10, 48, 2; 1, 117, 22; 1, 116, 12; 1, 119, 9; 9, 108, 4. Benfey, OO. 2, 245; Myriantheus, p. 142 f.

189. 1, 116, 3; 1, 182, 6; 1, 117, 14. 15; 1, 119, 4; 1, 116, 5. 4; 10, 143, 5: "Bhujyu tossed in the sea on the other side of the air"; 1, 116, 5: "home"; 1, 119, 4: "to the Fathers"; 1, 182, 5: "godward."—7, 68, 7, instead of Tugra's, "evil-minded companions" are named (4, 27, 4, appears to me corrupt).—The "vehicle swift as thought," the "animated ships floating in the atmosphere" (1, 182, 5: "Ye made in the floods that flying ship, endowed with life, for Tugra's son"), the "never failing, never tiring, never faltering, winged steeds," 7, 69, 7 recall the verses in Hom. Od. 8, 559 f., concerning the (cloud) ships of the Phaeacians: ἀλλ' αὐταὶ ἴσασι νοήματα καὶ φρένας ἀνδρῶν ‖ καὶ πάντων ἴσασι πόλις καὶ πίονας ἀγροὺς ‖ ἀνθρώπων, καὶ λαῖτμα τάχισθ' ἁλὸς ἐκπερόωσιν, ‖ ἠέρι καὶ νεφέλῃ κεκαλυμμέναι· οὐδέ ποτέ σφιν ‖ οὔτε τι πημανθῆναι ἔπι δέος οὔτ' ἀπολέσθαι. Vs. 565 οὕνεκα πομποὶ ἀπήμονές εἰμεν ἁπάντων. Sonne, KZ. 10, 337. With 1, 182, 7: "What was the tree, standing in the midst of the flood, which the son of Tugra seized in his need?" Sonne, KZ. 15, 109 f., compares Od. 12, 103, 431 f.: τῷ δ' ἐν ἐρινεός ἐστι μέγας, φύλλοισι τεθηλώς· . . . ἡ μὲν ἀνερροίβδησε θαλάσσης ἁλμυρὸν ὕδωρ· ‖ αὐτὰρ ἐγὼ ποτὶ μακρὸν ἐρινεὸν ὑψόσ' ἀερθεὶς ‖ τῷ προσφὺς ἐχόμην ὡς νυκτερίσ κτλ.—For the meaning of this sun-myth, see Sonne, KZ. 10, 335 f. Benfey, OO. 3, 159; Myriantheus, p. 158 ff.

190. 4, 43, 7; 10, 40, 12.—1, 116, 1; 1, 181, 7; 1, 180, 5. The Açvins, too, are praised for the miracle of the "soft milk in rough cows," above p. 27, with note 90; 1, 180, 3.—5, 73, 1; 8, 10, 5. 1:

"from front and rear, from above and below; from heaven and earth, from the sea; from plants, houses, from the mountains' peaks, and from foreign tribes," 7, 72, 5; 4, 44, 5; 7, 70, 3; 8, 10, 5; 1, 47, 7; *cf.* 1, 182, 3: "What do ye there, why sit ye where the people boasts unsacrificing?"

191. ***7, 69, 6*** (differently 4, 45, 4); 5, 76, 3. 2.

192. 1, 117, 4; *cf.* 1, 158, 3; 1, 181, 1; 7, 72, 2 (*cf.* 5, 76, 4 and 4, 44, 5: "Let not other devout men hold you fast when your old friends gather around you"); 1, 157, 4 *cd* = 1, 34, 11 *cd.* 1, 116, 25 with 1, 182, 3. 4; 10, 40, 13: "Give him a watering-place, with a good draught, and a resting-place on the journey"; 8, 8, 13; 8, 26, 7; 8, 35, 10 f., etc.

193. **Uṣas**: the "Irradiating." Muir, OST. 5, 181–198; GKR. 35 f.: ***1, 124; 7, 76.***—1, 92, 1; ***1, 124, 5; 7, 76, 2;*** 3, 61, 4; 4, 51, 1. 2; 7, 77, 2; 1, 123, 1; Homer: 'Ηὼς *φαεσίμβροτος*— and *χρυσόθρονον ἠριγένειαν* ‖ *ὦρσεν, ἵν' ἀνθρώποισι φόως φέροι.*—Max Müller, who traced a very large number of myths to the Dawn (*cf.* LSL. 2, 481 ff.), says, l.c. p. 517: "The dawn, which to us is merely a beautiful sight, was, to the early gazer and thinker, the problem of all problems. It was the unknown land from whence rose every day those bright emblems of a divine power which left in the mind of man the first impression and intimation of another world, of power above, of order and wisdom. What we simply call the sunrise, brought before their eyes every day the riddle of all riddles, the riddle of existence. The days of their life sprang from that dark abyss, which every morning seemed instinct with light and life. Their youth, their manhood, their old age, all were to the Vedic bards the gift of that heavenly mother who appeared bright, young, unchanged, immortal, every morning, while everything else seemed to grow old, to change, and droop, and at last to set, never to return. It was there, in that bright chamber, that, as their poets said, mornings and days were spun, or, under a different image, where mornings and days were nourished (10, 37, 2; 7, 65, 2), where life or time was drawn out (1, 113, 16). It was there that the mortal wished to go, to meet Mitra and Varuṇa. The whole theogony and philosophy of the ancient world centred in the Dawn, the mother of the bright gods, of the sun in his various aspects, of the morn, the day, the spring; herself the brilliant image and visage of immortality."

194. 1, 113, 3; 1, 123, 7; 6, 49, 3: "One decks herself with stars, with sunlight the other, relieving each other in their mutual courses" [instead of *sûro*, probably *sûrâ* should be read with Grassm. Dict. 1630]; 1, 113, 3 (in Note 200); ***1, 124, 9. 8*** (36); 1, 113, 1; 10, 172, 4; 4, 52, 1.

195. 1, 113, 1; 6, 65, 2; 6, 64, 3: "She drives away the darkness as a heroic defender chases the enemies, like a swift charioteer"; 1, 48, 8; 7, 81, 6; 10, 35, 3.—10, 35, 2, Uṣas drives away the guilt of sin; 8, 47, 18, the evil dreams.—For the dispute of Uṣas with Indra, ***4, 30, 8–11*** (73); 2, 15, 6; 10, 138, 5, *cf.* Sonne, KZ. 10, 416 f.; Müller, Chips, 2, 91 f.

196. 7, 81, 1; 7, 75, 1; 1, 92, 4. 11; 1, 48, 15; 1, 113, 4. 14; 4, 52, 5; 1, 92, 12: "Spreading out (her rays) like herds, as the river its waves, she is visible afar."

197. 1, 49, 1. 2; 1, 113, 14; 7, 78, 4; 7, 75, 6; 3, 61, 2; 4, 51, 5. —1, 124, 11; 5, 80, 3. The steeds or cattle of Uṣas are the light morning-clouds, "bright, shining, as the clear billows of the waters," 6, 64, 1. Theocr. 13, 11: λευκιππος 'Αώς 2, 147 f. ἵπποι ‖ 'Αῶ τὰν ῥοδόπαχυν ἀπ' 'Ωκεανοῖο φέροισαι, etc. Virg.: roseis Aurora quadrigis (bigis).—6, 64, 4. 1; 6, 65, 5; 5, 80, 1; 7, 79, 1.

198. 4, 51, 3; ***1, 124, 10***.—1, 92, 9; 7, 80, 2; 7, 77, 1; 1, 49, 3; 6, 64, 6 = ***1, 124, 12***; 7, 79, 1; 7, 75, 4. With the following verses *cf.* 1, 48, 5. 6 [where *padám ná vety ódatî* is obscure to me]:

> "She comes, and all the footed creatures rouses up,
> And stirs the birds to fly aloft.
> She sends men forth to battle, sends them to their toil . . .
> And never in their busy flight the birds seek rest
> When shines thy radiance, Bounteous One."

"All the five peoples" (*panca janâsas, kṛṣṭayas*, etc.), originally the five tribes of the Yadus, Turvaças, Druhyus, Anus, and Pûrus [1, 108, 8], afterward formulaic for men in general, "the whole world"; see Zimmer, AIL. 119–123.

199. 1, 92, 4; 1, 123, 10; 6, 64, 2; 5, 80, 5. 6; 1, 113, 15; 7, 81, 5; 7, 76, 7; 7, 75, 2.

200. 1, 123, 8. 9; 7, 76, 5; 1, 92, 12; 5, 80, 4 = ***1, 124, 3*** (35); *cf.* 1, 113, 3, of night and morning:

> "The sisters' paths are each alike, and endless,
> On them they journey, by the gods instructed;
> Unlike in color, but alike in spirit,
> They never halt nor strive, steadfast forever."

201. 1, 92, 10; 1, 118, 11: "in the ever renewed light of the Dawn"; 1, 123, 8; 4, 51, 6; 1, 113, 8. 15; ***1, 124, 2. 4***.

202. On *svadhâbhis* (1, 113, 13) *cf.* 3, 61, 1, *ánu vratám*, and 1, 113, 10; for the rest on pâda d, 4, 51, 6; 3, 61, 1; 1, 123, 2. 8. On 1, 92, 10. 11 (4, 51, 9, *ámîtavarṇâ*); Bollensen, OO. 2, 463 f., 465. For the thought, *cf.* Plut. Consol. ad. Apoll. 15, p. 110, B: *γενναῖον δὲ καὶ τὸ Λακωνικόν· νῦν ἁμές, πρόσθ' ἄλλοι ἐθάλεον, αὐτίκα δ' ἄλλοι, ὧν ἁμὲς γενεὰν οὐκέτ' ἐποψόμεθα.*

203. Sûrya: the "Gleaming, Shining."—Muir, OST. 5, 155–161; GKR. 55 f.: ***1, 115; 10, 189*** (sunrise)—***1, 115, 2*** (55); 10, 37, 1. 9. Mimnermus fgm. 12: Ἠέλιος δ' ἀμέγαρτ' ἔλαχεν πόνον ἤματα πάντα, ‖ οὐδέποτ' ἄμπαυσις γίγνεται οὐδεμία ‖ ἵπποισίν τε καὶ αὐτῷ, ἐπεὶ ῥοδοδάκτυλος Ἠὼς ‖ Ὠκεανὸν προλιποῦσ' οὐρανὸν εἰσαναβῇ.

204. 7, 63, 3. 2; 4, 13, 4; 7, 63, 1: "Sûrya, the fortune-giving, who, like a skin, rolls the darkness together."—1, 50, 2; ***10, 189, 2***: "He moves among the hosts of stars,—at his breath they fade."

205. Sûrya's Mares: ***1, 115, 4. 5;*** 10, 31, 8; 1, 121, 13; 5, 29, 5; 5, 45, 10; 10, 92, 8 (seven: 1, 50, 8; 4, 13, 3; 7, 66, 5; 7, 60, 3). Horses: ***1, 115, 3;*** 10, 37, 3; 10, 49, 7 (*saptâçva*; 5, 45, 9), *cf.* Eur. Phoen. 1 f.: ὦ τὴν ἐν ἄστροις οὐρανοῦ τέμνων ὁδὸν καὶ χρυσοκολλήτοισιν ἐμβεβὼς δίφροις Ἥλιε, θοαῖς ἵπποισιν εἱλίσσων φλόγα κτλ. Hom. Hymn. in Solem 9 f. (vs. 14: ἄρσενες ἵπποι), in Merc. 69, in Cer. 88. Soph. Aj. 845: σὺ δ' ὦ τὸν αἰπὺν οὐρανὸν διφρηλατῶν Ἥλιε κτλ. Ar. Nub. 571: Ἥλιος ἱππονώμας. Aesch. fgm. 192 D (186 N.), etc.

206. 1, 50, 2 (πανόπτης ἡλίου κύκλος. Ἠέλιος, ὃς πάντ' ἐφορᾷ, etc.); 10, 35, 8; 4, 1, 17; 5, 45, 9: "Sûrya goes to the field, which spreads out far and wide before him." 5, 45, 10, and 7, 60 4: "The bright flood of light." 7, 60, 2: "The herdsman of all things standing and moving, *i.e.* the immovable and the movable, of the inanimate and animate, looking upon right and wrong among men." 6, 51, 2; 10, 37, 5.—***1, 115, 4*** with 4, 13, 4 (*vihâran tántum*); ***1, 115, 5.*** "Dome" = "vault, arch of heaven," often.

207. 1, 115, 1 ("the moving and standing," see 7, 60, 2, in the preceding note); 5, 27, 6; 7, 63, 1. Matth. 5, 45: τὸν ἥλιον αὐτοῦ ἀνατέλλει ἐπὶ πονηροὺς καὶ ἀγαθούς, καὶ βρέχει ἐπὶ δικαίους καὶ ἀδίκους.—1, 50, 4. 2; 10, 170, 3; 4, 13, 2 (spoken of Mitra-Varuṇa, as usually; see above p. 59); 7, 83, 2; 7, 66, 2: "The bright eye, placed by the gods." *Cf.* p. 59 with Note 224.

208. Hillebrant rightly observes, Varuna und Mitra, p. 45: "To infer from the name that they were all personifications of various attributes of the sun, seems suspicious to me, in so far as we look upon it as a production of the Vedic poets themselves; for some, we may rather ask whether they were not originally sun-gods of different tribes, who gave them names as they appealed to their fancy; whether, then, in the consolidation of single tribes, the cults were not also brought over," etc.

209. Pûṣan: Muir, OST. 5, 171–180; GKR. 51 f.: ***1, 42.***—4, 3, 7; 8, 4, 15; 1, 89, 6; 6, 58, 4; 10, 26, 7: "The strong lord of refreshing, the strong friend of nourishing"; 1, 42, 8; *cf.* 10, 139, 2; ***1, 42, 6. 9*** (51): "Give richly, and with open hand"; 1, 89, 5: "We call him, that he may be a true defender and guardian for the increase of wealth"; 8, 4, 17. 18; 8, 29, 6; 6, 48, 15; 6, 54, 8; 6, 53, 3–6; 6, 56, 6:

> "We pray to thee for happiness
> From trouble free, in treasures rich;
> For full prosperity to-day,
> And for to-morrow highest good."

210. 10, 139, 2. 1 with 1, 23, 14 (*ā́ghṛṇi*, often), and 10, 17, 3; 2, 40, 5; 3, 62, 9.—Goads; 6, 58, 2; 6, 53, 9.—1, 89, 5; 10, 26, 6 (*cf.* Zimmer, AIL. 229); 6, 54, 5–7.—10, 17, 3: "The world-herdsman, who loses no cattle"; 6, 54, 10: "Pûṣan shall stretch his right hand far; he shall drive back the lost"; 1, 23, 13.—Pûṣan is drawn (like the Scandinavian Thôrr), not by horses, but by goats: 6, 57, 3; 6, 55, 6. 4. 3; 6, 58, 2; 10, 26, 8; only in 6, 58, 3 are "golden ships, which move upon the sea and in the air, with which Pûṣan does messenger's service for Sûrya," spoken of [instead of *dûtyā́m, dûtyàm* ought probably to be read; so also Ludw. Rv. 1, 157].—Pûṣan does not care for the Soma, but for the preparation of barley: 6, 57, 2.

Do the passages 6, 56, 1; 1, 138, 4; 1, 42, 10,

> Who mockingly of Pûṣan says:
> 'Behold the gruel-eater there!'
> His jeers the god will not endure.—
> For I do not disdain thee, Pûṣan, glowing god;
> Thy friendship I do not reject.—
> The god from us no chiding hears;
> We bring him praise in pleasing songs,
> The Helper we implore for wealth,

indicate mockery on the part of certain tribes towards those with other cults?

211. 6, 49, 8 (6, 53, 1: "Companion on the journey," Vâj.-Sanh.); ***1, 42, 7. 1. 2–4;*** 10, 17, 5; 6, 54, 1. 2:

> Bring us, o Pûṣan, to a man
> Who, wise, at once shall point the way,
> And say to us, "Lo, here it is."
>
> With Pûṣan joined let us go forth,
> Who points the houses out to us,
> And says to us: "Lo, here they are."

9, 67, 10.—Pûṣan also aids in battle, 10, 139, 3, and so becomes Indra's comrade, 6, 57, 4; brings the seasons, 1, 23, 14. 15.

212. 10, 17, 3–6; 10, 59, 71 (Ath.-Sanh. 16, 9, 2; 18, 2, 53); so Pûṣan ψυχοπομπός; *cf.* Notes 221 and 272.

213. Viṣṇu is the only Vedic god whose name has been preserved in the Hindu triad of divinities, while in the Veda he does not play an important part; Muir, OST. 4, 63–298; GKR. 53 f.: *1, 154.*— *1, 154, 3;* 1, 22, 16 f.; 1, 155, 4; 6, 49, 13; 7, 100, 1. 3; 8, 29, 7; *1, 154, 1;* 7, 99, 2. 3. The steps: rising, highest point, and setting of the sun.

214. 7, 99, 3; 7, 100, 4, with *1, 154, 2;* 6, 69, 5: "Indra and Viṣṇu, ye made the atmosphere wide, and stretched out the worlds for our existence."—Viṣṇu, more often than Pûṣan, is named as the ally of Indra: 1, 22, 19; 1, 156, 4. 5; *4, 18, 11* (63); 8, 89, 12; 6, 20, 2; 7, 97, 4 f.; *cf.* 6, 69, 8 in Note 65.—The epithet *çipiviṣṭa* is quite obscure in 7, 99, 7; 7, 100, 5: verse 6:

"What was to be descried in thee [Muir, what hadst thou to blame], o Viṣṇu, when thou declaredst, 'I am Çipiviṣṭa'? Do not conceal from us this thy beauty (disguise?), when in battle thou assumest another form."

[Çipiviṣṭa: Ludwig ad. loc. renders "bald-headed" (Rv. 1, 162); see his note, Rv. 4, 153, and Muir, OST. 4, 87 f.]

215. 7, 99, 1 with 1, 155, 5. 4.—1, 22, 20; *1, 154, 5; cf.* 10, 177, 1: "Sages behold with heart and mind the bird adorned by the power of the Asura," *i.e.* the sun pictured as a bird; see 10, 72, 8 in Note 226, and 10, 149, 3 in Note 370.

216. Savitar (from root *su, sû;* Pres. *suvati;* Aor. *ásavît*): Muir, OST. 5, 162–170; GKR. 46 f.: *2, 38; 5, 81.*—Savitar and Sûrya: *cf. e.g.* 4, 14, 2: "God Savitar raised his banner high, providing light for all the world; Sûrya has filled the earth and heaven, and the wide realm of air with beams." 10, 158, 1: "Sûrya protect us from heaven . . ."; v. 2: "Rejoice (?), o Savitar . . ."; v. 3: "Savitar, give us . . ."; v. 4: "We would see thee, o Sûrya . . ."; 1, 35, 1–11; 7, 63, 1 f.

217. *E.g.* 1, 157, 1: "*Savitar* enlightened (*prấsavît*) the world"; 1, 110, 3: "*Savitar* has awakened (*âsuvat*) immortality"; 3, 33, 6: "God *Savitar* has led us with beauteous hands, at whose impulse (*prasavê*) we flow"; 5, 82, 4: "Send (*sâvîḥ*) us to-day, god *Savitar*, the blessing with children; drive away (*parâsuva*) evil dreams" [10, 27, 4, *apa-suva*, of Sûrya]; *2, 38, 1* (46): "The divine inciter comes to arouse" (*devaḥ savitấ savâya*); numerous other examples in Muir, OST. 5, 165–168.

218. *5, 81, 4* (49), to Savitar: "Thou gladdenest thyself in Sûrya's beams"; 7, 63, 3: "This god (*sc.* Sûrya) seems to me to be a Savitar, never changing the same order." In 10, 139, 1, Savitar is called "Sûrya-beaming," 7, 66, 4; 1, 123, 3; 7, 45, 2; etc.

219. 5, 82, 8; 5, 81, 4.—5, 81, 2. 3; 6, 71, 5. 1; 7, 45, 2.—6, 71, 2; 8, 27, 12: "Savitar has raised himself up before you, desirable he stands high uplifted; the two-footed and the four-footed, the striving and the flying, have gone to rest"; 1, 35, 2; 7, 45, 1; *1, 124, 1* (35); 3, 38, 8.

220. 1, 35, 3. 2; 5, 81, 4 (in Note 218); 7, 38, 1 with 1, 73, 21 ("true like Savitar"; also 9, 97, 48); 7, 38, 2; 7, 45, 3; 1, 35, 3; *cf.* verse 10, and 671, 5; *5, 81, 2.*

221. 6, 71, 3; 7, 38, 3; 1, 35, 11; 7, 45, 4. 3; 6, 71, 6; 1, 24, 3–5 (1, 110, 3, in Note 217); 4, 54, 1 f., verse 3: "Whatever (offence) we have committed, by want of thought, against the divine race,—by feebleness of understanding, by violence, after the manner of men, either against gods or men,—do thou, O Savitar, free us from guilt."—10, 17, 4, Savitar is ψυχοπομπος, like Pûṣan; Note 212.

222. 4, 53, 2; 1, 35, 11; 4, 53, 4.—The following verses from the Evening Hymn, *2, 38* (46).—To Savitar is also addressed the celebrated Gâyatrî or Sâvitrî, the daily prayer of the Brâhmans (Rv. 3, 62, 10): ["Of Savitar, the heavenly, that longed-for glory may we win! and may himself inspire our prayers!" "No good and sufficient explanation of the peculiar sanctity attaching to this verse has ever been given; it is not made remarkable, either by thought or diction, among many other Vedic verses of similar tenor. Its meaning is a matter of some question, depending on the meaning given to the verb in the second páda, *dhímahi,* whether 'we may receive, gain, win,' or 'let us meditate.' If the latter be correct, the correspondence of root and meaning between this verb and the following noun, *dhiyaḥ,* in the third páda, cannot be accidental, and should be regarded in translating: we must read, "and may he inspire (or quicken) our meditations (adoring or prayerful thoughts)."—"Sâyaṇa gives no less than four different explanations of the *gâyatrî,* and leaves his readers free choice as to which they will accept." Whitney, Colebrooke's Misc. Essays, p. 111 f.].

223. Uṣas: above p. 54, with Note 200, where in 1, 113, 3 it is also said of Night and Morning that they "are taught by the gods to go their way." Savitar: 4, 13, 2.

224. 4, 13, 3 (above p. 55: "whom they have made," etc.); *cf.* 7, 62, 2; 7, 60, 1; 10, 12, 8; 7, 60, 3; 10, 37, 5.—6, 51, 1; 7, 61, 1; 7, 63, 1; 1, 115, 1; 1, 136, 2; *cf.* 5, 66, 2 and the hymn *1, 152,* especially vs. *3–5* (13 f.).—7, 63, 5; 7, 60, 5; *cf.* 8, 90, 2. Indra even says of himself, 10, 48, 11: "As god, I do not disturb the decrees of the gods, the Âdityas (Vasu, Rudriya): *they* made me for great might as unconquerable, unvanquished victor"; 10, 113, 5: "Indra darts his lightning for Mitra and Varuṇa"; 10, 89, 8. 9.—7, 63, 5; 7, 65, 1; 7, 66, 12 (Mitra-Varuṇa-Aryaman); *cf.* 5, 69, 3 (Aditi-Mitra-Varuṇa).

225. Aditi ('Eternity, Infinity'); M. Müller, Translation 1, 230–251, OGR. 233 f.; Muir, OST. 5, 35–53 = OO. 3, 462 f.; the monograph, Ueber die Göttin Aditi. A. Hillebrandt, Breslau 1876.—7, 10, 4; 1, 136, 3; 1, 185, 3; 1, 166, 12.—8, 25, 3.—4, 25, 5; 8, 18, 6; 8, 47, 9; 10, 36, 3; 8, 56, 10–12:

"And thee I summon to my side,
O mighty goddess, Aditi,
Thee, Merciful, to my defence.

In deep or shallow places save,
Thou mother of the gods, from foes,
Do thou our children keep from harm.

Far-searching thou, grant sure defence
To all our children, far and wide,
That, living, they may spread abroad."

1, 162, 22: "May Aditi grant us sinlessness"; 5, 82, 6: "guiltless before Aditi"; 4, 12, 4; 7, 93, 7; *2, 27, 14* (23); *7, 87, 7* (9); 10, 12, 8; 1, 24, 15: "Varuṇa, loose us from the uppermost, the middle, and the lowest bond. Then may we, O Âditya, in thy service, freed from sin, belong to Aditi."

(On Varuṇa's bonds, see p. 67 and Note 255.)

Aditi, viewed as a divinity, as the personification of 'the visible Infinite, the endless expanse beyond the earth, beyond the clouds, beyond the sky' (Müller, Translation 1, 230) may be younger than Varuṇa, Bhaga, Mitra, and Aryaman; but the group of the Âdityas, as the name itself proves, pre-supposes the proper name Aditi (Weber, JLZ. 1876, p. 652 = IStr. 3, 453). "It was, no doubt, the frequent mention of these her sons that gave to Aditi, almost from the beginning, a decidedly feminine character. She is the mother with powerful, with terrible, with royal sons. But there are passages where Aditi seems to be conceived as a male deity or, anyhow, as a sexless being." Müller, OGR. 236 f.

Aditi is praised in pantheistic fashion in 1, 89, 10: "Aditi is the heaven, Aditi the atmosphere, Aditi the mother; she (*sá*) is father, she son, all gods are Aditi, the whole world, Aditi is what is born, Aditi is what shall be born," recalling the familiar Orphic verses (Lobeck, Aglaophamus, p. 521 f.):

Ζεὺς πρῶτος γένετο, Ζεὺς ὕστατος ἀργικέραυνος,
Ζεὺς κεφαλή, Ζεὺς μέσσα, Διός τ' ἐκ πάντα τέτυκται,
Ζεὺς πυθμὴν γαίης τε καὶ οὐρανοῦ ἀστερόεντος,
Ζεὺς ἄρσην γένετο, Ζεὺς ἄμβροτος ἔπλετο νύμφη,
Ζεὺς πνοιὴ πάντων, Ζεὺς ἀκαμάτου πυρὸς ὁρμή,
Ζεὺς πόντου ῥίζα, Ζεὺς ἥλιος ἠδὲ σελήνη, κτλ., and the like.

226. The **Âdityas**: Roth, Die höchsten Götter der Arischen Völker. ZDMG. 6, 67–77; Muir, OST. 5, 54–57; GKR. 19 f.: ***1, 41; 2, 27; 10, 185.*** The long recognized identity of the Indian Âditya with the Iranian Amesha Çpenta, is followed out in details by J. Darmestetter, Ormazd et Ahriman, leurs origines et leur histoire. Paris 1877, pp. 7–84. For the most frequently mentioned, *cf.* Note 227.

Mitra and Varuṇa: Muir, OST. 5, 58–76; GKR. 13 f.: ***1, 152; 7, 61;*** the excellent monograph, Varuna und Mitra. Ein Beitrag zur Exegese des Veda, von Dr. Alfred Hillebrandt. Breslau 1877. On Mitra, Note 228; on Varuṇa, Note 241.

Seven Âdityas are mentioned, 9, 114, 3 (*cf.* Müller, Translation 1, 240 f.); for their names, *cf.* Note 228.—In AV. 8, 9, 21 Aditi is called the "mother of eight sons," with which *cf.* RV. 10, 72, 8. 9:

"Eight sons there are of Aditi,
Who from her body were produced.
With seven she approached the gods,
But the egg-born she cast away.

With seven only Aditi
Approached the former race of gods.
To birth at first, but then to death,
The goddess brought Mârtâṇḍa back,"

and the legend of the ÇB. attaching to these verses: Roth, ISt. 14, 392 f. The "egg-born" is the sun, pictured as a bird; *cf.* Note 215. [Ludw. Rv. 5, 443 and Muir, OST. 4, 13 f.]

The later period mentions twelve Âdityas, with distinct reference to the months.

227. The important hymn ***2, 27*** (21–24), in v. 1, names Mitra, Aryaman, Bhaga, Dakṣa, Añça, Varuṇa. The name of the seventh Âditya can not be discovered; it cannot be Indra, nor Savitar (7, 85, 4; Vâl. 4, 7; 8, 18, 3), though in isolated—always late—verses of the Rig (1, 150, 13; 1, 163, 13; 1, 191, 9; 8, 90, 11) the word *Âditya*, as afterwards, stands as an appellative for *sun*.

Very rarely appear

Añça (portion): the 'Apportioner,' and

Dakṣa (ability, strength, intellectual power): the 'Capable, Clever'; somewhat more frequently

Bhaga (portion): the 'Dispenser, Protector, Lord'; see espec. 7, 41, 2–4. His name as an appellative in the Iranian and Slavonic tongues means *God*.

The following are almost never mentioned separately:

Aryaman: the Bosom-friend; 5, 29, 1? ***6, 50, 1*** (126): "Aryaman, who gives without being asked" (*cf.* Matth. 6, 8), and

Mitra: the 'Friend'; the only hymn addressed to him is ***3, 59*** (17); but both, especially the latter, are very often connected with

Varuṇa (p. 61 f., Note 241).

The last three, or even the dual divinity Mitra-Varuṇa (*cf.* Note 226) serve as the representatives of the Âdityas in general. On this account, and to avoid too frequent repetitions in the following notes, the hymns to the Âdityas and to Mitra-Varuṇa are treated together, the latter distinguished by the sign *.

228. 8, 25, 17 (*okyā́ samrâjyásya*); 8, 90, 6: "Ye regard the immortal ordinances of mortals, inviolable." — 7, 65, 2 (*devā́nâm ásurâ*). "The laws of the moral are as eternal and unchangeable as those of the natural world. The same divine power has established the one and the other. This power is represented by a circle of divinities who may be most pertinently entitled the Gods of Heavenly Light. Human immagination was able to find no visible thing with which they could be compared, saving the light. They are and are named the Spiritual." Roth, JAOS, 3, 340 f.; *cf.* Roth, ZDMG. 6, 69 and Müller, OGR. 294 f.

229. *7, 66, 2 with 8, 25, 1 (*cf.* 8, 25, 3) and *6, 67, 5. The following verses, all from the above-named hymn ***2, 27,*** are in part taken out of their original sequence (11 ab with 9 cd, 14 ab with 11 cd etc.). This order will here excuse itself.

230. 8, 47, 11: "Ye look down, Âdityas, like watchmen from the battlements." — Mitra-Varuṇa at the shining of the dawn, at the rising of the sun mount their firm highest seat, the golden throne, which rests on a thousand brazen columns; from thence they look upon the infinite and the finite, they even look into the heart of man (*5, 62, 8. 7 with *2, 41, 5; ****7, 61, 1***); *cf.* *7, 65, 1: "The divine power of you twain is imperishable, ye hasten closely regarding each one in his course"; 10, 65, 5: "Not far away are the two all-rulers with their spirit." — In *6, 67, 5 cunning, never deceived spies are assigned to them; so ****7, 61, 3. 5*** (15):

"From the broad earth and from the heights of heaven
Ye send abroad your spies that never tire,

In every place, through field and house, their presence
Unceasingly keeps watch on each transgressor.

All your avenging spirits, O ye Mighty,
In whom can be perceived no form or token,
Unerringly the sin of men they punish;
And nothing is so hid as to escape you."

Cf. also ***2, 27, 16*** (23).

231. 7, 66, 11: "They ordered the years, months, days" (Gen. 1, 14; Psalm 74, 16. 17; 104, 19; Jerem. 31, 35; Yaçna 44, 3: Who ordered the path of the sun and the stars? Who (ordained) that the moon now waxes, now wanes? [on *thwat cf.* BR. sub 3 *tva*]; *6, 67, 6: "They extended earth and heaven as a dwelling of man"; *5, 69, 4: "You who are the supporters of the ether, the atmosphere and the earth-regions"; *cf.* v. 1, with ***2, 27, 8. 9*** (22); *5, 76, 2: "The supporters of the peoples"; 7, 64, 2: "Strong lords of the rivers send refreshing rain from heaven"; *7, 51, 2: "Guardians of the world"; according to *8, 90, 2 they guide the sun with their arms.—3, 38, 5 f.?

232. *7, 60, 5: "Avengers of much wrong they grew up in the house of the right"; *7, 66, 13: "Just, born and strengthened in right, hating wrong, terrible"; *6, 67, 4: "Their mother made them terrible to the deceitful man"; *7, 65, 3: "Binding wrong with many bonds not to be overstepped by the deceitful man"; *1, 139, 2: "For the sake of right they lay hold on wrong with the wrath of their spirit"; 8, 25, 4: "The just loudly proclaim the right."

233. "So their spies are called invisible ("in whom can be perceived no form or token"; *7, 61, 5 in Note 230); 1, 105, 16: "The path which is prepared for the Âdityas praiseworthy in the heavens is not, O gods, to be overstepped, ye cannot perceive it, O mortals."—8, 25, 9: "Seeing further than the eye with unclouded vision, even slumbering they observe attentively"; *10, 65, 5 (in Note 230); 5, 62, 6: "For the righteous, far-reaching protectors with hands clean from blood." With this *cf.* Indra's words 10, 48, 2 and 10, 113, 5 in Note 224 (*i.e.* Indra fights for them), also ***6, 68, 3*** and 7, 85, 3 in Note 242.

234. *6, 67, 6; *2, 41, 5; ****7, 61, 4****; 8, 56, 13; 1, 90, 2; *5, 69, 4 (see Indra's words, 10, 48, 2 in Note 224); ****7, 61, 4****: "The moons of the god-haters dwindle powerless"; ***1, 152, 1***: "Ye strike to earth every impiety and protect the right"; 5, 67, 3: "They follow the decree step by step"; 1, 136, 1: "Their dominion, their divinity no one can assail"; *7, 60, 10; *6, 67, 9.

235. 8, 18, 15 (*cf.* ***7, 61, 1;*** 6, 51, 7 = 7, 52, 2: "We do not do what ye, O good ones, punish"; 8, 56, 7; 8, 18, 5 (5, 67, 4; 1, 107, 1); 8, 47, 8.

236. 2, 29, 2. 6; 8, 56, 6; ***2, 28, 3;*** 8, 47, 13; 8, 56, 17 ('penitent' = "who returns from his sin," above p. 31 with Note 106); 8, 18, 18. 22; 8, 56, 20; 1, 89, 9: "When our sons are fathers, — do not (before) harm our life in the midst of its course"; ***2, 28, 5:***

"Let not the thread of my devotion sever,
Let not the laborer's staff too soon be broken."

237. Differently in 8, 47, 5: "May dangers avoid us as drivers (avoid) bad roads."

238. 1, 41, 4: "Well paved and thornless is the path for him who lives aright." — 8, 47, 2. 3: "As the birds their wings, spread over us your defence." Ps. 91, 4: He shall cover thee with his feathers, and under his wing shalt thou trust: his truth shall be thy shield and buckler. Ps. 17, 8: Hide me under the shadow of thy wings, etc. — Rv. 8, 47, 8: "We are united to you as a fighter to his armor"; see further Note 239.

239. 10, 63, 13: "Every mortal prospers unharmed, he propagates his line in child and grandchild, whom ye Âdityas guide with good guidance through all misfortunes to happiness." *7, 65, 4; *7, 62, 5: "Stretch forth your arms that we may live, and refresh our fields with rich nourishment; O youths, make us renowned in the people, hear my call, Varuṇa and Mitra." Their most excellent protection and defence guard from poverty and sickness, from snares and enemies, from dangers of all kinds: 7, 66, 13; *5, 70, 3. 4; 8, 18, 10. 11; 8, 56, 15. 21; 10, 126; *8, 90, 4 etc.; ***1, 41, 1-3*** (19); 8, 47, 7; 10, 126, 1; ***10, 185, 2. 3*** (25). — ***7, 82, 7*** (30); ***2, 27, 7. 12. 15*** (22 f.).

240. The passages 8, 18, 12; 8, 56, 17 f.; 10, 63, 8 and 8, 47, 8 above p. 30–31; 2, 29, 5; 7, 52, 2: "Let us not expiate another's transgression," etc.

241. Varuṇa; Roth, ZDMG. 6, 71 ff.; 7, 607 f.; JAOS. 3, 340 ff.; Muir, OST. 5, 61 ff., MTr. 159–163 and 313–317; Ludw. Rv. 3, 314 ff.; GKR. 1 ff.: ***2, 28; 5, 85; 7, 86. 87. 88. 89;*** *cf.* ***4, 42*** (26 f.).

The name *Varuṇa* (from root *vṛ*, *cover, envelop*) signifies the '*Enveloper*,' the '*Investor of All*,' and is, in spite of Ludwig's objection (Rv. 3, 314), etymologically identical with the Gk. Οὐρανός, which in Homer signifies not (as in Hesiod) a divinity, but also the sky as a region, as the container of everything. Though in the Veda the ethical relations of Varuṇa — displayed in Greece and Rome by the Father of Heaven Zeus-Jupiter — always stand in the foreground, yet the original signification of the god often appears; 8, 41, 7: "Like a cloak he spread himself over all the world, surrounding its regions"; v. 3: "He enclosed the nights and skillfully established the mornings; he is seen about all things" (*cf.* 1, 25, 18); ***7, 87, 5:*** "The three heavens are enclosed by him; three earths beneath, a series of six."

"The *eye* with which he beholds the zealous among men" (1, 50, 6) is of course the *sun* in the sky. *Cf.* Hesiod O.D. 267: Πάντα ἰδὼν Διὸς ὀφθαλμὸς καὶ πάντα νοήσας with Hom. Il. 3, 277: ἠέλιός θ' ὃς πάντ' ἐφορᾷς καὶ πάντ' ἐπακούεις. Soph. Ant. 879, Aristoph. Nub. 285: ὄμμα γάρ αἰθέρος ἀκάματον σελαγεῖται μαρμαρέαις ἐν αὐγαῖς etc. Macrob. Sat. 1, 21, 12: quia *Solem Jovis oculum* appellat antiquitas. "The *two* bright eyes that rule the earth and fill the three highest spaces, the sure abode of Varuṇa" (8, 41, 9; *cf.* 1, 72, 10: "They endowed him with beauty when they created the two immortal eyes of heaven"), *sun and* moon (νυκτὸς ὀφθαλμὸς, ὄμμα of the moon, Aesch. Sept. 390, Pers. 428 etc.); the adjective *four-faced* (*caturanîka:* 5, 48, 5) refers to the four quarters of heaven.

The above-mentioned (p. 59, Note 226 f.) frequent combination Mitra-Varuṇa brings out the two sides of the 'All-container,' the 'shining day-sky,' and the 'glimmering night-sky,' both of which moreover Varuṇa alone displays, *e.g.* 8, 41, 10: "Who made and enclosed the gleaming white and the black" (*i.e.* days and nights); ***7, 88, 2:***

> "When I obtain a vision of his features,
> His form appears to me like gleaming fire;
> So may the ruler let me view in heaven
> The wondrous glory of the light and darkness."

In later times Varuṇa is lowered to a mere *god of the waters,* which stream down from the sky to earth; *cf.* with Note 245 also 7, 34, 10 f.; 8, 41, 2: "Who stands at the source of the streams in the midst of the seven sisters," *i.e.* rivers; 8, 58, 11. 12; ***7, 49, 3*** (125), and in general Muir, OST. 5, 72 f. and Hillebrandt, Varuna und Mitra, p. 83 ff.

242. 10, 103, 9: "The host of Indra the hero and Varuṇa the king"; especially ***7, 82, 2. 4-6*** and ***7, 83, 9*** (29, 30. 33), and the passages 10, 89, 8. 9; 10, 113, 5 in Note 224; beside ***6, 68, 3*** (31) and 7, 85, 3:

> "The one destroys the fiend with might and lightning,
> The other is a counsellor of wisdom."—
> "The one protects the tribes, far separated,
> The other slays his enemies, the mighty."

7, 28, 4: "In these days help us, O Indra, for hostile champions come on in gleam (of weapons) [so with Grassm. and Hillebrandt, against GKR. 76]; the wrong, which He sinless beheld in us, may wise Varuṇa henceforward pass over"; 7, 84, 2: "May Varuṇa's wrath pass by us; may Indra open to us an ample space"; v. 4: "Âditya takes away wrong, the hero dispenses immeasurable wealth."—For the mutual relations of both gods the hymns ***4, 42*** (26) and 10, 124 are specially characteristic; *cf.* Muir, OST. 5, 116 f.; Hillebrandt, Varuna und Mitra, p. 104 f.

243. ***4, 42, 3-4*** with 8, 42, 1 (*viçvávedas*); ***5, 85, 1; 7, 87, 5;*** 8, 25, 18.

244. 8, 41, 5. 6: "The wise one brings many a wise work to completion .... in whom all wisdom is placed as the nave in the wheel," (differently by Hillebrandt, p. 81); *cf.* ***5, 85, 5. 6.***—8, 42, 1; 8, 41, 10: "With a prop he held the two worlds apart."—"Wisdom in the heart"; 8, 42, 3: "O God, increase this prayer of the learner, and his power, O Varuṇa, and knowledge."—1, 93, 6: "The eagle brought the Soma from the rock"; *cf.* Note 289.

245. ***7, 88, 1:*** "Who brings to us the great exalted sun-steed, that grants a thousand gifts."—1, 24, 8: "For King Varuṇa made that broad path for the sun to travel; he made feet for the footless to tread and scattered that which wounded the heart."

The Waters: 10, 75, 2: "Varuṇa opened for thee, O Sindhu, paths to flow"; 10, 124, 7: "Without trouble Varuṇa set the waters free"; *cf.* Note 241; ***4, 42, 4; 5, 85, 3.4*** (Amos 5, 8; 9, 6); ***5, 85, 6*** (Eccles. 1, 7: above p. 27); ***2, 28, 4:*** "The orderer of the worlds made the rivers run," etc.

246. 1, 25, 13. Avesta, Yt. 13, 3 (Note 285 a, 286 a): "This heaven above, gleaming and beautiful, like polished brass in appearance, shining over the three divisions of earth, which Mazda wears like a garment, spangled with stars, god-woven" (Roth).—***5, 85, 1*** (*samrâj*).—8, 25, 18; ***5, 85, 5;*** 8, 42, 1; 8, 41, 4.

247. ***4, 42, 3*** (.... *sám airayam dhârayamca*); 8, 41, 5 (*dhartâ bhúvanânâm*); ***7, 87, 2; 1, 115, 1,*** (Note 207); ***5, 85, 3.***

248. ***7, 88, 5; 7, 87, 5;*** 1, 25, 20 (three heavens [Note 283 a] and three earths; ***7, 87, 5*** in Note 241; 8, 41, 9 etc., and three air-regions; so "nine homes," as in the old Norse belief. Zimmer, AIL. 358).—***2, 27, 10; 7, 87, 6.*** Even the flying birds do not reach the bounds of Varuṇa's dominion, not the ceaseless moving waters, nor those that surpass the wind's swiftness: 1, 24, 6.

249. 1, 25, 10 etc.; 1, 24, 10 = 3, 54, 18 etc. (* 8, 25, 17: "The old statutes of the all-rulers," above p. 59; Ps. 148, 6).—***2, 28, 8;*** 8, 42, 1.—10, 11, 1: "He knows everything, like Varuṇa." "Ruler of all": ***5, 85, 1;*** 6, 68, 9; 8, 42, 1; 1, 25, 10; *cf.* 1, 25, 5.—Varuṇa brings the sun as the light of day; by his ordinance the stars know their path and the moon moves light-giving throughout the night: 1, 24, 10; *cf.* Ps. 136, 8 f.; Job 38, 31 f.; Jerem. 31, 35: Thus saith the Lord, which giveth the sun for a light by day, and the ordinances of the moon and of the stars for a light by night; Ps. 148, 3 f. 6: He hath also stablished them (sun, moon and stars) forever and ever: he hath made a decree which shall not pass.

250. 1, 24, 10; 8, 41, 5 (of Soma, 9, 87, 3; Note 304). — 1, 25, 7. 8. — 1, 25, 9. — 1, 25, 11; 8, 25, 16: "He only, the lord of the house, sees much and far"; 1, 25, 5. 16; *8, 90, 2; 7, 34, 10.

251. ***7, 49, 3*** (125); 8, 41, 1. — ***2, 28, 6.***

252. Roth, Der Atharvaveda. Tübingen 1856, p. 29; Müller, Chips, 1, 41, Introd. 243 f.; Muir, OST. 5, 64. 126; MTr. 163; Ludw. Rv. 3, 388. — In the last verse instead of *ní minoti*, 'he holds,' should perhaps be read with BR. 5, 764; 7, 409 *ví cinoti*, 'he surveys.'

253. ***2, 28, 6. 7. 10;*** 8, 42, 2. — 1, 24, 9 ("Varuṇa the lord of remedies," Vâj.-Sanh. 21, 40); 8, 42, 3 (in Note 244); 1, 105, 15: "Varuṇa creates prayers; we call to him as the inventor of songs; he calls forth devotion in the heart"; *cf.* *1, 151, 2. 6. — On ***7, 87, 4*** (mysteries of creation? GKR. 8 with n. 4); *cf.* Amos 3, 7: Surely the Lord God will do nothing, but he revealeth his secret unto his servants the prophets. Ps. 25, 14.

254. ***7, 86, 2*** (1, 25, 5. 19); ***2, 27, 10*** (22); *cf.* ***7, 89, 1*** and ***2, 28, 5. 7. 9;*** on the blessed life among the gods, p. 69 f. — The two footnotes after Roth, ZDMG. 7, 607 and JAOS. 3, 341 and 342.

255. 1, 24, 11; *1, 139, 2 (in Note 232); ***7, 86, 2.*** — ***7, 87, 3;*** 1, 25, 13; ***2, 28, 7.*** — 1, 24, 13. 15 (on p. 68: "In chains," and in Note 225); 1, 25, 21 ("Take away the undermost of the bonds"); 7, 88, 7. [*Cf.* 7, 89, 2. 4: "I go shaking like a puffed-up skin. . . . I stand in the midst of water, yet thirst consumes me; be merciful, o Lord, forgive," *i.e.* dropsy sent as punishment.] — *Cf.* ***2, 27, 16*** (23); 2, 29, 5; 8, 56, 8. — 6, 74, 4; 10, 85, 24; *7, 65, 3 (in Note 232) and 7, 84, 2 (to Indra-Varuṇa): "You who bind with bonds without cords." — 1, 25, 14; ***7, 28, 4*** (76; *cf.* Note 242). — Varuṇa himself is sinless and pure and just, he punishes every error; Levit. 11, 44: Ye shall be holy, for I am holy.

256. 7, 84, 2 (in Note 242; *cf.* 4, 1, 4; 1, 94, 12; 7, 93, 7. — *7, 60, 8; *7, 62, 4); 1, 24, 11: "Without wrath attend to us"; 1, 25, 3; 1, 24, 14. — Ps. 6, 2; 38, 1: O Lord, rebuke me not in thy wrath: neither chasten me in thy hot displeasure.

257. ***7, 86, 7; 7, 87, 7*** and ***2, 28, 1*** (penitent: p. 31 with Note 106 and p. 61 with Note 236); *cf.* Ps. 32, 5. 6; Prov. 28, 13: He that covereth his sins shall not prosper: but whoso confesseth and forsaketh them shall have mercy. Isaiah 12.

258. 1, 24, 14 (p. 68):

> "Do thou who hast the power, wise king eternal,
> Release us from the sins we have committed."

1, 24, 9: "Take away from us the sin accomplished"; ***2, 28, 5:*** "Loose sin as a cord from me."—*Cf.* 10, 37, 12: "If we have sinned grievously against you, o gods, with the tongue, by thoughtlessness (lit. 'absence of mind'), raising your anger"; 10, 164, 3: "If we have erred through wish, through turning aside, through blame, waking or sleeping."—Following verses GKR. 5. 6. 2. 5. 11.

259. See 6, 51, 7 = 7, 52, 2 in Note 240 and 4, 3, 13: "Do not visit the sin of an erring brother (on us)."—The verse is addressed to Agni, the best sacrificer; with this *cf.* above p. 36 with Note 124; 4, 12, 4 (in Note 261); 4, 1, 4: "O do thou, Agni, turn away from us the wrath of god Varuṇa, since thou canst"; similarly 1, 94, 12; 6, 48, 10; 7, 93, 7 (Agni, Aryaman, Aditi); 5, 2, 7 in Note 263.

260. Beside the above verses ***5, 85, 7*** ("If we to any loved companion . . ."), *cf.* ***7, 88, 6:*** "If, Varuṇa, thy friend who is dear to thee, if thy companion has offended thee, yet punish not . . ."; also 10, 37, 12 and 10, 164, 3 in Note 258 ("with the tongue," etc.).

261. ***5, 85, 8:*** (Whatever sin we have committed), "all that, o god, remove like flakes, and then may we be dear to thee again"; ***7, 87, 7:*** "Who shows mercy even to the sinner,—O that we were guiltless before Varuṇa"; 1, 25, 1–3: "However, O god Varuṇa, we have violated thy laws day by day, give us not over to the deadly weapon of the wrathful, nor to the fury of the raging; as the driver looses the horse from the harness, so we (loose) appease thy mind through songs, that thou mayst have mercy"; ***7, 89, 5*** (12) and ***7, 86, 6:*** "It is not our own will, Varuṇa, that leads us astray, but some seduction,—wine, anger, dice and our folly. The older remains in the errors of the younger; even sleep occasions sin."

Cf. further 4, 12, 4: "Whatever offence we have committed against thee, through folly, after human fashion, O Agni, make us free from sin against Aditi" (Note 259). "Sin after the manner of man," 7, 57, 4; 10, 15, 6. "In folly, in weakness of judgment, in human fashion," 4, 54, 3, Note 221.

262. See the fine lines ***7, 88, 3-5*** (10) and with the words, "What now has become of our friendship, who formerly enjoyed intercourse?" *cf.* Ps. 89, 50: Lord, where are thy former loving kindnessess which thou swarest unto David in thy truth? Ps. 77, 6–10.

263. After ***7, 86, 3. 4*** with ***2, 28, 6; 7, 88, 6*** (6. 2. 11); with the following verses *cf.* 5, 2, 7 (to Agni: Note 259):

> "And from a thousand pillars Çunaḥçepa
> The fettered thou didst loose; for he entreated.
> From us too take away, O God, the fetters."

264. 6, 51, 8: "By acts of devotion I seek to blot out sin already committed," GKR. 7.

265. Müller, Chips, 1, 44; *cf.* Roth, ZDMG. 4, 427. Müller in the 2d edition adds the words of Lessing (vol. 11, 63, Lachm.): "Without the belief in a future life, a future reward and punishment, no religion could exist," and those of Schopenhauer (Parall. vol. 1, 37) on the "real Jewish religion of Genesis and the historical books." Detailed proof that the belief in a personal immortality not only existed in the oldest Indo-Germanic period in general traits, but was also developed in many particulars must be reserved for another occasion; I confine myself in the following to a few indications (Notes 270–286 with the accompanying foot-notes) and refer, in addition to the general work of E. Spiess, Entwickelungsgeschichte der Vorstellungen vom Zustand nach dem Tode. Jena 1877, to the works of W. Geiger, Die Mythen vom Tod und Jenseits bei den Indogermanen, in Lindau's Nord und Süd, Vol. 11, Oct. 1879, p. 84–103;

On the Vedic belief, to Whitney, OLSt. 1, 46–64; Muir, OST. 5, 284–329; MTr. 186;

On the Iranian belief, to Hübschmann in the Jahrbücher für Protest. Theologie, 1879, p. 203–245;

On the belief of the Greeks, to Weisse in Fichte's Zeitschrift für Philos. und Spec. Theol. Vol. 2. 1838; E. Curtius in Altertum und Gegenwart. 1875, p. 219–236; K. Lehrs in the Populäre Aufsätze. 2d ed. 1875, p. 303–362; J. Girard, Le sentiment religeux en Grèce d'Homère à Eschyle.[2] 1879, p. 207 f., 247 ff.

266. For the first time in 10, 154, 2: "Who through penance are invincible, who through penance attained heaven, who accomplished mighty acts of penance—"; vs. 4. 5: "the righteous Fathers, singers."

267. After ***10, 18, 10. 12. 13*** (above p. 77 f.) and v. ***11*** (152).

268. The grave as house of the dead body: see p. 77 f. with Note 329.—Evidence that the soul is considered as coming from heaven and returning thither as its home: see Note 275.

269. ***10, 14, 1*** (146) with 10, 16, 4 d—Vivasvant, the god of the breaking light of day, the morning sun, is the personification of all phenomena of light, is called the father of Yama, and the gods are his race (***10, 14, 5;*** 10, 58, 1; 10, 60, 10; ***9, 113, 8; 10, 14, 1.*** — 10, 63, 1). That Yama is really looked upon as the first man is expressly stated in AV. 18, 3, 13, variants to AV. 18, 1, 49 = RV. ***10, 14, 1;*** Note 276, *cf.* Weber's ISt. 14, 393 and Zimmer, AIL. 415 * (in opposition to which Müller, LSL. 2, 529 f.).

270. GKR. 146 (*jajnânâs* belongs not to *jnâ*, but to *jan*, as Grassmann takes it in all passages except this, Ludwig in most passages). On pâda b *cf.* in the Avesta Yaçna 43, 13: "the desire for eternal life, which no one of you can assail, for the better existence which shall be in Thy kingdom." To the 'Fathers' (*pitṛ, pitaras*) *i.e.* the 'spirits of the departed righteous' (p. 70 *) correspond

the **Fravashis** among the Iranians (Note 283 *a* to 286 *a*);

the "**heroes of the past**" and the Θεοὶ πατρῷοι among the Greeks (Note 285 a);

the **Divi Manes and Lares** among the Romans (Note 283 *a*, 285 *a*).

271. After 10, 16, 2; ***10, 18, 13*** (152; above p. 78: "I settle firmly now the earth," etc.); ***10, 14, 8:*** "free from all imperfection"; (see Note 275); 10, 15, 14; 10, 16, 5 (in Note 278); 10, 56, 1 (in Note 275).

272. 10, 17, 3–6 (above p. 56 with Note 212; with Puṣan Savitar is mentioned in 10, 17, 4: Note 221).

273. That before the final entrance into the land of the blessed a stream was to be crossed is indicated by 10, 63, 10: "May we embark free from sin (*ánâgasas*, var. of AV. 7, 6, 3) on the divine ship with good oars." 9, 41, 2 (*cf.* the variant SV. 2, 3, 1, 3, 2 = 2, 243) seems to point to the bridge often mentioned in the Avesta: "May we succeed in passing over the bridge hard to reach, after conquering the godless enemy." More material on this subject is presented in the Iranian, Grecian and German sources.

274. Two broad-nosed, four-eyed, spotted (*çabála*) dogs, the offspring of Saramâ (p. 42, Note 149) occupy the path and guard the entrance of Paradise, in order that no godless person may steal into the region of the blessed, ***10, 14, 10:*** p. 70; ***10, 14, 11*** (*pathirákṣî:*

---

273 *a.* On the **Cinvat-bridge** ("Bridge of the Gatherer") of the Iranians, *cf.* the foot-notes 274 *a* and 283 *a*.

274 *a.* The **Iranians** believe according to Vendidad 13, 9 (25 Spiegel) that two dogs guard the Cinvat-bridge leading to Paradise, and passable only for the righteous. The name of the guardian Κέρβερος among the Greeks has long been recognized as identical with Skt. *çarvára*, 'varie-

variant of AV. 18, 2, 12: *pathiṣádî*); *cf.* 10, 15, 1: "The Fathers, who entered unharmed into the spirit world," and the fragment 7, 55, 2–4, which describes a scene at the entrance of the world of the dead. "A dead man, who has reached the confines of the shadow-kingdom, is stopped by Sârameya, who shows his teeth and is about to attack him. Then he conjures the monster to sleep; let him attack thieves and robbers, but the speaker is an adorer of Indra, and as such is entitled to admission." Aufrecht, ISt. 4, 342.

According to the other fragment ***10, 14, 11. 12*** the two never satisfied dogs ("in turn," if with Sâyaṇa 1, 29, 3 should be referred here) go about among men, search out those who are to die and accompany them surely. — *Cf.* Muir, OST. 5, 294, 439.

275. 10, 15, 14; 10, 16, 2; ***10, 14, 8*** (147; above p. 70). The heaven is, therefore, the home of the soul, to which, after death, it r e t u r n s purified ("free from all imperfections"); 10, 16, 5: "Dismiss him again, o Agni, to the Fathers"; 10, 56, 1: "When thou enterest thy (new) body, be welcome, be dear to the gods in the highest homes"; here belongs also 10, 135 (hymn to Yama at the funeral of a boy), v. 5: "Who gave life to the boy? Who made his car roll forth? Who to-day could tell us how he was given back?"

According to 10, 16, 3: "Let thy eye go to the sun, thy breath to the wind; go to the sky, to the earth, according to (thy) nature; go to the waters, if that is destined for thee; enter into the plants with thy members," man came from the edifice of the world; Zimmer, AIL. 403 points out analogous Germanic conceptions in Grimm, Mythol. 1, 464 ff., 4th ed.

---

gated, spotted,' an older dialectic by-form of the adjective *çabála* used of Yama's dogs above: Müller, *e.g.* Chips, 2, 180; LSL. 2, 497; A. Weber, ISt. 2, 298; *cf.* IStr. 2, 229 f.; Kuhn, KZ. 2, 314; Bréal, Hercule et Cacus p. 121. 130; finally Benfey, Gött. Gel. Anz. 1877, 8 f. = Vedica 149–163. "If anything is certain, the agreement of *çabala*, *çarvara* with Κέρβερος is assured. And yet, according to the decision of a competent judge, lately pronounced, 'no advantage for Grecian mythology is to be looked for from India.' We may therefore expect to see sillinesses like the comparison of Κέρβερος and ἔρεβος paraded once more," Aufrecht, ISt. 4, 342 (1858).

275*a*. Concerning the belief of the **I r a n i a n s**, we learn from the Bundehesh (a work quite young in its composition, but in contents of considerable antiquity): "The soul is created before the body." "It comes from heaven and rules the body, as long as it lives; when the body dies, it is mingled with the earth, and the soul goes back to heaven." (Bundehesh, c. 15, 17, ed. Justi, pp. 17, 23; *cf.* Spiegel, Eranishche Altertumskunde, 2, 149).

276. GKR. 147. Although both are 'princes of the blessed,' yet Varuṇa, the god, is expressly distinguished from Yama, who is 'as the first man (Note 269), so also the first to arrive in the realm of the Immortals, the natural head of those who are destined, each in his turn, to follow him thither' (Roth, ZDMG. 4, 426). Therefore he is called, 10, 135, 1, the 'lord of races, the father,' and 10, 14, 1 the 'Gatherer of the peoples'; *cf.* Athen. 3, 55, p. 99 B: *οἶδα δ' ὅτι που . . . εἶπεν τὸν Ἅιδην ἀγησίλαον.* Hesych.: *Ἀγήσανδρος ὁ Ἅιδης* (more in O. Schneider, on Callim. Lav. Pall. 130, vol. 1, 362 f.).

277. Saramâ's dogs: Note 274.—The Fathers are propitious also in 10, 15, 3. 9; 10, 17, 3; see p. 71 with Note 285, and *cf.* Hesiod's *πλουτοδόται*, OD. 126 in Note 285*a*.—"In bliss with Yama"; Note 280.

278. A syllable is wanting in the pâda, perhaps *te*, "thy body"? 10, 15, 14: "Shape thee a body at pleasure"; 10, 16, 5: "Restore him, Agni, to the fathers; him who, offered to thee, now goes in peace, clothing himself in youthful strength (seeking posterity?), and let him meet with a (new) body"; 10, 56, 1 in Note 275.

279. GKR. 53; ***1, 115, 1*** (55), the following after the beautiful hymn ***9, 113, 7–11***, GKR. 111: "In the inmost midst of the highest heaven," literally: "Where is the innermost space of the heavens—in threefold third heights of heaven—where is the sun's highest pinnacle."—Here refer 10, 56, 1: "Unite thyself with the third brightness"; 1, 35, 6: "There are three heavens, two spaces of Savitar, the third in the realm of Yama, containing men," the latter recalling the *ἄναξ πολυδέγμων, πολυδέκτης* in Hom. Hymn. in Cer. 17. 430.

Similarly the belief of the Greeks: Eur. Suppl. 1140 f.: *Βεβᾶσιν· αἰθὴρ ἔχει νιν ἤδη ‖ πυρὸς τετακότας σποδῷ.* Corp. Inscr. Att. 1, n. 442: *Αἰθὴρ μὲν ψυχὰς ὑπεδέξατο, σώ(ματα δὲ χθών).* Epicharm. in Plut. Consol. ad Apoll. 15: *συνεκρίθη καὶ διεκρίθη κἀπῆνθεν ὅθεν ἦνθεν, πάλιν γᾶ μὲν εἰς γᾶν, πνεῦμ' ἄνω.* Mosch. in Eur. Suppl. 531 ff.: *ὅθεν δ' ἕκαστον ἐς τὸ σῶμ' ἀφίκετο, ‖ ἐνταῦθ' ἀπελθεῖν, πνεῦμα μὲν πρὸς αἰθέρα, ‖ τὸ σῶμα δ' ἐς γῆν.* Eur. fgm. 836: *χωρεῖ δ' ὀπίσω, ‖ τὰ μὲν ἐκ γαίας φύντ' ἐς γαῖαν, ‖ τὰ δ' ἀπ' αἰθερίου βλαστόντα γονῆς ‖ εἰς οὐράνιον πάλιν ἦλθε πόλον.* C. I. G. 1, n. 1001: *γαῖα δὲ κεύθει ‖ σῶμα, πνοὴν δ' αἰθὴρ ἔλαβεν πάλιν, ὅσπερ ἔδωκεν.* (Eccles. 12, 7); so often in epigrams; *cf.* Kaibel, Epigrammata Graeca. Berlin 1878. p. 680, *s.v. anima*, and Roscher, Hermes der Windgott. Leipsig 1878. p. 58 f.

Among the Romans, Lucretius teaches, De Rerum Nat. 2, 999 f. (like Eur., however, in the last quoted passage, not only of the genus humanum): cedit item retro, de terra quod fuit ante, ‖ in terras, et quod missumst ex aetheris oris, ‖ id rursum caeli rellatum templa receptant; Macrob. Sat. 1, 10, 15 (of Egypt): "quod aestimaverunt antiqui, animas ab Jove dari et rursus post mortem eidem reddi."

9 and Aesch. Suppl. 157: τὸν πολυξενώτατον Ζῆνα τῶν κεκμηκότων, fgm. 229 D, 224 N, etc.

280. Beside the text, only passages which speak in general of a joyful life of bliss; see *10, 14, 3. 6. 9* (146 f.): "where waters flow, days and nights interchange"; *i.e.* the delights of earth are also found; 10, 56, 4; 10, 15, 8. 9 and the like; scattered passages 10, 56, 3: "Go to the lovely" (*sc.* women or maidens, acc. plur. fem.); 10, 135, 1: "Beneath what tree, with beautiful foliage, Yama drinks with the gods, there the Father, founder of our race, cares lovingly for our ancestors." — More of the same nature is found in the more popular Atharvaveda, and later: "There warm, grateful breezes blow, cooling rain falls gently; there there are basins of cream, brooks in which honey flows, streams filled with milk, carrying surâ instead of water; glistening cows giving milk at will, which do not kick out the foot, come up to the righteous, and the weaker has not to pay tribute to the stronger." Zimmer, AIL. 412 f.; Muir, OST. 5, 303–311. 314 f.

281. "What shall be the employment of the blest, in what sphere their activity shall expend itself — to this question ancient Hindû wisdom sought no answer. The certainty of happiness was enough for it." Roth, JAOS. 3, 344.

282. 1, 24, 1. 2: "Who shall give us back to the great Aditi? I would behold my father and mother"; Av. 6, 120, 3: "Where virtuous friends rejoice, — there we would see our parents and our children."

283. The data for the belief in a personal immortality, a happy

---

283 *a*. According to the testimony of Diog. Laert., Theopompus had already told that the Iranians believed in the immortality of the soul: ἀναβιώσεσθαι κατὰ τοὺς Μάγους φησὶ τοὺς ἀνθρώπους, καὶ ἔσεσθαι ἀθανάτους, or, with Aeneas of Gaza: ὁ δὲ Ζωροάστρης προλέγει, ὡς ἔσται ποτὲ χρόνος, ἐν ᾧ πάντων νεκρῶν ἀνάστασις ἔσται (C. Müller, Fgm. Hist. Gr. 1, 289, n. 71; Windischmann, Zoroastr. Stud. p. 233, 279). We now know much more, and more definitely from the Avesta, the sacred scripture of the Eastern Iranians, which, however, still presents great difficulties of interpretation; to defend here my translations of even the few passages from it would lead too far: videant periti! Vend. 9, 44 W.: "Announce to man as the reward of the other world the gain of (the best place) Paradise"; *cf.* 13, 8 (22). Yt. 1, 25 (37): "There are (imperishableness) completeness and immortality, which are the reward of the righteous who have attained to Paradise." Yç. 45, 5: "They will attain to completeness and immortality through acts of righteousness." Yç. 43, 2 f.: "The righteous shall gain the best thing; he who seeks Ahura

continuance of life in the other world, have been given in the preceding; see the foot-note 283 *a*.

Mazda, the most holy spirit, shall attain to the heavenly light (*cf.* Yç. 50, 5), and to the refreshment, which he gives really to the righteous, in fullness, all the days of an eternity. May that man prosper more who shows us the straight paths of this (embodied) earthly world and the spirit-world, to the true abodes where Ahura dwells." Yç. 51, 13: "The soul of the wicked perishes, but the soul of the upright is confirmed and, through its deeds, through its words, attains to the regions by the bridge of the Gatherer (Note 273 *a*), the paths of the righteous." — "When the spirit of the righteous over that bridge has come from the perishable to the imperishable world, it goes joyfully to the golden thrones of Ahura Mazda, of Amesha-Çpenta (*cf.* Note 230), to Garonmâna, the bright, gleaming Paradise, the dwelling of Ahura Mazda, of Amesha-Çpenta, of the other righteous" (after Vend. 19, 30 f. (101 ff.) with Visp. 7, 1 (8, 8)). — On the 'threefold third height of heaven' of the Veda (Note 248. 279); *cf.* the arrangement Yt. 22, 14 f., Mainjo-i-Khard, 2, 145; 7, 8 ff., ed. West.

On the Fravashis, corresponding exactly to the 'Fathers' (Note 270), it is enough to refer to Roth in Baur und Zeller's Theol. Jahrb. 8, 291 f. and Spiegel, Uebersetz. des Avesta 3, xxix. Eran. Alterth. 2, 91 ff., and to the following Notes, 284 *a* to 286 *a*.

If among the Greeks Homer's epic does not show this belief in immortality, yet the belief in a continued existence of the soul, in a better, happy life after death, lived among the people from the oldest times, not first as the teaching of philosophers, as no less a one than Aristotle distinctly informs us (Plut. Consol. ad Apoll. c. 27, p. 115 C): *διόπερ, ὦ κράτιστε πάντων καὶ μακαριστότατε, πρὸς τῷ μακαρίους καὶ εὐδαίμονας εἶναι τοὺς τετελευτηκότας νομίζειν καὶ τὸ ψεύδεσθαί τι κατ' αὐτῶν καὶ τὸ βλασφημεῖν οὐχ ὅσιον ἡγούμεθα ὡς κατὰ βελτιόνων καὶ κρειττόνων ἤδη γεγονότων. καὶ ταῦθ' οὕτως ἀρχαῖα καὶ παλαιὰ διατελεῖ νενομισμένα παρ' ἡμῖν, ὥστε τὸ παράπαν οὐδεὶς οἶδεν οὔτε τοῦ χρόνου τὴν ἀρχὴν οὔτε τὸν θέντα πρῶτον, ἀλλὰ τὸν ἄπειρον αἰῶνα τυγχάνει διὰ τέλους οὕτω νενομισμένα.* And Socrates says in Plato's Apol. 32 p. 40 C, that *τὸ τεθνάναι κατὰ τὰ λεγόμενα μεταβολή τις τυγχάνει οὖσα καὶ μετοίκησις τῇ ψυχῇ τοῦ τόπου τοῦ ἐνθένδε εἰς ἄλλον τόπον*, *cf.* p. 40 E and ibid. p. 41 C: *τά τε γὰρ ἄλλα εὐδαιμονέστεροί εἰσιν οἱ ἐκεῖ τῶν ἐνθάδε, καὶ ἤδη τὸν λοιπὸν χρόνον ἀθάνατοί εἰσιν, εἴπερ γε τὰ λεγόμενα ἀληθῆ ἐστιν.* On the 'Fathers,' the 'Fravashis' of the Greeks, see Note 285 *a*.

The belief of the Romans in a 'happy future' (see Kuhn's words in Note 315) finds its most eloquent expression in the renowned cult of the divi Manes and the Lares (to be connected, in spite of Preuner, Hestia-Vesta, 1864, p. 341), the Italic 'Fathers.' The *summa rerum* of ancient laws reads in Cic. De Leg. 2, 9, 22: Deorum manium iura sancta sunto; sos [*i.e.* suos. Vahlen with the Mss., nos] leto dato divos

284. 10, 15, 1. 2; 10, 13, 3 f.; 10, 16, 11 f.; 10, 56, 2; 10, 154, 2; 1, 164, 30. 38: "The immortal is of one origin with the mortal." For the ancestral cult of the Iranians, Greeks, and Romans, see the foot-note 284 *a*.

285. 1, 164, 30; 10, 15, 2; 10, 56, 5 ("With might they move through the whole atmosphere, measuring the old unmeasured re-

---

habento. Cornelia, the mother of the Gracchi, writes to her son: ubi mortua ero, parentabis mihi et invocabis Deum parentem (Corn. Nep. ed. C. L. Roth, p. 177); and according to Varro's testimony (Plut. Quaest. Rom. 14 p. 267 B) the words θεὸν γεγονέναι τὸν τεθνηκότα were spoken immediately after the burning of the corpse. Serv. ad Virg. Aen. 5, 47.

For the Germans, refer to Grimm, Mythol. 31, 132. 172 ff. Mannhardt, Germ. Mythen. p. 749, Index *s.v.* Seele.

Mannhardt observes that the Celts (*cf.* Caes. B. G. 6, 14) held the same belief as the Germans, and l.c., p. 320, 1, collects the testimony of the ancients.

284 *a*. The Iranians 'praise and honor all the true spirits of the righteous, that are, that have been, and that shall be, with hand furnished with flesh and covering, with devotion which attains uprightness,' with rich sacrifices, especially on fixed days (Yt. 13, 21. 31 f. 49 f.).

The libations and offerings for the dead among the Greeks are well known; there were, besides, 'public forefathers' days, on which all families celebrated the memory of their departed.'

Varro tells of the Romans (Plut. l.c.): ἐπὶ τῶν τάφων περιστρέφονται, καθάπερ θεῶν ἱερὰ τιμῶντες τὰ τῶν πατέρων μνήματα, and Tertullian makes them the reproach (Apolog. 13): Quid omnino ad honorandos eos (*sc.* deos) facitis quod non etiam mortuis vestris conferatis? aedes proinde, aras proinde; idem habitus et insignia in statuis . . . quo differt ab epulo Jovis silicernium?—Characteristically enough, the language of the Romans calls the act of burial an 'reverence,' the Latin *sepelio* being element for element identical with Skt. *saparyâmi*, honor, revere: Sonne, Kuhn, Schweizer-Sidler, KZ. 10, 327; 11, 262; 14, 147.

285 *a*. The Fravardin Yasht of the Avesta (Yt. 13) "describes the speed and strength, the majesty and kindness and friendliness of the spirits (fravashi) of the just; the strong, victorious, how they come to help, how they give support, the powerful spirits of the just" (vs. 1: Roth, ZDMG. 25, 217). Spread through all the atmosphere, through the families, through villages, districts, lands, they hasten to the offerings (εἰδώλων πλήρη εἶναι τὸν ἀέρα: Diog. L. Prooim. 6; Yt. 13, 21. 49. 68. 84); when with a believing spirit men call upon them and satisfy them with offerings, the good, strong, holy Fravashis come, mightier, more victorious, more healing, more favoring than one can tell in words (Yt. 13, 34. 47. 63. 64; *cf.* 75. 27: "They are prosperity, refreshing where they come"); vic-

gions"); 10, 15, 3 ff.; 10, 56, 5. 6; 10, 154, 3; 10, 15, 6; 10, 154, 4; 10, 16, 11.

286. 7, 76, 4: "They were the companions of the gods, the righteous singers of olden times; the Fathers found the hidden light, with true hymns they produced Uṣas." 10, 154, 5; 10, 68, 11. — More

---

torious to aid the pious, they fight bravely in battle at their abodes and homes against the enemies of the land, and bring for their children, for their village, their districts, their land, the fructifying water, for the Aryan regions, and growth to the trees (Visp. 11, 15 (12, 33); Yt. 13, 23 f. 27. 36 f. 67. 69 f. 66. 68. 43. 53. 55); in the sacrificer's house there will be an abundance of cattle and men, the swift horse and the firm wagon; but the Just ward off all evil for all time (Yt. 13, 52; 33. 76 f.).

In the popular belief of the Greeks, likewise, the heroes of old times, and according to the verses of Hesiod, OD. 121 ff. (cl. 252 f.), brought into this their proper connection by Roth, in his treatise on the myth of the five races of man in Hesiod, Tübingen 1860, "the men of the Golden Age after their peaceful death have become friendly demons or immortal guardians of mortals, who, wrapped in mist [*i.e.* "in the atmosphere"], everywhere pervade the earth" (Roscher). These verses are (according to the account in Plato Rep. p. 469 A. cl. Cratyl. 398 A. Plut. De Def. Orac. 39 p. 431 E and elsewhere, evidently better in spite of Lacth. Inst. Div. 2, 14): *αὐτὰρ ἐπειδὴ τοῦτο γένος κατὰ γαῖα κάλυψεν, || τοὶ μὲν δαίμονες ἁγνοὶ ἐπιχθόνιοι τελέθουσιν || ἐσθλοί, ἀλεξίκακοι, φύλακες μερόπων ἀνθρώπων, || οἵ ῥα φυλάσσουσίν τε δίκας καὶ σχέτλια ἔργα, || ἠέρα ἑσσάμενοι πάντῃ φοιτῶντες ἐπ' αἶαν || πλουτοδόται καὶ τοῦτο γέρας βασιλήιον ἔσχον.*

—Further, the Θεοὶ πατρῷοι correspond to the "Fathers," the "Fravashis."

That the Romans believed that their dead possessed divine power eternally, is distinctly told in a grave-epigram (Ritschl, Opusc. Philolog. 4, 244. 250. 252): Manes colamus, namque opertis Manibus || Divina vis est aeviterni temporis (opertis: *i.e.* rite sepultis). Men hope for their help and that of the Lares in the most various circumstances. The old Arval song begins: E nos Lases iuvate! (Lares placare: Hor.) In the letter quoted above (Note 283 *a*), Cornelia writes further to her son: In eo tempore non pudet te, eorum deum preces expetere, quos vivos atque praesentes relictos atque desertos habueris. Compare in general the Lares familiares, domestici, praestites (Ovid. Fast. 5, 134 fg.: quod praestant oculis omnia tuta suis. || Stant quoque pro nobis, et praesunt moenibus Urbis, et sunt praesentes, auxiliumque ferunt), viales, compitales, permarini. — Schoemann has already rightly shown (De Diis Manibus Laribus et Geniis, p. 10 f. Opusc. Acad. 1, 359 f.) that this belief was, among the Romans, a primitive popular superstition ("longe omni philosophia prior, . . . ipsis iam urbis Romanae primordiis aequalis").

plainly still the ÇB. 6, 5, 4, 8: "Whatever men go virtuous to heaven, these stars are their brightness"; ibid. 1, 9, 3, 10: "The righteous are the rays of the glowing sun." Similar declarations in the Mahâbhârata: Muir, OST. 5, 319 and n. 487. *Cf.* foot-note 286*a*.

287. After 4, 5, 5; 7, 104, 3 ("into the abyss, in endless darkness"); 10, 152, 4 ("to the undermost darkness"; Matth. 8, 12,

---

286*a*. According to the Iranian belief, Ahura-Mazda, by the aid and might of the Fravashis, ordered the heaven above, which, gleaming and beautiful, encloses in itself and round about that earth, which like a building stands raised, firmly founded, far-reaching, like polished metal in appearance, shining over the three parts (of the earth) [Roth]. Through their action and might, the divinely created waters flow onward in their beautiful paths; the trees grow forth from the earth, and the wind blows; through their action and might, sun, moon, and stars move on their paths, the heavens, the waters, the earth with its blessing, the whole world, remain established (Yt. 13, 2. 3. 53 with 14. 16. 57. 22. 9. 10 *cf.* 12). "All the unnumbered and innumerable stars which show themselves are called the spirits of men" (Mainjo-i-Khard. 49, 22, ed. West).

The analogy to the latter among the Greeks is proved by Arist. Pac. 832: *οὐκ ἦν ἄρ' οὐδ' ἃ λέγουσι, κατὰ τὸν ἀέρα || ὡς ἀστέρες γιγνόμεθ', ὅταν τις ἀποθάνῃ;*

For the Romans, we may compare *e.g.* Virg. Georg. 1, 32 f.: Anne novum tardis sidus te mensibus addas, || qua locus Erigonen inter Chelasque sequentis || panditur? ibid. 4, 225 f.: Scilicet huc reddi deinde ac resoluta referri || omnia; nec morti esse locum, sed viva volare || sideris in numerum, atque alto succedere caelo.

The greatest similarity to the Indian belief is seen in the Norse-German, in which "the stars are effects of the Elbs (*i.e.* souls of the departed)"; "stars are souls: when a child dies, God makes a new star; the soul of the righteous attains to Gimill, where, united with the Light-elves, *i.e.* the spirits of the just, it imparts light to the heavenly bodies"; "from the souls proceed the brightness of the sunbeams and the brightness of all heavenly bodies." Mannhardt, Germ. Mythen. p. 378. 310, 3; 439. 474.—Some related matter in H. Osthoff, Quaest. Mythol. Dissert. Philol., Bonn 1869, p. 22 f.

287*a*. Among the Iranians we read, Yç. 43, 5: "I think Thee holy, because I saw Thee, how from the beginning, for the creatures of the earth, Thou madest their acts and words to be accompanied by rewards: evil for the evil, a good allotment for the good, through thy excellent might at the last catastrophe of the creation." Yç. 45, 7: "Through his help all strive for reward, those who have been living and shall be; the passing over of the just is into immortality; but eternal woe is the fate of the wicked man." Yç. 49, 11: "In the house of the Druj are the lasting abodes of the soul of the wicked, who walk in an

τὸ σκότος τὸ ἐξώτερον) ; 9, 73, 8; 4, 5, 4; 1, 121, 13; 2, 29, 6; 4, 25, 6 in Note 163; *cf.* Zimmer, AIL. 420 f.

288. Soma: Muir, OST. 5, 258–271; GKR. 110 f.: ***9, 113; 10, 25*** and ***6, 74*** to Rudra-Soma. "It is now represented by a species of Sarcostemma, which, however, grows in more southerly regions than where the seats of the Vedic [or even, Note 293, Indo-Iranian] people lay; probably with the home the plant changed also." Roth, BR. *s.v.* In later Vedic writings (ÇB.), in case Soma should be wanting, substitutes are given. [Roth, Ueber den Soma, ZDMG. 35, 680 ff.; Wo wachst der Soma? ZDMG. 38, 134–139.]

289. 8, 89, 8; 4, 26, 6; 1, 93, 6; ***5, 85, 2*** (p. 63 and Note 244; the Soma of Mount Mûjavant was specially strong: ***10, 34, 1*** above p. 83), etc.; 9, 68, 5: "The wise saw the beauty of the Gladdening, when the falcon brought the herb from afar"; 9, 86, 24: "The well-winged brought thee from heaven, that art adorned with all songs." Differently ***9, 113, 3*** (110) and 9, 83, 4; 9, 85, 12; 8, 66, 4 f. [Roth, Der Adler mit dem Soma. ZDMG. 36, 353 ff.]

290. Soma *gavâçir* or *yavâçir*. *Cf. e.g.* (Plut. De Isid. et Osir. c. 46) Muir, OST. 2, 469 ff. Haug, l.c. and Essays on the Sacred Language of the Parsis, 2d ed. 1878, p. 282 f.; Grassmann, Transl. 1, 157; 2, 183 f.

291. *Cf.* the description in Zimmer, AIL. 272 f.—9, 2, 7; 1, 4, 7; 9, 24, 4; 9, 67, 2.

292. 8, 61, 17; 8, 48, 5. 4, *cf.* 11; 9, 96, 14; 9, 98, 4 (Note 299); 8, 48, 11. 6: "Make me bright like gleaming fire; enlighten us and make us richer. In thy intoxication, Soma, I think: *I shall now attain fortune, a rich man.*" *Cf.* 9, 4, 1–10; 6, 47, 3; in 9, 76, 4 Soma is called father; in 9, 96, 4 producer of the hymns; 8, 48, 3: "We

---

evil way . . ." Yç. 30, 10: "Then the fall into the place of rejection comes to liars." Vend. 5, 61 f. (174 f.): "In life he is not just, in death he has no part in Paradise; he comes to the place of the wicked, the dark, the darkest, to darkness." Yç. 51, 13: "The spirit of the wicked perishes."

That the Indo-Germanic (and Graeco-Aryan) period was acquainted with a place of torment for the wicked, Weber, ZDMG. 9, 242, has made probable from a legend of the ÇB. (Bhṛgu expiates his arrogance; the [etymologically identical] Φλεγύαι are condemned to hard pains of hell for their arrogance); Benfey even attempts (Hermes, Minos, Tartaros. Gött. Akad. Abhandl. 1877, p. 17 ff., 33 ff.) to prove the identity of Τάρταρος with Skt. *talâtala* (name of a hell in the Upaniṣads and Purâṇas).

have drunk the Soma, we are now immortal, we have entered into light, we have known the gods. What can an enemy now do to us? What can the malice of a mortal, O Immortal, now effect?"

The intoxicating effect of the drink upon Indra is described by himself in ***10, 119*** (81 f.).—With the passages mentioned, 6, 47, 3; 8, 48, 3, Muir, OST. 3 [2], 264 f., compares the verses Eur. Bacch. 294 f.: *Μάντις δ' ὁ δαίμων ὅδε· τὸ γὰρ βακχεύσιμον ‖ καὶ τὸ μανιῶδες μαντικὴν πολλὴν ἔχει. ‖ ὅταν γὰρ ὁ θεὸς εἰς τὸ σῶμ' ἔλθῃ πολύς, ‖ λέγειν τὸ μέλλον τοὺς μεμηνότας ποιεῖ,* ‖ and Cyclops 578 f.: *ὁ δ' οὐρανός μοι συμμεμιγμένος δοκεῖ ‖ τῇ γῇ φέρεσθαι, τοῦ Διός τε τὸν θρόνον ‖ λεύσσω, τὸ πᾶν τε δαιμόνων ἁγνὸν σέβας.* On Dionysos as 'the Grecian Soma,' *cf.* Muir, OST. 5, 259 f.

293. To the Indian Soma cult the quite analogous Haoma cult of the Eastern Iranians corresponds; *cf. e.g.* the translation of Yaçnas 9 and 10 by Geldner, Metrik des jüngern Avesta, Tübingen 1877, p. 122 f.; Plutarch tries to reproduce "*haoma*," the regular Bactrian form of the Skt. *sóma*, De Isid. et Osir. 46, p. 369 E: *πόαν γάρ τινα κόπτοντες ὄμωμι καλουμένην ἐν ὅλμῳ κτλ.*

294. "The simple-minded Aryan people, whose whole religion was a worship of the wonderful powers and phenomena of nature, had no sooner perceived that this liquid had power to elevate the spirits and produce a temporary frenzy, under the influence of which the individual was prompted to, and capable of, deeds beyond his natural powers, than they found in it something divine; it was to their apprehension a god, endowing those into whom it entered with godlike powers; the plant which afforded it became to them the king of plants. . . . Soma is addressed in the highest strains of adulation and veneration; all powers belong to him; all blessings are besought of him, as his to bestow, etc." Whitney, JAOS. 3, 299 f. = OLSt. 1, 10 f. — It has already been remarked (p. 21) that a large number of hymns are addressed to Soma, among others all those of the ninth book.— In many passages it can, of course, not be determined whether the word *soma* is to be taken as an appellative or as a proper name.

295. Of Indra, *e.g.* above p. 41, with Note 144; *cf.* also p. 31. He is pleasing to all gods, he intoxicates and gladdens all; see *e.g.* 9, 90, 5; 9, 97, 42, etc.

296. 9, 88, 3; 9, 96, 7; 9, 100, 3; 1, 91, 1; 9, 70, 9; ***10, 25, 6–8*** (114): "Thou best knowest paths and places"; on Pûṣan, p. 56.

297. 9, 66, 16–18; 9, 29, 4; 9, 70, 10; 9, 91, 4; 9, 94, 5; 9, 47, 2: "What he had to do he has done; the destruction of the enemies is plain"; 9, 97, 54: "Soma has sunk them in sleep and death"; 9, 88, 4:

"Like Indra, who performs great deeds, thou, Soma, overcomest the enemies and destroyest the strongholds."

298. 9, 70, 5; 9, 29, 5; 9, 79, 3; 9, 56, 4; 8, 48, 3 (in Note 292); 8, 48, 15: "Protect us in rear and front"; 1, 91, 8; 9, 104, 6; 9, 105, 6; 9, 110, 12; 9, 97, 16; 9, 85, 1; etc.

299. 9, 36, 5; 9, 14, 8; 9, 19, 1.—9, 66, 17: "more generous than rich givers"; 9, 32, 6: "grant splendor to me and the lord of the sacrifice"; 9, 98, 4: "thousandfold gift with hundredfold life"; 1, 91, 7.—"Food and drink for man and beast, for animals and plants": 9, 86, 35; 9, 94, 5; 9, 11, 3; 3, 62, 14.

300. 9, 107, 7; *cf.* 9, 97, 31 and 1, 93, 5: "Full of wisdom, Agni-Soma, ye placed those stars yonder in heaven"; 8, 68, 6; 9, 71, 7; 8, 68, 2: "He clothes what is naked, heals all that is sick, the blind see, the lame walk."

301. 9, 41, 1; 9, 73, 5; 9, 63, 5 with 6, 52, 3.

302. 9, 96, 10; 9, 97, 40. 56; 9, 101, 7; 9, 86, 29; 9, 87, 2 (*cf.* 9, 65, 11); 9, 89, 6.

303. 1, 91, 3; 9, 64, 9; 9, 86, 29: "Thy brightness, O Radiant, is (like) the sun."

304. 1, 91, 3; 6, 47, 4 (‖ Varuṇa: above p. 63, with 8, 41, 10 in Note 244); 9, 87, 3; 9, 97, 10: "king of the race" (‖ Varuṇa: 6, 68, 3: above p. 62, Note 242); 9, 71, 9; 9, 96, 7 (‖: p. 64 with Note 251); 9, 87, 3: "He knows what is hidden in them, the secret, concealed names of the cows (dawns)" (‖: 8, 41, 5: p. 64 and Note 250).

305. 9, 73, 4; 9, 47, 2; *cf.* 7, 104, 12. 13; 9, 85, 1; ***9, 113, 4;*** 9, 110, 1: "To conquer the haters thou hastenest as the punisher of sin."

306. 8, 48, 2; 1, 91, 4; 8, 68, 8; 1, 179, 5.

307. Delbrück, Altind. Tempuslehre, Halle 1877, p. 29.

308. 8, 68, 6; 8, 48, 7; 9, 4, 6; 1, 91, 7. 6: "Mayest thou will that we live; then shall we not die."—***9, 113, 7–11;*** 9, 108, 3: "For thou hast called the races of the gods to immortality."

309. **Bṛhaspati**: Roth, ZDMG. 1, 66 f.; Muir, OST. 5, 272–283; GKR. 107 f.; ***4, 50.*** Bṛhaspati is not to be taken only as a name of Agni, and to be identified with him; *cf.* Muir, l.c. 281–283.

310. ***4, 50, 1;*** 2, 24, 11; 6, 73, 1. 2.—2, 24, 3; ***4, 50, 5;*** 10, 68, 3–10; 2, 23, 18; 2, 24, 3 f.; 6, 73, 3.

311. 2, 23, 4. 8. 11; 2, 26, 13; 6, 73, 3.—2, 23, 11. 17; 2, 24, 13.

312. 2, 26, 3 f.; 6, 73, 2.—1, 18, 3 f.; 2, 23, 5; 2, 25, 5 etc. 2, 23, 9. 15; 2, 24, 10; 1, 18, 2; 3, 62, 4; 1, 190, 8.—2, 23, 10. 19; 2, 25, 2; ***4, 50, 6;*** Bṛhaspati's blessings, 2, 25.

313. 1, 90, 1; 2, 24, 10; 1, 40, 5.—2, 23, 2.

314. 2, 23, 2; 2, 24, 1. 15; 2, 23, 10.—***4, 50, 1*** (107); 1, 18, 7: "May he, without whom even a sage's sacrifice is fruitless, further the course of prayers." 2, 24, 9: "A high priest, who unites and scatters."

315. 2, 23, 6 Bṛhaspati is called *pathikṛt*, "*Path-preparer*"; and so ***10, 14, 15*** (148) "the Ṛṣis of former times, who prepared the way." What way is meant in this cannot be doubtful after the above, especially from ***9, 113, 7*** f. (111).—"With this meaning of *pathikṛt*, *pontifex* (identical in its first part) coincides exactly, and so much more, because we know what high reverence was paid to the Manes by the Romans (*cf.* above Note 283 f.); so they agree, at least for the older period, with Indians and Germans, in their conception of a happy future life, to which their Pontifex alone holds the key." A. Kuhn, KZ. 4, 76 f.

316. Viçve devâs (p. 34): in GKR. 126 f.: ***6, 50*** and ***8, 30***.—10, 100, 7.

317. The **Wedding Hymn** 10, 85 is treated by Haas, Die Heiratsgebräuche der alten Inder, nach den Grihjasûtra (*cf.* Note 24), in ISt. 5, 267–412, which is prefaced by Weber, ibid., pp. 177–266, Vedische Hochzeitssprüche, with a translation of 10, 85, and a number of related texts of the Atharvaveda.

318. For the analogy among the Greeks and Romans, the ἱερὸς γάμος of the highest god of the heaven, Zeus, and the moon-goddess, Hera, see Roscher, Studien zur vergleich. Mythologie 2, Juno und Hera, Leipzig 1875, p. 70 ff.

319. 10, 85, 18 f.: "Following each other, these two glad children encircle the air-region (instead of *adhvarám*, the variant *arṇavam*, AV. 7, 81, 1; 13, 2, 11; 14, 1, 23); the one surveys all creatures, the other, dividing the seasons, is born again. Ever new he is born again; as the standard of day he goes before the Dawns; he gives the gods their portions (regulates the times of sacrifice) by his course; the moon lengthens life."

320. Haas, l.c. p. 273.—In the text the subject could only be treated briefly after Çânkh. Gṛhya-sûtra 1, 13 (Oldenberg, ISt. 15, 27 f.), Pâraskara 1, 6, 3; *cf.* Âçv. 1, 7, 3 f.; see Zimmer, AIL. 311 f.

321. We cannot enter here upon the many and far-reaching coincidences; it is sufficient to refer to the treatises just mentioned (Note

317), especially the index l.c. 410–412, and the few observations in Jbb. 121, 457.

322. Pada c.: *Puraṁdhi:* "the rich"? or with Sâyaṇa, Pûṣan? or a special genius? *cf.* BR. s.v. — "With his right hand the right hand of the bride"; *cf.* ***10, 18, 8*** (above p. 77, bottom): "Who took thy hand once and espoused thee": the *dexterarum junctio* of the Romans.

323. I have already shown in Jbb. 121, 457, 28 that the corresponding Roman *quando (ubi ὅπου) tu Gaius, ego Gaia* was originally used at the marriage, and not (as it is given in most of the manuals) on entering the new home.

324. "From left to right" (*pradakṣiṇam*)*: ἐπιδέξια*: Jbb. ibid. 27. Team of heifers: ibid. 29.

325. Zimmer, AIL. 313.

326. The following hymn, ***10, 18*** (see the beautiful rendering of Roth, ZDMG. 8, 467 ff. and GKR. 150 ff.), presupposes the burial, on the other hand *e.g.* 10, 16; 10, 17, 3 ff., the burning of the corpse. — The ritual is treated by M. Müller in the supplement to ZDMG. 9, 1 ff.

327. Trees are frequently mentioned as coffins (AV. 18, 2, 25. 3, 70), which recalls the Allemanian 'Todtenbaum.'

328. This stanza has a very special interest, because with a very slight forgery it would give the highest sanction, the Vedic authority, for the custom of burning the widow on the grave of the husband; *cf.* Colebrooke, On the duties of a faithful Hindu widow, in his Misc. Essays, 1, 132 f. ed. Cowell, and Fitzedward Hall, JRAS. NS. 3, 183 f. (from *ā́ rohantu yónim ágre*, "let them first approach the place," the forgery *ā́ rohantu yónim agnéh*, "let them enter the place of fire").

329. The grave is thus the dwelling of the body (above p. 69); so also among the Greeks and Romans: "The grave, according to the universal view of antiquity, is a dwelling into which the dead enter, there to begin another and better existence; it has, therefore, the character of a house, which requires a certain arrangement," etc. Becker-Marquardt, Römische Altertümer. 5, 1, 367 f. For German antiquity, it suffices to refer to Weinhold, Altnordisches Leben. p. 490 f. ("here a regular house was built for the dead . . .").

330. Here is already seen the present usage; "by the Roman pontifical law the most essential ceremony at every burial is the *glebam in os inicere;* whoever omitted throwing a handful of earth on an unburied corpse was guilty of a piaculum." Marquardt, l.c. 5, 1, 375; *cf.* Soph. Antig. 256, with the scholium and the Interpr. on Hor. Ode 1, 28, 30 f.

331. For the historical relations, Roth, ZLGW. p. 87 ff.; Lassen, IA. 1², 421 ff.; Ludwig, in the 'Nachrichten' (above p. 94), now enlarged in the "Mantralitteratur" = Rigveda, vol. 3, 167–177 and 203–256, and Zimmer, AIL. 100–138; 185–217; 430 f.; among the hymns are those already quoted by Roth, l.c. ***3, 33*** (132); 7, 18; 7, 33; ***7, 83*** (32) by Belang; details in 6, 26; 6, 47; 10, 48; 10, 49; 10, 102; etc.

332. *Cf.* above pp. 17, 19; Zimmer, AIL. 104 f. Pretenders, ibid. p. 165, 175–177 (Jbb. 121, 446).—Violence: 10, 166, 4: "I have come here overpowering with an all-subduing host; I make myself master of your intention, your resolve, your assembly."—Coalitions: *e.g.* against Sudâs in the battle of the ten kings, p. 80: ***7, 83, 4–8*** (32 f.).—Contests of the warlike nobility against the Brâhmans: Zimmer, AIL. 197 f.

333. 7, 26, 1. 2: "Soma not rightly pressed (*i.e.* without song) does not please Indra, nor draughts poured without prayer the Mighty; I make him a song that he may rejoice in it, a mighty, new one, that he may hear us"; 8, 58, 14: "The young hero disdains the food prepared without a song"; 10, 105, 8: "A sacrifice without prayer does not greatly please thee."—1, 53, 1; 7, 32, 21: "With a poor song a mortal gains no good, no riches fall to the imperfect." 2, 33, 4: "May we not wake thy anger, O Lord, by a bad song."

334. After 3, 53, 9. 11 (according to Roth's rendering, ZLGW. 121); the fine hymn ***3, 33*** (132 f.); 3, 53, 12.—7, 33, 2. 6. "The final outcome is, however, different: while in later time the Tṛtsus have disappeared, the Bhâratas shine forth in bright light." Zimmer, AIL. 128.

335. 7, 18, 5.

336. 7, 33, 3; ***7, 83, 4;*** 7, 18, 18. 19. 13. 14; ***7, 83, 4–8;*** in verse 4 Vasiṣṭha boasts: "Our mediation for the Tṛtsus has prevailed."

337. 6, 47, 22; 6, 26, 4. From a comparison of this passage with 1, 33, 14; 6, 20, 8; 10, 49, 4 I conclude that Vetasu is the name of the gens to which Daçadyu belonged; so too now Zimmer, AIL. 128.

338. 7, 8, 4; 6, 27, 5. 6. *Harîyûpîya* and *Yavyâvatî*, otherwise unknown, are probably rivers. (Probably not *one hundred and thirty; cf. e.g. catuḥçatam* Vâl. 7, 4, etc.)

339. The Dânastutis are quite numerous, especially in the eighth book; *cf.* Ludw. Rv. 3, 274 f.; Zimmer, AIL. 170 f.; for the later time, Weber, ISt. 10, 47 ff.—Note 341. [Oldenberg, ZDMG. 37, 83 ff.]

340. So for those of the families of princes; in the gens of Trasadasyu we get the line Mitrâtithi, Kuruçravaṇa, Upamaçravas (Note 94); in the Tṛtsus, Vadhryaçva, Divodasa, Atithigva, Pijavana, Sudâs; further details can be gained from Ludwig's collections, Rv. 3, 100–167.

341. 5, 30, 12–15 (*pravṛje:* see R. Garbe, ZDMG. 34, 321). Some further examples, interesting in matter, follow: 6, 47, 22 (each ten caskets, steeds, the spoils of Çambara, chests, garments as presents; lumps of gold, chariots with horses, a hundred cows).—8, 1, 32 ff.; 8, 4, 20 ff. a singer drives away, as the reward of his songs, sixty thousand, whole herds of cows, so that the very trees rejoice where he rests.—8, 5, 37 f.: "Kaçu, the Cedi, gave a hundred buffaloes and ten thousand cattle, ten coverings adorned with gold (*tvaco* instead of *râjno* with Delbrück in Grassmann 1, 558); for the tribes subject to the Cedi princes are tanners; none walk in the path in which the Cedis go, no other lord of the sacrifice, no other people is reputed more generous"; 8, 6, 46 (hundreds from Tirindira, thousands from Parçu, among the Yadus; three hundred steeds, ten thousand cattle, double teams of buffaloes). 8, 21, 18: "Citra is a true king, obscure kings are those there (*isti*) on the Sarasvatî; as Parjanya gives rain with thunder, he gave a thousand myriads."—8, 63, 13 ff.—Vâl. 7, 2 ff.: "A hundred white heifers gleam like the stars in heaven; by their greatness they support the heaven. A hundred bamboo reeds, a hundred dogs, a hundred soft tanned skins, a hundred fabrics of Balbuja grass are mine, four hundred ruddy mares. Then the sevenfold team was praised: great is the renown of the not yet fully completed; the brown mares rush along the way so fast that the eye cannot follow them."—Vâl. 8, 1 ff.: "Thy rich gift, O Dasyavevṛka, is displayed; thy renown is high as the heavens. Dasyavevṛka, the son of Pûtakratâ, gave me ten thousand from his own possessions. A hundred asses, a hundred sheep, rich in wool, a hundred slaves, and wreaths of flowers; moreover, an adorned mare was brought forward for the Pûtakratâs (*i.e.* as their present), which did not belong to the steeds of the herd."—10, 62, 8: ". . . and two slaves, well trained for service, together with many cattle, Yadu and Turva gave me."—8, 46, 22 ff., 3: "And this excellent wife, adorned with ornaments, is brought to me (the singer), Vaça Açvia."—1, 126, 1 ff. Kakṣîvant piously brings joyful songs of praise, because a king dwelling on the Sindhu, striving for renown, has given him rich presents, and thereby raised his own imperishable renown to heaven: A hundred golden ornaments, a hundred steeds at one time, a hundred cattle, ten chariots with maidens, a thousand and sixty cattle fell to my share at the departure of day. Forty ruddy steeds lead the train of a thousand with their ten spans; the Kakṣivants, the race of the Pâjras, bore away spirited racers adorned with pearls.—6, 27, 8 (a double chariot team, twenty cows with maidens, a gift of the Pârthavas hard to attain).—7, 18, 22.—8, 19, 36.—8, 57, 15, and others. (Against Roth, BR. 6, 663, Grassmann Dict. 1203 and Transl., and Delbrück, Chrestom. 21, after Durga in the last five passages, I take *vadhû* in the usual signification; that women were given as slaves is shown in 8, 46, 33. So Ludw. Rv. 2, 622, 653. 655; 1, 427; 2, 218 and Zimmer, AIL. 107 ff., on linguistic evidence.)

342. ***7, 103,*** GKR. 169 f.; *cf.* Müller, ASL. p. 494; Muir, OST. 5, 435. MTr. 194. Haug, Brahma und die Brahmanen, p. 12. 40 f. does not consider the hymn a satire; frogs and priests are mentioned together only because both have reference to rain; so G. Buhler. I cannot agree with Gubernatis or Bergaigne, Revue Critique, 1875, 2, 393, "que les grenouilles dont il s'agit ici sont des grenouilles mythiques." [This is one of the three rain-bringing hymns, the others being 7, 101 and 7, 102.]

343. ***9, 112,*** GKR. 167; Muir, OST. 5, 424. MTr. 190.

344. ***10, 97,*** translated by Roth, ZDMG. 25, 645 f. and GKR. 172 ff.

345. ***10, 127,*** GKR. 138 f.; Muir, OST. 4, 498. *Cf.* the beautiful prayer to Night for protection, AV. 19, 47, translated by A. Kuhn, KZ. 13, 131 f.; Muir, OST. 4, 498–500; and Zimmer, AIL. 179 f.

346. ***10, 146,*** GKR. 140 f. Muir, OST. 5, 423. MTr. 189.—Broad humor is shown in the soliloquy of the intoxicated Indra, ***10, 119,*** GKR. 81 f. Muir, OST. 5, 90.

347. GKR. 158 ff. Muir, OST. 5, 425. MTr. 190. R. Heinzel, Stil der altgermanischen Poesie, Strasburg 1875, p. 53.

348. The hymn ***10, 117*** (155 f.) is a collection of sayings; to verses 1–6, which describe the blessing of well-doing, other passages have been added; *cf.* also the so-called Song of Wisdom, ***10, 71*** (162 f.).

349. How much speaking, but not silence, brought in gold to the Brâhmans is shown *e.g.* in Note 341; the blessing of the 'reward of sacrifice' is, therefore, praised in the highest strains in a special hymn, 10, 107 (Muir, OST. 5, 433; verses 8–11 MTr. 192); in the late verses, 1, 18, 5; 10, 103, 8, it is addressed directly as a god (dakṣiṇâ), together with Indra, Soma, Bṛhaspati, and the Maruts. 10, 107, 5 ff.: "Whoever gives dakṣiṇâ goes before as the chief of the clan (*cf.* ***4, 50, 7–9*** (108); 1, 40, 7. 8; 1, 190, 5 etc.). I consider him the king of the peoples who first introduced dakṣiṇâ. The generous die not, they fall not into ruin, they suffer no harm, and are not moved; all that this whole world and the heavens contain dakṣiṇâ brings to the givers. They gain splendid homes, beautiful as a lotus-pond, adorned like the dwellings of the gods; the maiden, clad in beautiful garments, waits upon them"; with this 5, 37, 3: "Here comes a woman, seeking a husband for herself; who shall lead home the blooming wife? His (*sc.* the righteous) chariot hastens by, rumbling, and many thousands direct their gaze to him" (*i.e.* the righteous wins the most desirable wife).

350. ***10, 117, 9*** (156) and 10, 32, 7 (*srutim;* Müller's texts *stutim.* Sâyaṇa, *mârgam*).

351. 8, 33, 17: For Indra himself even said: "Woman's . . ." like Simon. Amorg. fgm. 1, 16 f. 44 f.: ἡ σύν τ' ἀνάγκῃ σύν τ' ἐνιπῇσιν μόγις ‖ ἔστερξεν ων ἅπαντα καὶ πονήσατο ‖ ἀρεστά and fgm. 7, 1 (after Meineke): χωρὶς γυναῖκας θεὸς ἐποίησεν νόου ‖ τὰ πρῶτα. 10, 95, 15: "There can be no friendship with women, their hearts are those of hyenas"; on the other hand, the more favorable verdict, 5, 61, 6. 7: "And many a woman is often better than the man, the godless, impious; she, who knows well how to distinguish the weary, the thirsty, and lovers (*i.e.* helps and assists each in the right way), and has turned her mind to the gods." Ibid. v. 8: "And many a man, because he is unloved, is called a Paṇi (child of the devil, miser); but he remains the same even in his revenge" (*i.e.* can control himself; is better than his reputation. Differently Grassmann 1, 543, and Ludwig 2, 621).

352. 10, 27, 12: "To how many a maiden does the wooer, who desires to become her husband, show affection for the sake of her admirable treasures; but if a woman is pure and beautiful, she can of herself (even without treasure) find her mate in the people." 6, 28, 5: "Ye cows make even the lean fat, the ugly even ye make beautiful in countenance."

353. ***4, 24, 9*** (70) and 10, 107, 3; *cf.* v. 7: "Whoever is wise, makes the rewards of sacrifice his armor."

354. Here, already, is the wheel of fortune spoken of by Croesus to Cyrus, in Hdt. 1, 207: εἰ δὲ ἔγνωκας, ὅτι ἄνθρωπος καὶ σὺ εἷς καὶ ἑτέρων τοιῶνδε ἄρχεις, ἐκεῖνο πρῶτον μάθε, ὡς κύκλος τῶν ἀνθρωπηΐων ἐστὶ πρηγμάτων, περιφερόμενος δὲ οὐκ ἐᾷ αἰεὶ τοὺς αὐτοὺς εὐτυχέειν. Tibull. 1, 5, 70: versatur celeri Fors levis orbe rotae, etc.

355. After *10, 117, 1–6* (155 f.).

356. *10, 71, 7.* The whole hymn in GKR. 162 f.

357. *4, 33, 11* (122); 5, 48, 5: "We know not in our human wisdom where the Dispenser Savitar will give the desired good"; 10, 12, 8: "We do not understand the mysterious council in which the gods agree." *Cf.* also 1, 105, 16 in Note 233, and 10, 149, 2 in Note 370.—8, 18, 22 with 1, 164, 30 and 1, 116, 3.

358. 10, 60, 12; 10, 137, 12.—10, 137 is translated by Aufrecht, ZDMG. 24, 203 ff.; v. 1: "Ihr Götter hebt Gesunkene ans Land, ihr Götter, wieder auf; Und Götter, schuldbeladenen, weckt Ihr zu neuem Lebenslauf"; v. 7: "Ob zähngezacktem Händepaar flüstert die Zunge heil'gen Spruch; das leg' ich auf, das löse dich von deiner Uebel Wucht und Fluch."

359. 8, 80 *e.g.* tells how Indra heals a woman, Apâlâ, who is afflicted by a skin disease, by drawing her "through three apertures of his car," a remedy which Aufrecht, ISt. 4, 1–8, in agreement with Kuhn, connects with German superstition.—10, 163 (translated by Kuhn, KZ. 13, 66 f.); 10, 162, 1 f. (KZ. 13, 149); *cf. 10, 97, 12* (173); 10, 103, 12; 10, 164, 1.—7, 50, etc.

360. 10, 161, 2. 5; *10, 18, 14* (152); 10, 60, 7 f.; *cf.* in general the Gaupâyana hymns, 10, 57–60, treated by M. Müller, JRAS. NS. 2, 426 ff. (translated p. 457 ff.).

361. 10, 164, 5; 10, 162, 3 f.; charm against vermin, 1, 191 *cf.* 7, 50, 2 f.; 10, 165 is for the purpose of warding off the injury, probably death, announced by a dove (? *kapota*); v. 1: "Ye gods, for that which the dove, seeking, came hastening as the messenger of Nirriti, we will sing, we will propitiate, may it be well with us, with man and beast. The dove shall be propitious to us." In v. 4, beside the *kapota*, the owl is mentioned as the messenger of death (*cf.* AV. 6, 29, 2), in which function it is known also to German popular superstitions.—In 2, 42, 3 and 43, the wish is made that "a prophetic (ominous) bird may lift his voice on the right of our houses" ('*taschenhalb*,' as Hartlieb said); Homer, Il. 24, 319 f.: εἴσατο δέ σφιν ‖ δεξιὸς ἀΐξας ὑπὲρ ἄστεος. οἱ δὲ ἰδόντες ‖ γήθησαν, καὶ πᾶσιν ἐνὶ φρεσὶ θυμὸς ἰάνθη. So Il. 10, 274 f.; 13, 821 f.; 24, 292 f.; Od. 24, 311 f. Grimm, Deutsche Mythol. p. 1083 ff. Gesch. d. Dtsch. Spr.[1] p. 983 ff.—The Romans in part differently.

362. In 10, 145 (German by A. Weber, ISt. 5, 222. Zimmer, AIL. 307), a girl seeks to drive off a successful rival, and to bind a man to herself (Ἶυγξ, ἕλκε τὺ τῆνον ἐμὸν ποτὶ δῶμα τὸν ἄνδρα); *cf.* the inverse of this in the passage from the Çat. Br. in Kuhn, Herabkunft,

p. 75 f. — 10, 159 (German by Delbrück, Altind. Tempulsehre, p. 14) is the song of triumph of a woman after a successfully accomplished charm, which was to make her the only wife of her husband (much related matter from the AV. in Weber, ISt. 5, 218-266); in 7, 55, 5–8 (see Aufrecht, ISt. 4, 337–342; Zimmer, AIL. 308 f.) a maiden awaiting her lover seeks to put the whole household to sleep, from the grandfather to the faithful watch-dog. — Through 10, 19 it is sought to bring back cows which have wandered off, etc.

363. GKR. 129 f.; Indra, p. 41; Rudra, p. 38; Viṣṇu, p. 56. The two Açvins with Sûryâ, p. 50.

364. Haug, Vedische Rätselfragen und Rätselsprüche, Sitzungsber. der Philos.-Philol.-Histor. Classe der Königl. Bair. Akad. der Wissenschaften zu München. 1875, II. p. 459 f. (above Note 116*). Haug translates there, RV. 1, 164, a mixtum compositum of such questions. Ludw. RV. 3, 390 f. [Roth, Lösung eines Räthsels im Veda, ZDMG. 37, 109 ff.]

365. Beginnings of Philosophy: *cf.* Weber, HIL. 232 f.; Haug, Die Kosmogonie der Inder. Ausburger Allgem. Zeitung, 1873, p. 2373 f., 2390 f.; more in detail, Muir, OST. 4, 3 f. and 5, 350 f.

366. I mean *e.g.* the personification of abstract conceptions to genii, as of

Anumati ('agreement') to the genius of divine purity and mercy (10, 59, 6: "Long may we see the sun rise; O Anumati, be gracious to us"; 10, 167, 3: "In Soma's decree and King Varuṇa's, in Bṛhaspati's and Anumati's protection");

Çraddhâ ('confidence, faithfulness,' *crêdo* = *çrad-dhâ*) to the genius of faith (10, 151, 1–5; Muir, MTr. 330 f., v. 1: "Through faith the fire is kindled, through faith the oblation is offered, with our words we proclaim faith (to be) upon the head of good fortune"; v. 5: "We invoke faith in the morning, at noon, and at the setting of the sun; O Faith, inspire us with faith"; *cf.* ***9, 113, 2–4,*** GKR. 110).

367. 1, 164, 5 with 10, 82, 7 (above p. 88: "Him ye can never know, who formed," etc.).

368. *E.g.* of Indra; above p. 45, with Note 155. — 10, 88, 17 (*upaspij?*); 1, 185, 1. — 10, 81, 4 = 10, 31, 7 (*cf.* the Norse 'World-ash' Yggdrasil); 10, 81, 4. 2.

369. 10, 5, 7: "Existence and non-existence are in the highest heaven, in Dakṣa's home, in the bosom of Aditi"; 10, 72, 2: "In the former races of the gods, being was born from not-being"; ***10, 129, 1. 4;*** above p. 90.

370. 10, 149, 2 f.: "Where once the firmly founded sea sprang forth, that Savitar alone knows (so we need inquire no further concerning it; see 5, 48, 5 and 10, 12, 8, in Note 357); then from it the world and the realm of air arose, from thence heaven and earth spread forth; on it came into being Savitar's revered bird, with beautiful wings in the heaven" (the sun; Notes 215, 226).

371. According to 10, 72, 2. 6. 7, in the time of the first race of gods, existence was born from non-existence; then Brahmaṇaspati welded the world together, like a blacksmith; the gods stood in the flood; dust rose from them as from dancers. They lifted forth the sun, lying hidden in the sea, and caused the earth to swell. — 10, 81, 3: "Everywhere present, Viçvakarman creating welds earth and heaven together." — 10, 149, 2 f. in Note 370; 10, 190, 1 f. in Note 372.

372. 10, 190, 1 f.: "Law and Truth arose from kindled fire (*tapas: perhaps 'penance'?*); thence night was born, thence the surging sea (of air?); dividing day and night, he rules all that close the eyes. Sun and moon the creator formed in turn; heaven and earth, the air-space and the realm of light." — To this I refer ***1, 161, 9*** (118): of the Ṛbhus who, full of wisdom, entertain each other at work with sayings (***4, 33, 10:*** 122), one holds water for the most important thing (*bhū́yiṣṭha*), another considers fire the most essential.

It was stated (p. 13) that the waters are praised very loudly on account of their healing and refreshing powers; *cf.* (together with Notes 241 and 245) 1, 23, 16–23; 7, 47; 10, 9 and ***7, 49*** (125). They are often called "motherly," or, "most motherly, very motherly"; *cf.* ***6, 50, 7*** (127): "O ye waters, friendly to man, grant us unending favor, prosperity for child and grandchild. For ye, most motherly, are our physicians, ye bear all things, animate and inanimate." Water appears in the Brâhmaṇas, more often than in the Rig, as the starting-point of all animal creation (see Weber, ISt. 9, 2, n. 2 and 9, 74). In the Taitt.-Sanh. 7, 1, 5, 1 (ISt. 12, 245) it is stated that "in the beginning was the expanse of water, and upon it Prajâpati moved (p. 76*) in the form of a wind, of a breath," which recalls the *rûach elohîm* of Genesis 1, 2.

373. Translated by Müller, OGR. 300 f.; the following verses translated by Müller, OGR. 301 f.; Muir, OST. 4, 16; Monier Williams, Indian Wisdom, p. 23. (Müller, v. 6, reads *rodasî*, "heaven and earth," instead of *krandasî*, "the two armies.") V. 7 seems not to have belonged originally to the hymn. That v. 10: "Prajâpati, no other than thou is lord over all these created things: may we obtain that, through desire of which we have sacrificed; may we become masters of riches," appears to have been incorporated into the Rig text later, only after the formation of the Pada text, was remarked in Note 79.

From the beginning of the refrain *Kásmai devấya* (*cui deo, to what god*) the native tradition evolved at an early period a special highest unknown god, *Ka* (*Quo, Quis*), a new illustration of the degree to which the understanding of the texts had been lost: above p. 10 *.

374. Single verses; **1, 164, 46**: "Indra, Mitra, Varuṇa, Agni, they call him, and then he is that celestial, well-winged bird; that which is one they call by different names: they call it Agni, Yama, Mâtariçvan" (a verse with which the Brâhmans seek to invalidate the accusation of polytheism); 10, 114, 5: "Inspired singers represent under many forms the well-winged, who is one" (although he is but one).

To Viçvakarman: 10, 81 and 10, 82; often made use of above: Notes 367, 368, and 371; pp. 88 and 89.—Indra is called *viçvakarman*, 8, 87, 2.

375. GKR. 165 f.; Müller, ASL. 559; Muir, OST. 4, 3 f.; 5, 356 f.; MTr. 188; Monier Williams, Indian Wisdom, p. 22 (I abandon the theory of a hiatus between verses 4 and 5 (with Bergaigne, Rev. Crit. 1875, II. 393), and refer *eṣâm* to *kavayas*). [On this hymn see Whitney, Am. Or. Soc. Proc., May 1882. "The general character and value of the hymn are very clear. It is of the highest historical interest as the earliest known beginning of such speculation in India, or probably anywhere among Indo-European races. The attitude of its author and the audacity of his attempt are exceedingly noteworthy. But nothing can be said in absolute commendation of the success of the attempt. On the contrary, it exhibits the characteristic weaknesses of all Hindu theosophy; a disposition to deal with words as if they were things, to put forth paradox and insoluble contradiction as profundity. . . . The unlimited praises which have been bestowed upon it, as philosophy and poetry, are well-nigh nauseating."—Verse 2: "Whether 'fervor' (*tapas*) means physical heat or devotional ardor, penance, according to the later prevalent meaning of the word, admits of a question; but it is doubtless to be understood in the latter sense. For no such element as heat plays any part in the Hindu cosmogonies, while penance, the practice of religious austerities, is a constant factor in their theories."—Verse 5: "But the next verse is still more unintelligible; no one has ever succeeded in putting any sense into it, and it seems so unconnected with the rest of the hymn that its absence is heartily to be wished. 'Crosswise [was] stretched out the ray [line] of them: was it, forsooth, below? was it, forsooth, above? impregnators were, greatnesses were; *svadhâ* below, offering beyond.' The word rendered 'offering' is literally 'forth-reaching,' and, as sometimes also, as perhaps here, the signification 'straining, intentness.' . . . Who the 'they' are, unless the sages of the preceding verse, it is hard to guess" (Whitney, l.c.). Brunnhofer, Geist der Indischen Lyrik, p. 16, translates v. 5*a*: "And to these sages a ray of light appeared"; Ludwig: "From one to another was drawn the bond of these"; Muir: "The ray [or cord] which stretched across these [worlds]."]

Finally, we may mention:

a. The song to the twins **Yama and Yamî**, the first human beings, ***10, 10,*** GKR. 142. [Muir, OST. 5, 288.]

b. The so-called **Song of Wisdom**, ***10, 71,*** GKR. 162 (*cf.* above p. 85 and Note 348).

c. The hymn to the **Goddess of Speech**, Vâc (*voc-s*) ***10, 125,*** GKR. 136 f.; on *vâc* and λόγος (in St. John), *cf.* Weber, ISt. 9, 473–480; Schlottman and Weber, ISt, 10, 444 f., point out Biblical parallels.

d. The hymn to the **Genius of the House, Vâstoṣpati**, 7, 54 GKR. 135, to be recited, according to Pâraskara, Gṛhyaṣ. 3, 4 (with 7, 55, 1), after the entrance into the house.

e. The modern, pantheistic **Puruṣa-sûkta**, 10, 90, 'the Magna Charta of Brahmanism' (Haug), which tries to explain and justify the already existing division of the state into the four castes (v. 11 f.: "When they divided the original creature, Puruṣa (*i.e.* 'man'), the Brâhman was his mouth, the *Râjanya* became his arms, the *Vaiçya* was his thighs, from his feet sprang the *Çudra*"); see Weber, ISt. 9, 1–10; Muir, OST. 1, 7–15; 2, 454 ff.; 5, 367 ff.; Zimmer, AIL. 217 f.

f. And finally, the **Dialogue of Purûravas and Urvaçî**, 10, 95; see Roth, Erl. zum Nirukta, p. 153 ff., 230; Müller, Chips, 2, 98 ff.; Hehn, Herabkunft, p. 78 f., 85 f.

Müller's LSL.

Note	141,	English	Edition,	2, 430.
"	149,	"	"	2, 462.
"	172,	"	"	2, 495.
"	187,	"	"	2, 506.
"	193,	"	"	2, 462, 498.
"	269,	"	"	2, 510.
"	274 *a*,	"	"	2, 478.

I.

INDEX OF MATTERS, NAMES, AND WORDS.

[Figures refer to pages. N. = Note. Skt. *c* is placed before j, ç and ṣ after s, ṛ before r. Names of divinities are in heavy type.]

Abode (see *Home*, *House*) of the blessed, righteous, 31, 56, 57, 61, 66, 69 f., 73, 78, N. 273 f., 279 f., 283 *a*, etc.

Abodes of the Vedic people, 11 f.; Indo-Germ., 11, N. 36.

Aborigines (see *Barbarians*), 19, 30, 36, 43, 72, 78.

Accent, 7; Vedic and Greek, N. 18 *a*; verbal, N. 84 *d*.

Adbhuta-Br., N. 14 *a*, 2; 79 *a*.

Adhvaryu, 82 *.

Adhyâya, N. 71.

Aditi, 59, 61, 70, N. 225, 259, 282, 369.

Âditya = Varuṇa, 61, 68, N. 225.

Âdityas, the, 58–69, N. 226–264; names, N. 227; number, N. 226.

Adoption, 16, N. 48.

Age, 30 (N. 103), 41, 43, *cf.* 38, N. 159; *cf. Life, long; Death, before the time;* relative A. of the Maṇḍalas, N. 73.

Aged, 43; their treatment, 16 with N. 50.

Agnâyî, N. 148.

Agni, 35–37 (N. 119–126), 70, 80 f.; often in the Notes, N. 133 (Rudra?); N. 309 (Bṛhaspati?), 374, etc.; production of A., 35.

Agni-Purâṇa, N. 26.

Agohya, 37 with *.

Agriculture, 13.

Ahi, 40, N. 148.

Ahura-Mazda, N. 283 *a*.

Air, region, 34, 35, 87, 89 f.; distinguished from light, 34, N. 118; gods, 37–49.

Aitareya-Âraṇyaka, -Brâhmaṇa, -Upaniṣad, N. 14 *a*, 1.

Aja, 80.

Alexander the Great, 3, N. 39, 50.

All gods, 34, 74, N. 316.

Altar, 75, N. 75.

Amesha Çpenta, N. 226, 283 *a*.

Ancestors, 71 (see *Fathers*); Yama, N. 276, 280.

Ancestral worship, cult, 70 f.; Iranian, Greek, and Roman, N. 283 *a*, 284 *a*.

Andra (Iran.), N. 142.

Anger, N. 261; of the gods, 66, 67, 73, 74, N. 242, 259, 261.

Angiras, 42, N. 114.

Ângirasa, N. 73.

Animals, 53, 56, etc. (see *Man*); A. and plants, N. 299.

Animate and Inanimate, N. 206.

Anniversary, 71, N. 287 *a*.

Ança, N. 227.

Anu, 80, N. 198.

Anukramaṇî, N. 26, 85.

Anumati, genius, N. 366.
Anuvâka, N. 71.
Apâlâ, N. 359.
Âpastamba, N. 10, 1; 23; 23 *a*, 3; 24, 3; 25.
Apollo-Rudra, N. 133.
Âprîsûkta, N. 126.
Âptya, N. 112 *d*, 114; *cf.* *Trita*.
Âraṇyaka, 5, N. 16. — Ait.-Â., N. 14 *a*, 1; 16. Bṛhad-Â., N. 14 *a*, 4. Kauṣ.-Â., N. 14 *a*, 1. Taitt.-Â., N. 14 *a*, 3.
Âranyaṇî, hymn to, 83.
Arrangement of hymns in the books, 21 f.; chronological A. of books, 21, N. 73.
Army, 17, N. 54; both armies, 89, N. 152.
Arrow, 19, 47, 80.
Ârṣeya-Br., N. 14 *a*, 2.
Arts, 14, 20.
Aryà, árya, N. 37.
Aryaman, 61, 73, 75, 76, N. 225, 227, 259.
Aryan (etym. N. 37), 44, 72, 78, N. 54. A. = Indian and Iranian, 11; = Indo-Germanic, N. 37.
Asiknî, 12, N. 39.
Ass, N. 341.
Assembly, 17, 18, 78.
Astronomy, 6, 20, N. 68.
Âçáyâna, N. 145.
Âçrama, N. 15.
Âçvalâyana, N. 23 *a*, 1; 24, 1; 320.
Âcvinî, N. 148.
Açvins, 37, 49–52 (N. 171–192), 58, 72, 74, *cf.* 86.
Aṣṭaka, N. 71.
Atharvângiras, N. 11.
Atharvaveda, 4, 6, 86, N. 11–13 (AV. 4, 16: 65 f., N. 252). Brâhm., N. 14 *a*, 5; Çrautasûtra, N. 23 *a*, 5; Gṛhyasûtra, N. 24, 5; Prâtiçâkhya, N. 20.
Âthwya (Iran.), N. 112 *d*.
Atithigva, N. 340.
Atmosphere, 90 (see *Air*).
Âtreya, Atri (poet), 21, N. 73.
Atri (protegé of the Açvins), 51, N. 182.
Aurora, see *Uṣas*.
Autumn, 13, 66.
Avaricious, 42, 47, 53, 56, N. 198.
Avesta, N. 91, 106, 142, 226, 246, 270, 273, 274 *a*, 283 *a*, 284 *a*, 285 *a*, 286 *a*, 287 *a*, 293.

Babhru, 81.
Balbuja, N. 341.
Ballads, 22; Indo-Germ., N. 85.
Banishment, 18, N. 57.
Barbarians, 36, 43 f., 72; see *Aborigines*.
Barley, Puṣan's food, N. 210.
Barter, 14.
Battle, 17, 39, 42 f., 44, 46, 71, 78 f., N. 211, etc. B. of the elements, 42, etc.
Baudhâyana, N. 23 *a*, 3; 24, 3; 25; 26.
Beginning of things, 88, 90.
Being and not-being, 87 f., N. 369, 371.
Belief, Vedic, 32 f.
Beverages, 14, 72.
Bhaga, 75, N. 83 *b*, 225, 227.
Bhagavadgîtâ, N. 4.
Bhâgavata-Purâṇa, N. 26.
Bharadvâja, 21, N. 73. — N. 23 *a*, 3.
Bharata, 79, 80, N. 80, 334, 340.
Bhâratî, N. 80.
Bhârgava, N. 73.
Bheda, 80.
Bhikṣu, N. 15.
Bhṛgu, 35, N. 120, 287 *a*.
Bhujyu, 51, N. 189.

Bird, 53, 58, 64, N. 198, 220, 238, 248; see *Eagle*. B. = Sun, N. 215, 226, 270.
Birth, of a girl, N. 48; ritual, N. 24, *cf.* N. 49.
Blessed, 31, 56, 66, 69; see *Abode*.
Blessing, 59, etc.; of reward of sacrifice, N. 349; of instruction, well-doing, 85; of the dead to the living, 70 f., N. 285 *a*, 286 *a*; formulas of B., 86, N. 115.
Blind, 50 (*cf.* 52), 72, N. 177, 300.
Body (see *Corpse*), in the other world, 69 f., N. 278.
Bond of being and not-being, 90.
Bonds of Varuṇa and the Âdityas, 20, 67, N. 225, 255; of Soma, 72.
Books of the Rig, arrangement, relative age, 21 f., N. 73.
Bow, 78, N. 63, etc.
Bṛhad-Âr., N. 14 *a*, 4; B.-devatâ, N. 26, 72.
Brahma, 3, N. 26.
Brahmacârin, N. 15.
Brahmán (masc.), 84, N. 14, 82.
Bráhman (neut.), 4, 5, N. 14.
Brâhmaṇa (masc.), 31 f., 81 f., N. 110, 332, 349, 374, 375 *e*; stages of B., N. 15; their literary work, N. 27, 76.
Brâhmaṇa (neut.), 5, 32, N. 372; etymology, N. 14; importance and period, 5, N. 14; list of B., N. 14 *a*.
Brahmaṇaspati, Bṛhaspati, 32, 37, 73 f., N. 87, 309–315, 349, 366, 371.
Brahmaveda, 4.
Brahmodya, 86.
Bride, 74 f., N. 324; purchased, 15.
Bridge to the other world, N. 273, 274 *a*.
Bukka, 9.
Buffalo, 52, N. 341.
Burial (see *Funeral*), 76 ff., N. 326.
Burning of corpse, N. 326.

Case, 22, N. 84 *a*.
Caste, 17, N. 56, 375 *e*.
Cattle, 13, 58, 80 f., 82; C. of Uṣas, 53, N. 197.
Chaos, 90.
Chariot, of Agni, 36; of the Açvins, 50, 51, N. 176, 178, 189; of the Maruts, 39; of Pûṣan, N. 210; of Savitar, 57; of Sûrya, 55, N. 205; of Soma, 72; of Uṣas, 53, N. 197; of Vâyu, 38. Chariots given to singers, N. 341. C.-race, 19, N. 61.
Charms, spells, 4, 20, 86, N. 12, 358–362.
Childish conceptions, 27 f., N. 66.
Children, blessing of, 30, 52, *cf.* 67, 74, 76, N. 217, 239, etc.
Chronology, Indian, N. 38. Chronological order of the books, N. 73.
Cities, 13, N. 42.
Civilization, Vedic, 11; history of C., 74, N. 24, 47 f., 317, 321 f., 324, 327–330.
Climate, 12, 37, N. 40, *cf.* 136.
Clothing, 14, 56, N. 341.
Clouds, 39, 40, 42, 52, 63, *cf.* N. 143.
Collection of Vedic texts, 2–8, N. 8–26; of hymns, 22, N. 75.
Command, see *Ordinance*.
Commentary, native, 8, 9. C. of Sâyaṇa and Mâdhava, 8, N. 8, 27; *cf. Tradition.*
Composition, of the Vedic hymns, 11, N. 38; of the Brâhmaṇas, N. 14; of the Sûtras, N. 17; of the commentaries, 8.

Conjugation, 22, N. 81 *d*.
Contests, 19, 81, 86, N. 61.
Corpse, 69, 76 f.; buried and burned, 76, N. 326.
Cosmogony, 20, 87 f. Cosmogonic gods, 89; C. hymn, 90.
Cow, 13, 27, 81, N. 90, 190, 280, 341. C. as monetary unit, 14, N. 46. Cows = clouds, 42.
Creation, song of C., 90; theories of C., 88 f.
Creator, 45, 88–91, N. 372, 374, etc. (see *Viçvakarman*); Indra, 45; Varuṇa, 62 f.
Cult, ancestral, 70; Iran., Greek, Roman, N. 284 *a*, 285 *a*.
Cults, transferred, combined, N. 208; opposed, N. 210.

Dadhyanc, N. 188.
Dakṣa, N. 227, 369.
Dakṣiṇa, N. 349.
Dânastuti, 80, N. 339–341.
Dance, 19, 77, *cf.* 53, N. 371.
Danger, 61, N. 237, 239, etc.
Darkness, in the beginning, 90; of night, 33, 50, 52, 71, N. 195; unending D., 71, N. 287, 287 *a*.
Dasra, N. 172.
Dasyavevṛka, N. 341.
Dasyu, 19; see *Aborigines, Barbarians*.
Daçadyu, 80, N. 337.
Dawn, 28, 52 f., 71, 87; see *Uṣas*.
Day prolonged into Night, 45. D. and Night, see *Night*; propitious days, 31; D. guided by Varuṇa, 63.
Dead, see *Ancestors*, etc.
Death, 61, 66, 67, 69 f., 76 f., N. 159, 274; D. before the time, 61, N. 103, 236; D. and Immortality, 89; messenger of D., N. 361.
Decree, see *Ordinance*.
Demons, 40–43, *cf.* 36, N. 150.
Departed, see *Ancestors, Death*.
Deva, 32, 34.
Devatâdhyâya-Br., N. 14 *a*, 2.
Devotion, devout, *e.g.* 29, 47, 66, 70, 73 (see *Righteous*); haters of D., 47, 48, 81 (see *Unsacrificing*); Lord of D., see *Brahmaṇaspati*.
Dharmasûtra, -çâstra, 8, N. 25, 25*a*.
Dialect, 22; traces of D., N. 73.
Diaskeuasts, 22, *cf.* N. 79, etc.
Dice (see *Play*), 18, 54, 67, 83, N. 261; D.-song, 83 f.
Dionysos, the Grecian Soma, N. 292.
Dioskuroi, 49, N. 171.
Disease, see *Sickness*.
Division of the gods and universe, 34, N. 117, 118; D. of the year, N. 68.
Divodâsa, 80, N. 340.
Dogs, N. 341, 362; Yama's, 69 f., N. 274, 274 *a*.
Doubt, doubters, 32, 48, N. 168.
Dove, as messenger of death, N. 361.
Dṛdha, N. 149.
Dragon, 40 f., etc.
Drâhyâyana, N. 23 *a*, 2.
Dream, N. 195, 217, 261.
Druhyu, 80, N. 198.
Dual divinities, 33, N. 114.
Durga, N. 19.
Dwelling, see *Abode, Home, House*.
Dyaus, 28, 33, N. 112 *a*.
Dyâvâpṛthivî, N. 112 *b*.

Eagle, 59, 83; falcon, 72, N. 148, 289.
Earth, mother E., 69, 78; E. as region, 35 f., etc.; as goddess, N. 112 *bc*; home in E., 78.

Egg, son of the E., 58, 226.
Elephant, 39, N. 146.
Eos, see *Uṣas.*
Erratic verses, pieces, N. 79 *a.*
Etymology, 6, 7 (*cf.* the Greek, Latin, and German words on p. 195 f).
Evolution, 87 f., 90, N. 370–372.
Exegesis, Vedic, 9 f., N. 29, 34; methods, 9–11, N. 29–34.
Exposure, of new-born children, 16, N. 49; of the aged, 16, N. 50.
Eye, of the Lord, 65, 89; of Mitra-Varuṇa, 59; of Varuṇa, N. 241; of Night, 83.
Ezour-Veidam, 1, N. 2.

Faith, Genius of F., N. 366.
Family, family life, 14 ff., 74 ff., N. 47; numerous F., see *Children.*
Father, representative of a dead F., 15.
Fathers = Ancestors, 70*, 71, 78, N. 270, 275, 286; *cf.* 283 *a*, 286 *a*; see *Ancestors.*
Feast, 19, 43, etc.
Feet, 46, 53, 57, N. 198, 219, etc. F. of the sun, N. 245.
Ferîdun (Iran.), N. 112 *d*
Fetters, 20; see *Bonds.*
Figures, rhetorical, 23, N. 83 *a.*
Fire, 35, 75, 87; production, 35, N. 121; F. as original matter, 88, N. 372; see *Agni.*
Fish, 13, 58.
Flood, legend, N. 14 *a*, 4.
Food, 13, etc.
Footprints of Viṣṇu, 56.
Formulaic in language, 23, N. 83 *a.*
Formulas, liturgical, N. 95; F. of incantation, see *Charm.*
Forms, Vedic, N. 81, 81 *d.*
Fortune, 30, 75, 85, N. 209, 366; wheel of F., 85, N. 354.
Fravashi (Iran.), see *Ancestors, Fathers.*
Friend, friendship, 18, 52, 84, N. 282; Agni, 37; Indra, 47, N. 166; Varuṇa, 66, 68, etc.
Frog Song, 81, N. 342, *cf.* N. 140.
Funeral ceremonies, 71, 76 f., N. 24, 284 *a*; see *Burial.*
Future, 69, 70, 77, 85; see *Abode, Blessed, Life.*

Galita, N. 83 *c.*
Gandhâri, 12.
Gangâ, Ganges, 12, N. 39.
Garonmâna (Iran.), N. 283 *a.*
Gaupâyana, N. 360.
Gautama, N. 25, 73.
Gâyatrî, N. 222.
Genealogy, 80, N. 340.
Genius, individual, 25. — G. of Faith, N. 366; G. of the house, N. 375 *d*; G. of Night, of the woods, 83; G. of the seasons, 37 (see *Ṛbhus*).
Germ, original G., Gold-G., 9, 88 f.
Ghanapâṭha, N. 77.
Ghoṣa, 51, N. 186.
Gifts, 30, 31, 43, etc., N. 108; G. of princes to singers, 80 f., N. 341.
Gobhila, N. 24, 2.
Gods, 28 f., 32 f., 34–74, 88 f., etc. G. among men, 32, 35; All G., 34, 74, N. 316; older and newer, 33 f., N. 114, 369, 371; classified, 34, N. 114, 117; various G. identical, 34, N. 114, 133, 374; invisible, 87, 88, N. 233; anger of G., 36, N. 259, 261, etc.; cup of G., 37 f.;

images, N. 79 *a*; wives, 41, N. 131, 148; mother of the G., N. 225, 227; triad, 3, N. 26, 217.
Gold, golden ornament, 14, 55, 57, N. 230, 283 *a*, 341. Gold-germ, 88.
Gomal, Gomatî, 12, N. 39.
Gopatha-Br., N. 14 *a*, 5.
Gṛhastha, N. 15.
Gṛhyasûtra, 8; list, N. 24, *cf.* N. 23.
Gṛtsamada, 21, N. 73.
Grammar, Indian, 6 f., N. 22; Vedic, N. 81, 84.
Grave, 69, 76 f., N. 329 (see *Burial, Funeral*).
Guardians of the path, world, 56 f., 65, see *Spies*.

Hand, uplifted in prayer, 49, N. 173; laid on, to heal, 86, N. 358; grasped in marriage, 75, N. 323.
Haoma-cult of the Iranians, N. 293.
Harîyûpîya, 80, N. 338.
Harvest, 13, see *Autumn*.
Healing, ceremonies, 86, N. 358, 359, see *Medicine*, etc.; herbs, 83.
Heaven, region, 34 f., 58 f., 87, often. H. as garment of God, N. 246; home of the soul, 69, N. 275; dwelling of the blessed, 31, 57, 66, 69, 73; personified, 28, 33, 61, N. 112; H. and earth, 33 (N. 112), 87 f., often; three heavens and three earths, N. 241, 248; *cf.* 279, 283 *a*.
Hell, N. 287 *a*; *cf.* p. 71, N. 287.
Henotheism, 33, N. 113.
Herbs, see *Plants*.
Herds, 13, 43, 48, 56, 72, 81, etc., N. 362.
Hexameter, Homeric, N. 85.
Himâlaya, 12, 83.
Hiraṇyagarbha, 88 f.
Hiraṇyahasta, N. 178.
Hiraṇyakeçi, N. 23 *a*, 3.
Historical hymns, 78–81, N. 331–341; H. relations, ibid., *cf.* 11–20, N. 36–69.
Home, 15, 75, 76. H. of the soul, 69 f., N. 275 (see *Heaven*); longing for H., 58.
Honor, 30, 66, etc., see *Renown*.
Horse, steed (see *Mare*), 63, 71, 79, N. 341, etc. Horses of the Açvins, 50, 51; of Indra, 37; of Savitar, 57; of Sûrya, 55, N. 205; of Uṣas, 53. Horses' heads as tribute, 80, N. 188; hoof as spring, 51, N. 185.
House, 12. Varuṇa's H., 63 f., 68; H. of the dead, 78, N. 329. Genius of the H., N. 375 *d*.
Human fashion, 71, N. 221, 261; H. wisdom, 85, N. 357.
Humorous pieces, 81.
Hunting, 13.
Hymns, 3, 22 f., 26, N. 79 *a*, 87, 333; form and language, 22 f.; contents, 24 f.; see *Poetry*.

Immortal, 70 f.; poets think themselves I., 72, N. 292.
Immortality, of the gods, 57, *cf.* 41, N. 308; I. of the human soul, 31, 57, 66, 69–71, N. 265–287, 14 *a*, 4; Iranian, Greek, Roman, German, Celtic belief, N. 265, 273 *a*, 275 *a*, 283 *a*, 287 *a*, 315.
Incantation, see *Atharvaveda, Charm*.
India, migration into I., 11, *cf.* N. 38.
Indo-Germanic abodes, 11, N. 36; numbers, N. 65; poetry, N. 12, 82, 85.

Indra, 13, 21, 33, 39, 40–49 (N. 141–170), 72, 79, 80, 85, 86, N. 87, 131, 211, 214, 224, 227, 374.
Indrâṇi, N. 148, 159.
Indus, 12, N. 39.
Infinitive, N. 81, 84 *c*.
Inheritance, 15, 85, N. 352. Law of I., N. 25; widow's right, N. 51.
Inspiration of the texts, 5, 24, 25, N. 23, 87.
Intercalary days, 37*, N. 68; month, 20, 64, N. 68; period, 20.
Intercourse of India with the West, 14, N. 46.
Interpolations, 22, N. 79 *b*.
Irâvatî, 12, N. 39.
Îçâ-, Îçâvâsya-Upan., N. 10, 2; 16.
Itihâsa, N. 26.

Candrabhâga, N. 39.
Caraṇa, 3, N. 23.
Caraṇavyûha, N. 26.
Caturanîka, N. 241.
Cedi, N. 341.
Chandas, 6, N. 18.
Chandogya-Br., -Upan., N. 14 *a*, 2.
Cinâb, N. 39.
Cinvat, N. 273 *a*, 274 *a*, 283 *a*.
Citra, N. 341.
Cyavâna, 51, N. 183.

Jaiminîya-Br., N. 14 *a*, 2.
Jajnâna, N. 270.
Jâṭapâṭha, N. 77.
Jumna, 12.
Jyotiṣa, 6, N. 18.

Ka- (*kasmai devâya*), N. 373.
Kabul, Kabulistan, 12.
Kakṣîvant, 51, N. 185, 341.
Kalâpin, N. 10, 1.
Kali, 50, N. 179.
Kalpa, 6, N. 18, 23, 26.
Kaṇva, Kâṇva, 21, N. 73.
Kâṇva-çâkhâ, N. 10, 2.
Kâṇva (protegé of the Açvins), N. 177.
Kapota, N. 361.
Kaçu, N. 341.
Kaṭha, Kâṭhaka, N. 10, 1.
Kathenotheism, 33, N. 113.
Kâtyâyana, N. 20, 23, 23 *a*, 4; 26.
Kauçika, N. 24, 5; 79 *a*.
Kauṣitaki-Br., -Âr., -Upan., N. 14 *a*, 1.
Kauthumaçâkhâ, N. 9, 23 *a*, 2.
Kautsa, 10*.
Kena-Upan., N. 14 *a*, 2.
Khela, N. 180.
Khila, N. 8, 72.
King, kingdom, 17, 78–81.
Kramapâṭha, N. 77.
Krumu, Kurum, Kubha, 12, N. 39.
Kuruçravaṇa, N. 94, 340.

Lame, 50 f., 72, N. 300.
Language of the hymns, 22 f.; wealth of forms, N. 81 *d*.
Lâtyâyana, N. 23 *a*, 2.
Laugakṣi, N. 24, 3.
Law (see *Ordinance*), ideas of L., 18; literature, N. 25 *a*. Law-books, 8, N. 25. L. in Nature, N. 92 f.
Levirate marriage, N. 51.
Life, long L., 30, 52, 61, 66, 72, 73, 75, 77, N. 103, 236. L. after death, 31, 69–71, N. 275–287. Eternal L., 69 f. Stages of L. of the Brâhmaṇa, N. 15.
Light, 29, 34, 35, 57, 62, 70. L. and air distinguished, 34, N. 118; L.-region, the bright heaven, 34 f., 57, 58, 70, 89; gods of L. 49–58.

Lightning, 32, 41, 45, N. 147, 224, etc.
Lion, 40, N. 146, 160.
Liturgical sanhitâs, 3; L. hymns in the Rig, 22, N. 126.
Love, charms, 86, N. 362.
Lunar phases, N. 67 (see *Nakṣatra*); L. year, 20.

Mâdhava, 9, N. 27.
Madhyadeça, N. 39.
Mâdhyandina, N. 10, 2.
Maiden, Girl, 15, 19, 53, 85, N. 352, *cf.* 349. G. not desired, 16, N. 48; maidens given as slaves, N. 341; M. = Dawn, 51, N. 183, 186.
Maitrâyaṇî-Sanhitâ, N. 10, 1.
Man, 28, 60, 85, N. 230, 275, 351, etc. (*cf. Human*). M. and beast, 53, 57, 76, 89, N. 299, 316, etc. Men of olden time (*cf. Fathers*, etc.), N. 285 *a*.
Mânava, N. 23 *a*, 3; 24, 3; 25.
Maṇḍala, 21, N. 71.
Mantra, 2–4, 86.
Manu, 8, N. 25 *a*, 79 *a*.
Manuṣa, 28.
Mares, 79, N. 341. M. of the Maruts, 39; of Sûrya, 55, N. 205 (see *Horse*).
Markaṇḍeya-Pur., N. 26.
Marriage, 15, N. 24. M. of Soma and Sûryâ (Zeus and Hera), 75 f., N. 318. M. of brothers and sisters, N. 48.
Maruts, 39 f. (N. 136 f.), 41.
Maçaka, N. 23 *a*, 2.
Mâtariçvan, 35, N. 144, 374.
Mathematical treatises, N. 26.
Measure, 20. Measuring staff, cord, 36, 63.
Medicine, 20, 38, 39, 50, 66, 72 (see *Physician, Sickness*).
Melody, 3, N. 9.
Memorizing method, N. 76.
Mercy, 38 (Rudra), 47 (Indra), 56 (Viṣṇu), 66, 67, 68 (Varuṇa).
Messengers of gods and men, 36; Varuṇa's, 65, 67; see *Spies*.
Metempsychosis, 71.
Metre, 6, 7. M. of Indo-Germ. poetry, N. 85; of the Vedic hymns, 24, N. 85.
Milk, 13, 27, 63, 52, N. 90, 190.
Mina (μνᾶ), 14.
Miser, see *Avaricious*.
Mitra, 59, 73, N. 226, 227.
Mitra-Varuṇa, 59, N. 226, 227, 230, 241; hymns to M., see N. 227.
Mitrâtithi, N. 340.
Mocker, N. 163.
Modes, 23, N. 84 *b*.
Monarchy, 17.
Money, 14.
Monogamy, 15.
Monotheism, 33, 34, 89, 90, N. 374.
Moon, 28, 45, 46, 64, 74 f., 87, N. 231, 234, 249, 286 *a*; *cf. Sun*.
Mountains, 12, 37, 39, 42, 50, 63, 89, etc.
Mûjavant, 83, N. 289.
Music, 19, 39.
Mythology, Vedic, 34, N. 115.

Naigeya, N. 9.
Nakṣatra, N. 67.
Nârada, N. 25.
Nâsatya, N. 172.
Nature, laws, course of N., 28 f., N. 91, 92, 97; phenomena, 28, 29, 33, 40, N. 143; philosophy, 87 ff.
Navigation, 14.
Nighaṇṭu, N. 19.

Night, 28, 55, N. 68*. N. and morning, 28, 52, N. 241; N. and day, 28, 57, 64, 68, 87, 90 (see *Day*); N. personified, 28, 52, 55, 83; hymns to N., 83, N. 345.
Nirriti, N. 361.
Nirukta, 7, N. 19.
Nirukti, N. 19.
Number, 20, N. 65, 116; play on N., N. 83 *b*; N. of the Âdityas, 59, N. 226; gods, N. 117; hymns, 21, N. 72; Brâhmaṇas, 5, N. 14 *a*; Upaniṣads, N. 16.
Nuts as dice, 83.

Occupations, 14, 53, 55.
Offering, see *Sacrifice*.
Old age, 61, 75, N. 50; see *Age*.
Omen, 86, *cf.* N. 14 *a*, 2.
Omniscience of the godhead, 89; of Varuṇa, 66 f.
One, the, 88, 90.
Ophir, N. 46.
Oral transmission of the texts, 22, N. 64, 76.
Order (see *Nature*) of the books, 21 f.; chronological O., N. 73; O. of the hymns, 21 f.
Ordinances of Savitar, 57 f.; Mitra-Varuṇa, 59, 71; Âdityas in general, 59, 60, N. 224, 228, 234; Soma, 72, 73; Varuṇa, 20, 62, 64, 66, 70, N. 249.
Origin of things, gods, 88 f.
Original matter, 87 f., N. 370, 372.
Ornament, 14, 53, 75, 77, N. 341, etc.
Orphic pantheism, N. 225.
Outcast, 18, 50, N. 57.
Owl as messenger of death, N. 361.

Padapâṭha, N. 77, 78.
Paippalâdiçâkhâ, N. 13.
Pajra, N. 341.
Pajrid, 51.
Paṇi, 42, N. 149, 351.
Pâṇini, 7, N. 21, 79 *a*.
Pancanada, 12, 14.
Pancavinça-Br., N. 14 *a*, 2.
Panjab, 12, 14.
Pantheism, *cf.* N. 225, 375 *e*.
Paradise, N. 274, 274 *a*, 283 *a*, 287 *a*.
Paradox, N. 160.
Pâraskara, N. 23; 24, 4; 78 *a*, 105, 320, 375 *d*.
Parâvṛj, N. 57.
Pariçiṣṭa, 8, N. 26.
Paritakmyâ, N. 176.
Parjanya, 40, N. 139 f., 341.
Parçu, N. 341.
Pârthava, N. 341.
Paruṣṇî, 12*, 79, N. 39.
Path of the Âdityas, N. 233; righteous, 61, N. 238; wind, 64; stars, N. 286 *a*; P. to the next world, 69.
Pâṭha, Pada-, Sanhitâ-, etc., N. 77.
Pathikṛt, N. 315.
Pedu, 51, N. 181.
Pegasus, N. 185.
Penance, 67, N. 259, 266, 372, 375.
People, 17; 'Five Peoples,' 53, N. 198.
Period, Indo-Iran., 72, N. 293; Graeco-Aryan, N. 84 *d*, 65, 95.
Phallus-worshippers, N. 62.
Philosophical poetry, 87–91.
Phonetics, 7, 22.
Physician, 38, 50, 83; *cf.* N. 344, 372 (*cf. Medicine, Sickness*).
Pijavana, N. 340.
Pitaras, N. 270 (see *Fathers*).
Place of torment, see *Hell*.
Planets, 20, N. 67.
Plants, 37, 45, 63, 72; healing plants, 20, 83.

Play, gambler, 18, 67, 83 f.
Pleiades, 20, 27, 64, N. 67.
Plough, 13, 84.
Poets, 31, 45, 54, 68, 87 (*cf. Singers*), N. 169. P. of the separate books, 21.
Poetry, 20, 23, 25, 26. Didactic-gnomic P., 84 f.; historical, 78 f.; humorous, 81 f.; liturgical, 22, N. 126; philosophical, 87 f.; religious, 26–74; secular, 74–91.
Polygamy, 15.
Polytheism, 33, N. 374.
Pontifex, 74, N. 315.
Pṛthivî, N. 112 *c*.
Praise, 78, etc.; see *Singers, Song.*
Prajapati, 76, N. 372 f.
Prâkrit, 22 *.
Pramanthana, N. 121.
Prâtiçâkhyas, 7 (*cf.* 22), N. 78; list, N. 20.
Praudha-Br., N. 14 *a*, 2.
Pravṛje, N. 341.
Prayer, sacrifice, Soma, without P., 79, N. 333, *cf.* 314; P.-books, 4; Lord of P., see *Brahmaṇaspati.*
Prayers, contents of the P., 30, 67, 73; *cf.* N. 96, 166, 192, 209, 211, 217, 221, 225, 236, 239, 258, 261, 263, 282, 292, 298 f., 306, 372, 373, etc.
Priest, 31, 32, 35, 73 f., 77, 81 f., 86 (see *Brâhmaṇa*). P.-class, 78, *cf.* 31 f.; schools, 81.
Princes, 17, 78 f., 80 f., 86, N. 341.
Prometheus, 35 (etym., N. 121).
Pronunciation, 6, 7.
Prosperity, 30, 75, 85, N. 209, 366.
Proverbs, 84 f.
Psalms, 62 ff.; *cf.* II.
Ψυχοπομπός, N. 212, 221, 272, *cf.* 274, 315.
Punishment, after death, 70, N. 287.
Purâṇas, 8, N. 26.
Puramdhi, 50, 75, N. 178, 322.
Puru, 80, N. 198.
Purumitra, 50.
Purûravas, N. 375 f.
Puruṣasûkta, N. 79 *b*, 375 *e*.
Pûṣan, 28, 55 f. (N. 209–212), 69, 72, N. 272 f.
Pûtakrâta, N. 341.

Quail, 51, N. 187.

Ṛbhus, 37 f. (N. 127–131), 50.
Ṛta, order, 28, N. 92, 94, 98.
Ṛtu, N. 92.
Rain, 40, 63, 81 f., 87, N. 139, 143, etc.
Râjanya, N. 375 *e*.
Rânâyanîya, N. 9, 23 *a*, 2.
Rebha, 51, N. 184.
Recensions, see *Atharva-, Rig-, Sâma-, Yajurveda.*
Refrain, 23, N. 83 *a*.
Regularity in nature, 28, N. 92.
Religion, significance of the Indian R., N. 89.
Religious thought, 27; poetry, 3, 24 f., 26–74.
Renown, 53, 78 f., N. 239, 341, 349, 351.
Rhetorical figures, 23.
Rich, the, 85, N. 352.
Riches, 30, 31, 67, 71, 85, etc.
Riddles, 86, N. 364.
Right, 71, N. 47, 92, 232. R. and wrong, 60, 64. R. hand, 75 f., 77, N. 322, 324; leading from left to R., 75, N. 322.
Righteous (*cf. Blessed*), 47, 52, 55; 56, 62, 66, 69, 73, 74, N. 238, 239, 274 *a*, 283 *a*, 284 *a*, 287 *a*.

Rigveda, 3, 21 f. (*cf. Hymns, Poetry*). The collection, 21 f., 25, N. 71 f.; time of collection, 22, N. 75; time of composition, 11, N. 38; recensions, 21, N. 72, *cf.* N. 14 *a*, 1.—Brâhm., N. 14 *a*, 1; Sûtra, N. 23 *a*, 1; 24, 1; Prâtiç., N. 20.—Editions of the text, N. 8; translations, N. 116. —Importance of the R., 26, 91, *cf.* N. 89.
Rinamcaya, 80 f.
Ritual, 5, 8. R. works, 8, N. 23–25 *a*.
Rivers of the Panjab, N. 39.
Rodasî, N. 148.
Rûach Elohîm, N. 372.
Rudra, 33, 38 (N. 133–135), *cf.* 86. R. ident. with Agni? related to Apollo, N. 133.
Rudriya, N. 114, 131.
Ruler of the Universe, Indra, 45 f.; the Âdityas, 59 f.; Varuṇa, 65 f.

Sabhâ, N. 59.
Sacrifice, 3, 29, 35, 36, 43 f., 88. Rewards of S., 80, *cf.* N. 341, 349, 353; place of S., N. 26.
Sacrificial carrier, 36; gifts, 30 f., 44, 79, N. 16, 333; posts, N. 126.
Sahasra, N. 67.
Sâman, 3, N. 9.
Sâmayâcârikâ-sûtra, N. 25.
Sâmaveda, 3; Sanhitâs, N. 9; Brâh., N. 14 *a*, 2; Sûtra, N. 23 *a*, 2; 24, 2.
Sâmavidhâna-Br., N. 14 *a*, 2.
Sâmi, N. 67.
Samnyâsin, N. 15.
Samudra, N. 39.
Sanhitâ, 2 f., 22, N. 8; S.-pâṭha, N. 77, 78.
Sanhitopaniṣad-Br., N. 14 *a*, 2.
Sanskrit, 22, 23.
Saparyâmi, N. 284 *a*.
Saramâ, 42, N. 149; dogs of S., 70, N. 274.
Sârameya, N. 149, 274.
Sarasvatî, 11, N. 39, 341.
Sarcostemma, N. 288.
Satlaj, 12.
Savitar, 28, 56–58 (N. 216–222), 59, 74, N. 227, 272, 279, 357, 370. S. and Sûrya, 56 f., N. 216–218.
Sâvitrî, N. 222.
Sâyaṇa, 8 f., N. 8, 27, 38.
School (see *Caraṇa*) instruction, N. 76.
Sciences, 20.
Sea, ocean, 12 (N. 39), 27, 64, 65, 89, N. 370–372; both seas, 65.
Seasons, 37, 82, 86, N. 68, 127, 211. Genii of the S., N. 127 f.
Secret, 61, 64, 65, 66, 73, N. 253.
Serpent, 41, N. 145, etc.; S.-smiter, 58.
Sheep, 56, N. 341.
Shepherd, 56.
Ship, 49, 52, 64, N. 152, 273. S. of Pûṣan, N. 210; of the Phaeacians, N. 189.
Sickness, 20, 50, 67, 72, N. 358, 359 (see *Medicine, Physician*).
Sin, 61, 67, 68 f., 73, N. 106, 195, 221, 225, 258, 260, 261, etc.
Sindh, Sindhu, 11, N. 39.
Singers (*cf. Poets*), 31, 48, 88. Families of S., 21, 79, 80, N. 73; speech, 23.
Sirius, 20, N. 67.
Sleep, 80, N. 297.
Smârtasûtra, 8.
Smṛti, 8.
Soil, 12, N. 40.

Solar year, 20.
Soma, plant, 63, 72, N. 244, 288, 289; drink, 3, 14, 26, 38, 41, 43, 47, 71, 79 (S. without prayer), N. 144, 188, 210, 290 f., 294, 333. God, 21, 72 f., 74 f., N. 155, 288–308, 349, 366. S.-cult, 72, N. 293; sacrifice, 3, N. 333; intoxication, 72.
Song-books, 3.
Songs, see *Hymns*.
Sons, desired, 6, 15, 76; see *Children*.
Soul, 56, 69 f., N. 274, 274 *a*, 275, 275 *a*; see *Home*.
Speech, goddess of S., N. 375 *c*.
Spell, see *Charm*.
Spirit life, world, 69 ff. Spirits of the dead, 69.
Spoils, 19, 36, 79, etc.
Spy, Sûrya called a S., 55; the Âdityas, N. 230. Spies of Mitra-Varuṇa, N. 230; of Savitar, 57; of Soma, 73; of Varuṇa, 65.
Stars, heavenly bodies, 20, 45, 54, 57, 71, 83, N. 194, 204, 249, 286, 286 *a*, 300, 341.
State, 16.
Steps of Viṣṇu, 56, N. 213.
Stream, 11, 37, 48. S. held back and passed over, 44, 79; into the other world, 69, N. 273.
Stronghold, 36, 66, N. 149, 297.
Strophe, 24, N. 86.
Sudâs, 44, 79 f., N. 340.
Suitor, 15, 35, N. 352.
Sûkta, N. 71.
Sun, 14, 27 (N. 91), 28, 37, 39, 54–58, 62, 87, N. 179, 189, 286, 286 *a*, etc. S. stands still, 45; S. brought by Indra, 41, 45; by Varuṇa, 63, N. 245, 249; by Soma, 72; by the Fathers, 71, N. 286 *a*; by the gods from the sea, N. 371. S. guided by the Âdityas, N. 231. S. = eye of Mitra-Varuṇa, 59, *cf.* N. 207; of Varuṇa, N. 241. S. represented as a bird, see *Bird*. How many suns? 87. S. and Moon, 75, N. 249, 286 *a*, 318, 319. Eclipse, N. 67. Course of S., 87; chariot, 45, 55, 57. S.-god, 37, 50, 54 (see *Pûṣan*, *Savitar*, *Sûrya*, *Viṣṇu*). Sunrise, 54, 55, 57, etc. Sunset, 55, 58, N. 182.
Surâ, 14, N. 280.
Sûrya, 28, 54 f. (N. 203–207), 57, 59, 73, N. 216–218 (see *Savitar*).
Sûryâ, 50, 74 f., *cf.* 86; N. 148, 176.
Suçravas, 44.
Sûtra, 6, N. 23. Dharma-S., N. 25; Gṛhya-S., N. 24; Çrauta-S., N. 23 *a*. S.-period, N. 17.
Sûtracaraṇa, N. 23.
Suvastu, Swat, 12, N. 39.
Synopsis of Vedic Sanhitâs, N. 8.
Syntax, 23; comparative, Greek S., N. 84.

Çabala, N. 274, 274 *a*.
Çâkala-, 21, N. 72.
Çâkaṭâyana, N. 21.
Çâkhâ, 3, 21, N. 9, 10, 13, etc.
Çambara, 80, N. 341.
Çânkhâyana, N. 14 *a*, 1; 23 *a*, 1; 24, 1; 72; 320.
Çarvara, see *Çabala*.
Çatam, N. 67.
Çatapatha-Br., N. 14 *a*, 4; 286; 287 *a*.
Çaunaka, N. 13, 20, 26.
Çigru, 80.
Çikṣa, 6, N. 18.
Çimyu, 79.

Çipivișța, N. 214.
Çiva, 3, N. 26, 133.
Çyâva, N. 178.
Çraddhâ, N. 366.
Çrautasûtra, 8, N. 23, 23 *a*.
Çruti, 5.
Çudra, N. 375 *e*.
Çulvasûtra, N. 23, 26.
Çunaḥçepa, 68, N. 263.
Çușṇa, 40.
Çutudrî, 12 *, 79, N. 39.

Sadvinça-Br., N. 14 *a*, 2.

Tacitus, 17, N. 54.
Taittirîya-Sanh., N. 10, 1, etc. T.-Br., -Âr., -Upan., N. 14 *a*, 3; T.-Prâtiç., N. 20.
Talâtala, N. 287 *a*.
Talavakâra-Br., -Upan., N. 14 *a*, 2.
Tâṇḍya-Br., N. 14 *a*, 2.
Tapas, N. 266, 372, 375.
Tense, N. 84 *b*.
Texts, Vedic, 2 ff., 6. Editions (see the various classes of works), N. 8–27. T. become unintelligible, 10 *, 22, N. 373; enlarged, N. 79 *a*, 348. Transmission of T., 22, N. 76 f.; oral, 22, N. 64, 76; written, N. 76. Forms of T. (pâṭhas), 22, N. 77.
Thieves, 18, 42, 54.
Thrâetana (Iran.), N. 112 *d*.
Three heavens, three earths, N. 241, 248, *cf.* 279, 283 *a*. Number Three in superstitions, N. 117.
Threefold division of the universe, 34 f., N. 117 f., 286 *a*.
Throne, 78, N. 332. T. of Mitra-Varuṇa, N. 230; of Amesha Çpenta, N. 283 *a*.
Thunderbolt, 40, 41, 86, N. 144, etc.
Time (see *Composition*, *Period*) of the Collection, 22, 26, N. 75; of Pâṇini, 7, N. 21.
Tirindira, N. 341.
Tṛtsu, 44, 79, N. 334, 340.
Tradition, in exegesis, 9 f., N. 29 f., 34, 373; in ritual, 5, 15, 75, N. 24, 317, 321–324, etc.
Traitana, N. 112 *d*.
Translations of the Rig, N. 116.
Trasadasyu, N. 340.
Trayî vidyâ, 4, N. 11.
Tree, 42, 87, N. 189, 280, 285 *a*, 327, 341.
Tribe, political unit, division, 17. Tribes of the Aryans, N. 54; of the Dasyus, N. 62.
Trita, 33. T. Âptya, N. 112 *d*.
Triumph, songs of T., 78.
Tugra, 51, N. 189.
Turva, N. 341.
Turvaça, 45, N. 198.
Turvîti, 44.
Tvaṣṭar, 38, 41, N. 131, 144, 188.
Twilight, N. 171.

Union in the next world, 31, 70, N. 282 f.
Unsacrificing, 43, 47, N. 164, 190, etc.
Upalekha, N. 77.
Upamaçravas, N. 94, 340.
Upanișad, 5, 8; list, number, purpose of the U., N. 16.
Urvaçî, N. 375 f.
Ușas (*cf. Dawn*), 28, 52–54 (N. 193–202), 57, 59 (N. 223), 64, N. 286. Dispute of U. with Indra, N. 195.

Vadha, vadhar, N. 147.
Vadhryaçva, N. 340.
Vadhû, N. 341.

Vaiçya, N. 375 *e*.
Vaiçvâmitra, N. 73.
Vaitânasûtra, N. 23 *a*, 5.
Vâc, N. 375 *c*.
Vâja, N. 127.
Vâjasaneyi-Sanh., N. 10, 2; 14 *a*, 4; 16; 23 *a*, 4; 24, 4.
Vala, 42, N. 149.
Vâlakhilya, N. 72.
Vâmadeva, 21, 85, N. 73.
Vânaprastha, N. 15.
Vandana, 51, N. 179.
Vança-Br., N. 14 *a*, 2.
Vâra bhár, N. 95.
Variety in hymns and conceptions, 24 f., 26.
Vartika, N. 187.
Varuṇa, 20, 28, 36, 59, 61–69 (N. 226 f., 241–264), 70, 73, N. 142, 366, 374. Eyes of V., N. 241. V. and Indra, 33, 62, N. 114, 242. V. and Mitra, 59–61, 71, N. 225–240, 241. V. and Yama, 69 f., N. 276.
Varuṇânî, N. 148.
Vasiṣṭha, 21, 79, N. 336.
Vâsiṣṭha, N. 73. —N. 25.
Vâstoṣpati, N. 375 *d*.
Vasu, N. 114, 131.
Vaça Açvya, N. 341.
Vâṣkala, N. 72.
Vâta, **Vâyu**, 33, 38, 72, N. 72.
Vayya, 63.
Veda, 2 ff.; see *Atharva-*, *Rig-*, *Sâma-*, *Yajurveda*.
Vedá, N. 102.
Vedânga, 6–9.
Vedânta, 6, *cf.* N. 16.
Vedârthayatna, N. 33.
Vedic civilization, 11–20; V. belief, 32–34; V. homes, 12 f.; V. period, 11, N. 38.
Verses interpolated, 22, N. 79 *a*, 83 *c*. Index of first lines, RV., N. 8; AV., N. 13; SV., N. 9. V. repeated, 23, N. 83 *ac*; crowded out, N. 83 *c*.
Vetasu, 80, N. 337.
Vibhvan, N. 127.
Victory, 19, 78.
Vijayanagara, 9.
Village, 13, 17, 19, 71, N. 59.
Vîlu, N. 149.
Vimada, 50, N. 178.
Vipâç, 12 *, 79, N. 39.
Viçpalâ, 51, N. 180.
Viçvakarman, 89, N. 371, 374.
Viçvâmitra, 21, 79, N. 73.
Viçve devâs, 34, 74, N. 316.
Viṣṇu, 3, 56, 86, N. 26, 213–215.
Viṣṇu-Dharmasûtra, N. 25; V.-Purâṇa, N. 26.
Vitastâ, 12, N. 39.
Vivasvant, 69, N. 269.
Vṛka, N. 187.
Vṛcîvant, 80.
Vṛtra, 40, 43.
Vyâkaraṇa, 6, N. 18.
Vyâsa, N. 75.

Wanderer, 49, 58 (the sun, 28).
War, 19, 43 f., 78 f.
Warmth, cosmogonic force, 90.
Water, waters, 13 f., 31, 40, 41, 63, 65, 80, 90, N. 248. W. loosed by Indra, 41; guided by Varuṇa, 63. W. as original matter, 87 f.
Way, of the gods, 74, N. 233.—N. 211 (see *Path*).
Weapons, 19; W.-song, N. 63.
Weaving, 14, 56, 58.
Wicked, place of the W. in the other world, 71, N. 287, 287 *a*.
Widow, 16, 77, N. 51; right of inheritance, re-marriage, burning, N. 51, 328.
Wife, 15, 16, 75, 77, N. 47.

Wind, 37, 38, 40, 52, 63, 64, N. 248, 372.
Wine, 14, N. 261.
Winged steeds of the Açvins, 50, 51, N. 189.
Winking of an eye, 50, 64, 66.
Wisdom, Wise, 63, 69, 90, etc. Song of W., 85, N. 348, 375 *b*.
Wish, 29, 70, N. 96.
Wolf, 52, N. 187.
Woman, 16, 71, 85, N. 351.
Word, formation, 23, N. 81 *b*. Play on words, 23, N. 83 *b*.
World, worlds, 28, 42, 45 f., 49, 60, 62 f., 65, N. 92, 157, 163, 214, 244, etc.; W. of the righteous, 66, 69 (see *Abode*, *Righteous*).
Writing, 20, N. 64. Texts committed to W., N. 77.

Yadu, 45, N. 198, 341.
Yâjnavalkya, 8, N. 14 *a*, 4; 25, 79, etc.
Yajurveda, 4, N. 10. Black Y., N. 10; 14 *a*, 3; 20; 23 *a*, 3; 24, 3. White Y., N. 10, 2; 14 *a*, 4; 20; 23 *a*, 4; 24, 4.
Yajus, 3.
Yakṣu, 80.
Yama, 69, 70, 78, N. 269, 275, 276, 279, 280, 374. Yama's dogs, 69, N. 274, 274 *a*; his bright realm, 70. Y. and Yamî, N. 375 *a*.
Yamî, see above.
Yamuna, 12.
Yâska, 7, 10 *, N. 19, 28.
Yavyâvatî, 80, N. 338.
Year (*cf.* *Autumn*, *Seasons*), 37, 46, 82, 86, N. 231, 372.
Yûpa, N. 126.

Zeus and Hera, N. 318.

ἄγγελοι, 42 *.
ἀήρ, αἰθήρ, N. 118.
Ἀθάνα, N. 112 *d*.
Ἀκεσίνης, N. 39.
Ἀρια-, Ἀριο-, N. 37.
ἄρρινες, ἄστομοι, N. 62.
Βίπασις, N. 39.
-βοιος, N. 46.
Βράγχο-, Βραγχίδαι, N. 82.
Γανδάριοι, 12.
γλῶσσαι, 7.
Δαρδανία, N. 149.
δωτῆρες ἐάων, N. 95.
ἑκατόν, N. 65.
ἐπιδέξια, N. 324.
Ἑρμείας, N. 149.
Ζαδάδρης, Ζάραδρος, N. 39.
Ζεύς, 33, N. 112 *a*.
ἡμι-, N. 65.
ἦρα φέρειν, N. 95.
θεοὶ πατρῷοι, N. 285 *a*.
Ἴλιον, N. 149.
Ἰνδός, N. 39.
Ἰωβάρης, Ἰωμάνης, N. 39.
Κέρβερος, N. 274 *a*.
κλέος ἄφθιτον, N. 95.
Κωφήν, N. 39.
λεύκιππος Ἀώς, N. 197.
λύκος, λυκοκτόνος, N. 187.
μείς, μήν, 28.
μένος ἠΰ, N. 95.
ὄμωμι, N. 293.
Οὐρανός, N. 241.
πόλις, N. 42.
Προμηθεύς, N. 121.
Ῥουάδις, N. 39.
Σανδαβάγα, Σανδαροφάγος, Σόαστος, N. 39.
Τάρταρος, N. 287 *a*.
Τριτωνίς, N. 112 *d*.

Ὑαρώτης, Ὑδάσπης, Ὑδραώτης, Ὕφασις, N. 39.
ὑλόβιοι, N. 15.
Φλεγύαι, N. 120, 287 *a*.
χίλιοι, N. 65.
ὠκεανός, N. 145.

Cantabas, N. 39.
Centum, N. 65.
Credo, N. 366.
Depontani, N. 50 †.
Dexterarum junctio (p. 75), N. 322.
Diespiter, 33.
Flâmen, N. 82.
Gaius, ego G., tu Gaia, N. 323.
Glebam inicere, N. 330.
Lares, Manes, N. 270, 283 *a*, 285 *a*.
Mars, N. 133.
Mille, N. 65.
Pontifex, N. 315.
Ratus, N. 92.
Semi, N. 65.
Sepelio, N. 284 *a*.
Sexagenarii de ponte, N. 50 †.
Sindus, N. 39.

Arbeit, N. 127.
Hundert, N. 65.
Mensch, 28, N. 93.
Recke, N. 57.
Sippe, N. 59.
Tausend, N. 65.
Wetter, N. 147.
Wuotan, N. 132.
O. Norse, *brag-r*, *Bragi*, N. 82.
Goth, *faírguni*, *Fiörgyn*, N. 139.

II.

BIBLE PASSAGES.

GEN. 1, 2: N. 372.
1, 7: P. 65.
1, 14: N. 231.
15, 1: P. 66.

EXOD. 14, 21: P. 45.
20, 5: P. 67.

LEVIT. 11, 14: N. 255.

DEUT. 10, 14: P. 65.

JOSHUA 10, 13: P. 45.

1 SAM. 16, 7: P. 60.

1 KINGS 8, 39: P. 64.

EZRA 9, 13: P. 67.

JOB 5, 10: P. 63.
9, 7: P. 64.
9, 8: P. 62.
9, 11: P. 60.
10, 5: P. 46.
13, 23: P. 67.
26, 10: P. 63.
28, 24: P. 65.
31, 4: P. 65.
34, 21: P. 65.
38, 4: P. 62.
38, 5: P. 63.
38, 12 f.: P. 53.
38, 18: P. 63.
38, 25: P. 63.
38, 31: N. 249.
38, 33: P. 62.
38, 36: P. 63.
39, 19: P. 63.

PSALMS 1, 3: P. 61.
6, 2: N. 256.
17, 8: N. 238.
19, 13: P. 67.
22, 2: P. 68.
24, 1: P. 65.
25, 14: N. 253.
31, 2: P. 67.
32, 5 f.: N. 257.
33, 13: P. 65.
38, 2: N. 256.
50, 11: P. 64.
51, 3: P. 67.
59, 16: P. 66.
71, 2: P. 67.
72, 6: P. 63.
74, 15: P. 63.
74, 16 f.: P. 63, N. 231.
77, 6 ff.: P. 68, N. 262.
78, 13: P. 45.
79, 8: P. 67.
88, 2: P. 68.
89, 11: P. 64.
89, 12: P. 62.
91, 1 ff.: P. 66.
91, 4: N. 238.
91, 14: P. 66.
91, 16: P. 66.
102, 24: P. 61.
102, 26: P. 62.
103, 10: P. 67.
104, 2: P. 62, 63.
104, 3: P. 64, N. 143.
104, 5: P. 62.
104, 7: P. 58.
104, 10: P. 63.

PSALMS 104, 13 f.: P. 63.
104, 19: P. 63.
104, 22: P. 55.
107, 29: P. 58.
109, 15: P. 67.
113, 5: P. 65.
121, 4: P. 60.
135, 7: P. 64.
136, 8: P. 62, N. 249.
138, 6: P. 65.
139, 2: P. 65.
139, 3: P. 65.
139, 7 ff.: P. 65.
143, 1, 11: P. 67.
147, 4: P. 64.
147, 8: P. 63.
148, 3 f.: N. 249.

PROV. 21, 2: P. 64.
28, 13: N. 257.
30, 18: P. 64.

ECCLES. 1, 7: P. 27, N. 245.
11, 5: P. 62, 64.
12, 7: N. 275 *a*.

ISAIAH 12: N. 257.
19, 1: N. 143.
40, 22: P. 62.
41, 10: P. 66.
44, 24: P. 62.
50, 2: P. 58.
63, 12: P. 45.

JEREM. 10, 12: P. 62.
10, 13: P. 63, 64.
17, 8: P. 61.
17, 10: Pp. 60, 64.
23, 23: P. 65.
23, 24: P. 62.
31, 35: P. 62, N. 231, 249.
32, 18: P. 67.
32, 19: P. 65.
51, 15: P. 62.
51, 16: P. 63.

EZEK. 18, 20: P. 67.

DAN. 7, 13: N. 143.

HOS. 6, 3: P. 54, 63.

AMOS 3, 7: N. 253.
5, 8: N. 245.
9, 1 ff.: P. 65.
9, 6: N. 245.

HABAK. 3, 8: N. 143.

MATTH. 5, 45: N. 207.
6, 8: N. 227.
8, 12: N. 287.
8, 27: P. 58.
10, 30: P. 66.
18, 20: P. 65.
24, 30: N. 143.
26, 64: N. 143.

LUKE 12, 7: P. 66.

JOHN 1, 1: N. 375 *c*.
3, 8: P. 38, 64, N. 132.

HEB. 4, 13: P. 65.